当代国际商务文化阅读丛书

Readings for Modern International Business Culture

拥抱新欢亚马逊

——『电子商务』篇

Embraces Amazon Service E-Commerce

【英汉对照】

吴斐 编著

武汉大学出版社
WUHAN UNIVERSITY PRESS

图书在版编目(CIP)数据

拥抱新欢亚马逊:"电子商务"篇:英汉对照/吴斐编著.—武汉:武汉大学出版社,2016.5
当代国际商务文化阅读丛书
书名原文:Embraces Amazon Service:E-Commerce
ISBN 978-7-307-13997-8

Ⅰ.拥… Ⅱ.吴… Ⅲ.电子商务—英、汉 Ⅳ.F713.36

中国版本图书馆 CIP 数据核字(2014)第 181972 号

责任编辑:郭园园 金 军 责任校对:鄢春梅 版式设计:韩闻锦

出版发行:武汉大学出版社 (430072 武昌 珞珈山)
(电子邮件:cbs22@whu.edu.cn 网址:www.wdp.com.cn)
印刷:武汉中远印务有限公司
开本:880×1230 1/32 印张:10.375 字数:227 千字
版次:2016 年 5 月第 1 版 2016 年 5 月第 1 次印刷
ISBN 978-7-307-13997-8 定价:28.00 元

前　言

人类社会进入21世纪后， 国家间的商务往来更加频繁， 商务交际手段随着互联网的诞生和电子信息的进步日新月异， 国际化企业的文化和理念千差万别， 商务话题的表达和沟通能力无疑是人们所遇到的最大障碍。 在我们熟知的生活英语、 学术英语之外， 商务英语不仅是我国目前从事或即将从事涉外商务人员英语实际应用能力不可多得的辅助工具， 更是商务工作人员在这个国际化的高科技时代商务竞争能力、 外贸业务素质和英语水平的重要体现。《当代国际商务文化阅读》（英汉对照）丛书以从事国际商务活动所必需的语言技能为经， 以各种商务活动的具体情景作纬， 将商务精神和商务元素巧妙融合， 展示时尚而又经典的商务文化世界流行风， 为广大读者提供一套语言规范、 内容新颖、 涉及面广、 趣味性强、 具有实用价值、 富于时代精神的读物， 既注意解决人们在国际商务环境中因遇到不熟悉的专业词汇而无法与外国合作者就工作问题交流沟通的难题， 又着力解决人们学外语单纯地学语言而缺乏商务专业知识的弊端。

《当代国际商务文化阅读》（英汉对照）丛书由10个单行本组成：《拥抱新欢亚马逊（Embracing Amazon Service）——电子商务篇（E-Commerce）》、《华尔街梦魇 （Nightmare on Wall Street）——商界风云篇（The Business Circles）》、《路易斯·波森的朋克摇滚（The Punk Rock of Louis Posen）——商界精英篇（Business Elites）》、《希波克拉底誓言（Hippocratic Oath）——商务交际篇（Business Communication）》、《强烈的第一印象（A Powerful First Impression）——商务礼仪篇（Business Etiquette）》、《企业帝国继承权之争（Corporate Empires' Grappling with Succession）——商务文化篇（Business Culture）》、《紫色血液（The Purple Blood）——商务心理篇（Business Psychology）》、《多米诺骨牌效应（The Domino Effects）——商务知识篇（Business Knowledge）》、《公开的赌注（Public Stakes）——商务演讲篇（Business Speeches）》、《伊斯特林悖论（The Easterlin Paradox）——感悟财富篇（Comprehension of Wealth）》。这套丛书的编写旨在帮助读者在国际商务环境下，能够读懂英文的商务信息和商务新闻，并能对某一商务话题的知识有全面透彻的了解，领悟当代时尚商务文化成长的环境和思维方式，提高在全球化高科技时代的商务竞争能力、外贸业务素质和英语交际水平。丛书中的阅读材料力求做到题材广泛、内容精辟、语言规范，遵循趣味性、知识性和时效性原则，培养读者在商务环境下的英语竞争能力和综合应用能力。丛书融时代性与经典性为一体，内容经得起时间考验，文字经得起反复咀嚼，保证其可读性。读者在阅读过程中接收大量的语言输入，为合理组织和娴熟运用英语语言表达自己的思想打下牢固的基础。丛书的单行本包括以一个主题为中心的30篇文章，每篇文章包括题记、英语原文、汉语译文、生词脚注和知识链接。“题记”用丰富生动的语言点评文章的精髓，对文章的内容起到提炼和画龙点睛的作用。“英语原文”主要摘自当代国际主流报纸杂志，具有语言规范、内容新颖、涉及面广、趣味性和时代感等特点。“汉语译文”力求准确流畅，既关注译文的文化语境及其内涵，也重视译文的外延和现当代标志性语言符号。“生词脚注”的难度把握在大学英语六级和研究生英语词汇程度，以帮助读者及时扫清阅读障碍。“知识链接”根据文章内容，或精解一个专业术语、或阐释一种新的商务理念、或介绍叱咤商界的企业或公司，以帮助读者培养游弋商海、运筹帷幄的能力，具备洞悉中西文化的国际视野。

《拥抱新欢亚马逊》（Embracing Amazon Service）——“电子商务”篇（E-Commerce）给读者展示了一个璀璨斑斓的电子商务世界。电子商务，英文是 Electronic Commerce，简称 EC，它指使用各种电子工具从事商务活动。这些工具包括从初级的电报、电话、广播、电视、传真到计算机、计算机网络，到 NII（国家信息基础结构——信息高速公路）、GII（全球信息基础结构）和 Internet 等现代系统。随着全球互联网使用人数的增加，利用互联网进行网络购物、并以银行卡付款的消费方式已日渐流行，电子商务的市场份额正在迅速增长，电子商务网站也层出不穷。如果说一百年前电的发明为工业提供了历史机遇，使资本主义国家在不到 100 年的时间里创造的生产力远远超过了以前几个世纪的总和，给人类带来了进步和幸福，那么电子商务是人类文明史上科技领域里信息技术的又一次重大飞跃。这次科技革命不仅极大地推动了人类的社会经济、政治、文化领域的变革，而且也影响了人类生活方式和思维方式，使人类社会生活和人的现代化向更高境界发展。互联网开创的电子商务时代，不仅仅是某种跨越式的技术，而是

前 言

利用互联网技术创造出前所未有的商业模式。B2B、C2C、B2C、C2B四位一体的产业群生态链垂直循环营销模式打破了传统垂直的商业模式，对传统企业的发展、运营及赢利具有革命性的颠覆，为电子商务发展创造了新的契机。本书的主要阅读文章包括：电子商务（E-Commerce），数字化营销（Digital Marketing），网络购物（Internet Shopping），在线销售（Online Selling），数字钱夹（Digital Wallets），虚拟企业（Virtual Enterprise），虚拟网络（Virtual Internet），数码产品（Electronic Gadgets），网上营销（Web-based Marketing），网站集资（Web-site Fundraising），以及互联网交易（Internet Business）等。今天，互联网正在以迅雷不及掩耳之势催生无数的新兴产业，君不见网路漫漫其修远兮。阅读风靡全球的电子商务，让我们跟随时代潮流，追赶互联网信息化、数字化、网络化、智慧化、娱乐化的商业脚步，享受世界流行文化创造的快乐、荣誉、价值和成就感！

作 者

2016年1月

目　　录

目　录

目 录

题　记

音乐电子商务交易平台横空出世，受到各路豪侠的青睐。亚马逊(Amazon)的β版Amazon MP3赢得了“自由斗士”的美称和业界分析人士的赞许。许多人认为Amazon MP3将把苹果的iTunes拉下马，还将开启音乐界无DRM的新纪元。四大主要唱片公司对亚马逊提供歌曲下载服务，百事和亚马逊的合作扩展了唱片公司网上销售空间。但是，这并不意味着亚马逊就会踏上一帆风顺的坦途。迫使苹果继续销售有权限的音乐就好像穿着里面塞有小石子的鞋一样难受。正当亚马逊轰轰烈烈地拉开iPod销售业务的帷幕之时，苹果却强调将迎来一个没有DRM的新世界。音乐行业和苹果公司持续不断的紧张关系继续剑拔弩张。实际上，无论对于苹果还是亚马逊——甚至整个行业而言——机遇与挑战并存。亚马逊正在穿越商业竞争的重峦叠嶂，迎来下一轮经济大发展的曙光。

Embracing Amazon: A New Comer

At the Super Bowl next month, the music industry will be switching teams — from Apple to Amazon.com. The major record labels lined up with Pepsi-Cola and Apple four years ago to give away 100 million songs through Apple's online store, unveiling the promotion in a Super Bowl commercial with music from the band Green Day. The effort helped spread the word about Apple's iTunes[1] offerings. Pepsi's promotion is back this year on a much bigger scale — but with the star wattage provided by Justin instead of Green Day, and Amazon in place of Apple.

The switch is an indicator of the continuing tension between the music industry and Apple. Pepsi's earlier ad, set to Green Day's version of the song "I Fought the Law," prodded[2] music fans to quit pirating music online and instead buy songs — legally — from Apple's then -

---

① Apple iTunes：Apple iTunes是整理、共享、聆听电脑里的音乐最简单的方法，轻松享用iPod的最佳伴侣，免费下载，适用PC或Mac。Apple iTunes是一个个性播放器，同时也是一个商店。

② prod [prɔd] *vt.* 刺激；激励

拥抱新欢亚马逊

在下个月即将举行的美国橄榄球超级碗大奖赛上，音乐行业将会抛弃旧爱苹果，转而投入新欢亚马逊的怀抱。四年前，几个主要的唱片品牌与百事可乐和苹果集团联手，通过苹果网上商店发售了 100 000 000 首单曲，而这一骄人的业绩就始于绿日乐队演奏的音乐在超级碗电视广告中的促销。这一举措使苹果集团的 iTunes 产品变得家喻户晓。百事今年的促销活动又如约而至，而且规模更大，不过，这次闪亮登场的巨星由绿日变成了贾斯汀，苹果也被亚马逊取而代之。

这个转变昭示了音乐行业和苹果公司持续不断的紧张关系。绿日乐队出品的“我与法律之战”作为音乐背景的百事早期广告，促使歌迷不再选择从网上下载侵权的免费歌曲，转而使用苹果新开发的 iTunes 合法地从网上购得喜爱的音乐。四年之后，iTunes 已成为数字音乐市场的龙头老大，但从今年 9 月开始，整个行业却将橄榄枝伸向了其竞争对手亚马逊。尽管 iTunes 开启了网上付费购歌的先河，唱片总监们仍然怨声载道，认为苹果的首席执行官斯蒂文·乔布斯在商品定价和有关条款等方面施加了过多的影响。眼下备受关注的问题是自己的品牌能否帮助普及一个更有利于行业发展的服务，以及加快数字产品销售的步伐。透过行业成员转换合作伙伴的

fledgling[1] iTunes. Four years later, iTunes is by far the biggest digital music store, and the industry is taking a liking to Amazon's rival music service, introduced in September. Though iTunes blazed[2] a trail in encouraging fans to pay for music online, record executives now complain that Steven P. Jobs, Apple's chief executive, wields too much clout in setting prices and other terms. At issue now is whether the labels can help popularize a more industry-friendly service and accelerate the pace of digital sales. Behind this strategy is a growing desperation: sales of digital albums and songs are rising far too slowly to offset the rapid decline of the CD, the industry's mainstay product. CD sales slid 19 percent last year; after adding in the 50 million digital albums sold last year and counting every 10 digital songs sold as an album, overall music sales were still down 9.5 percent, according to Nielsen SoundScan.

In trying to nurture Amazon's service, the four major record companies have offered it one potential edge. One by one, they have agreed to offer their music catalogs for sale on the service in the MP3 format, without the digital locks that restrict users from making copies of the songs. All of the companies except the EMI Group still require Apple to sell their music wrapped in digital rights management software, or DRM[3], which is intended to discourage rampant copying. Some consumers say D.R.M. creates confusing problems, like a lack of compatibility

---

① fledgling [ˈfledʒliŋ] *n.* 新手

② blaze [bleiz] *v.* 照耀,激发

③ DRM:英文全称 Digital Rights Management,内容数字版权加密保护技术。

表面现象，我们能隐约窥见业内不断增长的悲观情绪：CD一直都是音乐行业盈利的重要支柱，而数字唱片和单曲销量的缓慢增长并不足以弥补CD销量的急剧下滑。尼尔森音像公司统计的数据显示，去年CD的销售量下滑了19个百分点；即使把50 000 000网上数字专辑销量和总单曲销售量除以10为计的专辑销量一并计入总销售量，也不能改变其下滑9.5个百分点的事实。

在推动亚马逊网上服务的进程中，四大主要唱片公司功不可没。它们纷纷向亚马逊提供音乐销售目录，并同意以MP3格式向用户提供不受数字密码限制的歌曲下载服务。除了EMI集团之外，所有其他唱片公司仍然要求苹果通过捆绑数字产权管理软件或者DRM销售唱片，抵制猖獗的盗版行为。一些用户抱怨使用DRM反而会产生许多麻烦，比如他们下载的绝大多数歌曲与苹果和微软提供的播放器不兼容。实际上，就连管理层也在2月份公开呼吁整个行业放弃一直以来所坚持的软件捆绑销售，指出这种方式无法有效地控制盗版。不管怎样，整个行业都在观望，看亚马逊是否能很快取代iTunes，成长为值得信赖的合作伙伴。

这是一场硬碰硬的较量。业内总监们认为，如果两者在获得部分单曲和特别促销活动的独家代理权方面展开竞争，这场较量将愈演愈烈。一名不愿透露姓名的另一家唱片公司高层执行官指出，他将在亚马逊筹建网上歌曲下载服务的6个月到1年的时间内保留其在iTunes的歌曲下载权限。苹果一直坚持以99美分的价格出售旗下的所有单曲，而亚马逊的价格却是89美分到1美元以上。一名策划本次“百事可乐套餐”的商业促销活动市场营销代理商认为，

between most songs and the devices sold by Apple and Microsoft. In fact, it was the management who, in February, called on the industry to drop its longstanding insistence on the use of the software, saying it had failed to rein① in piracy. In any case, the industry is waiting to see whether — and how quickly — Amazon can grow into a credible alternative to iTunes.

This is really a stare-down! Industry executives say the rivalry could intensify if the two services jockey over who will be given exclusive rights to some songs or special promotions. A senior executive at another record company, who requested anonymity, said he was prepared to keep copy restrictions on his label's songs on iTunes for six months to a year while Amazon establishes itself. Apple insists on selling all single tracks for 99 cents, while Amazon sells them for 89 cents to over a dollar. One of the marketing agencies that developed the promotion "Pepsi Stuff" said the industry's collective shift away from DRM would unleash a new age in the music business, and it's sorely needed. So to speak, Pepsi's alliance with Amazon reflected in part the record companies' desire to increase the retail space online and help level the playing field. In the promotion to be announced, consumers who buy Pepsi drinks will receive points that can be redeemed② for music downloads at a special section of the Amazon site.

The biggest of the four music companies, the Universal Music Group, has declined to join the offer but it will still sell music through

---

① rein [rein] *vi.* 控治,支配

② redeem [ri'di:m] *vt.* 恢复,补偿

此次业内对 DRM 立场的集体转向将开启音乐行业的新纪元，这是绝对必要的。由此可见，此番百事和亚马逊的合作在一定程度上反映出唱片公司扩展网上销售空间以及促进行业平衡发展的期望。在这项即将发布的商业宣传活动中，凡是购买百事饮品的顾客均可获得在亚马逊网站特定单元下载歌曲的相应点数。

四家唱片公司中最大的环球唱片公司尽管已经谢绝参与该活动，但仍然计划通过亚马逊销售音乐。华纳唱片也期待与亚马逊的合作。亚马逊可望为百事促销活动中的每张单曲付款约 40 美分，而通常的付款单价为 65~70 美分。行业分析家认为，他们预计苹果只会把这种情形视作小事一桩。数字音乐市场的扩张也同时提高了 iPod 的销售量，而 iPod 正是数字播放器市场的主宰，其利润空间远远大于 iTunes。有一位分析家说，迫使苹果继续销售有权限的音乐就好像穿着里面塞有小石子的鞋一样难受。对苹果来说，保持对等的竞争力在某种程度上来说十分重要，但说到底，他们卖的主要还是 iPod。亚马逊也开展了 iPod 销售业务。苹果的一名发言人拒绝谈论其竞争者，但却强调苹果将迎来一个没有 DRM 的新世界。亚马逊撤销音乐文件权限的做法是否一定有利，现在还很难说。有人调侃说 DRM 应该表示“无关紧要”的意思，而且，多数 iTunes 用户可能会被版权限制所恼，转而投奔亚马逊购买无版权限制音乐。不过，这将是亚马逊全面扩张的好时机。他们更大的目标应该是所有尚未使用数字下载的用户。如何说服他们相信数字音乐是个良好开端？亚马逊目前处于一个十分有利的位置来做到这一点，但这将是一场长期的努力。

the Amazon service. The Warner Music Group is also expected to participate. Amazon is expected to pay the record companies around 40 cents for each track that is given away in the Pepsi offer; Amazon's usual payment ranges from 65 to 70 cents. Industry analysts said they expected Apple to treat the situation as a minor annoyance. And an expansion of the digital music market is likely to increase sales of iPods, which are more lucrative① than the iTunes store and dominate the digital player market. An analyst said that forcing Apple to continue selling restricted music is kind of like a couple of pebbles in the shoe. Apple maintaining parity is probably somewhat important, but in the end, they're still selling iPods. And Amazon also sells many iPods. An Apple spokesman declined to discuss the company's competitors but pointed that Apple would embrace a DRM-free world. It is far from clear that Amazon's unrestricted music files will be an advantage. Someone joked that DRM should stand for "doesn't really matter", and many iTunes customers were bothered by copy restrictions or would defect to Amazon to buy unencumbered music. But, Amazon may find an opportunity to expand the overall market. The much bigger target is all of the people who don't do digital downloading yet. But how to convince them digital music is a good thing to begin with? Amazon is in a good position to do that, but it's a long struggle.

(901 words)

---

① lucrative [ˈluːkrətiv] *adj.* 有利润的

知识链接

四大主要唱片公司　文中的四大主要唱片公司是指世界上的四大唱片公司，它们分别为：索尼贝图斯曼公司（SonyBMG）、华纳唱片公司（WEA: Warner ElektraAtlantic）、EMI 唱片公司（电力及音乐集团 Electrical and Musical Industries. Ltd）以及环球音乐集团（Universal Music. Ltd）。这四大唱片公司分别以美国最大的本土唱片公司、全世界最大的唱片集团、当今世界历史最悠久的唱片公司以及“唱片帝国”驰名于美国乃至全世界，且旗下拥有众多当今世界歌坛巨星。他们的一举一动几乎影响着全世界音乐界和唱片业的发展及动向。其中，索尼贝图斯曼公司是 2003 年由前全球五大唱片公司中的索尼公司和德国贝图斯曼集团两家合并而成。

数字音乐市场　数字音乐是用数字格式存储、通过互联网和无线网络传输的音乐。它可以很方便地拷贝、播放，并保证音乐的质量。数字音乐分成两大类：一类是铃声、彩铃类非原声的不完整歌曲；一类是原声类、由人声演唱的完整歌曲。德国率先于 1987 年研究出一种音频文件压缩技术 MP3（MPEG Audio Layer 3），音乐文件大小只相当于没有压缩前的十分之一，使音乐变得很方便携带。现在，时尚的 MP3 播放器逐渐变得更加精巧，MP3 变得越来越流行。数字音乐的发展，让音乐产业产生更多的赢利模式，并降低了音乐制作、传播和经营的门槛：蓝海市场“口水歌”让中小唱片公司有了广阔的生存空间，单曲时代让更多的歌手和小唱片公司加入竞争；音乐网站的包装、定位和推广成为专业音乐人才的孵化器；彩铃平台通过网通、电信等运营工具形成关联消费、互动分享和音乐交友等诸多互联网的功能。手机用户音乐下载拓展了短信搜索、语音搜索、模糊搜索等无线音乐类的搜索和订阅。据调查机构 Forrester 的数字音乐报告，预期数字音乐将呈现 23% 的年增长率，而数字音乐的收益增长仍不能弥补 CD 销量的持续下跌。音乐订阅服务将迅猛增长，无 DRM 的音乐下载将继续扩展至 iTunes 等更多数字音乐市场，包括在 SNS 社区中向好友销售自己喜欢的歌曲等衍生服务市场。

题　记

在线拍卖如今已发展成世界互联网的时尚垂直门户群体，致力于慈善事业和公益活动。在线拍卖在形式上、内容上都与传统的拍卖方式有极大的不同。它在形式上采用内部全部用互联网的手段执行；在内容上以社会责任为主题。它不仅加快了世界运作的速度，更提高了效率，使越来越多的人享受到与人文主义以及慈善的理念息息相关的意外惊喜：为玻利维亚西部的马迪迪国家公园发现的新的猴子物种命名的权利、与股神沃伦·巴菲特共进午餐的权利等超出了所有人的目标，吸引了世界各地的兴趣。慈善拍卖不再是俊男靓女们身着漂亮的晚礼服，在高谈阔论和杯箸交错中给琳琅满目的拍品出价的专利，也是网络虚拟世界结合自身平台的独特优势和用户特点，为高尚的慈善拍卖事业筹集资金、呈现多元文化的一种方式。

Online Charity Auctions

Nonprofits can raise more money in less time by offering their Warren Buffett lunches and Michael Jordan sneakers for bidding on the Web. It used to take Cynthia Thomashow as long as six months to raise the $ 100,000 or so her nonprofit organization needs to run for a year. But with the help of an online charity site, she can raise that sum in as little as a month. "It changed our lives," says Thomashow, executive director of the New Hampshire Center for Environmental Education, a group that provides environmental educational tools to schools. "It's a quick and efficient way to raise an operating budget." Since 2004, Thomashow has raised about $ 500,000 with the help of online charity sites.

The Web has wrought a sea change in the way nonprofits raise funds through auctions. Charities have long hawked① donated items through live auctions, where bidders try to outbid each other publicly, often with the help of a fast-talking auctioneer, or through so-called silent auctions that let potential donors browse through items, then submit bids in writing. But with online auctions, nonprofits say they can raise more money in less time, selling a coveted item or service, often donated by a

① hawk [hɔːk] *vt.*沿街叫卖

在线慈善拍卖

通过网上拍卖与沃伦·巴菲特共进午餐的权利或者拍卖迈克尔·乔丹的私人物品，非盈利组织可以在更短的时间里筹集更多的钱。过去森莎·托马肖需要长达 6 个月的时间才能筹集大约100 000美元，以供她的非营利组织运行 1 年。但现在有了在线慈善网站，她仅需要 1 个月就可以凑足这么多钱。新汉普郡环境教育中心的执行总裁托马肖认为，“在线慈善网站改变了我们的生活，它是一种快速高效筹集运行预算的方式”。托马肖的公司是一个为学校提供环境教育工具的机构，自 2004 年以来，托马肖在在线慈善网站的帮助下已经获得 500 000 美元的捐款。

在线慈善网站给非营利机构通过拍卖筹集资金的方式带来了彻底的改变。慈善机构长期以来通过现场拍卖兜售捐赠物品，投标人在花言巧语的拍卖主持人帮助下彼此公开竞标，或者通过所谓的缄默拍卖，即让潜在的捐赠者浏览捐赠物品后写下报价竞拍。有了在线拍卖，非营利机构说他们可以在更短的时间里筹钱，出售让人羡慕的物品或服务，这些物品或者服务通常由名人或社交名流捐赠——比如说与沃伦·巴菲特共同进餐或者迈克尔·乔丹的运动鞋收藏——都能通过网络找到更高报价的竞拍者。

各大网站——包括开办“奉献工程”项目的易趣网——提供的数据表明，在线慈善拍卖金额至少高达 2.5 亿美元。其他网站包括

celebrity or socialite—say, a meal with Warren Buffett or Michael Jordan's sneaker collection—to the highest bidder from across the Web.

Online charity auctions have raised at least $ 250 million, according to figures provided by the largest sites, including eBay (EBAY), which runs a program called Giving Works. Others include Charity Folks and Charitybuzz. The biggest player, eBay, has raised $ 150 million for charity since 1999. Of that total, $ 50 million was raised in the last year alone. Its Giving Works helps more than 84 million eBay users "support the causes most important to them" and gives 15,000 nonprofits "direct access to this key constituency①," says Kristin Cunningham, general manager of eBay Giving Works.

No item, it seems, is off-limits for auction. Online casino② site Goldenpalace.com placed the winning bid for the right to name a new species of titi monkey discovered in Bolivia by the Wildlife Conservation Society. With $ 650,000, the casino outbid Ellen DeGeneres to name the monkey callicebus avrei palatti, or "Golden Palace." Other prizes that have been auctioned for a cause include a 90-foot Ferris wheel and five days on a 157-foot private yacht. Two auctions have even reached seven figures: The most recent lunch with Warren Buffett fetched $ 2. 11 million, and a letter signed by 41 Senate Democrats demanding that Rush Limbaugh apologize for calling antiwar veterans③ "phony soldiers" hauled in $ 2.1 million.

The auction-hosting sites get a share of loot, too. CMarket's

---

① constituency [kən'stitjuənsi] *n.* 支持者,赞助者

② casino [kə'siːnəu] *n.* 赌场;娱乐场

③ veteran ['vetərən] *n.* 老兵,退伍军人

"民间慈善"和"慈善闲谈"。自 1999 年以来，在线慈善拍卖最大的参与者易趣已经为慈善事业募集了 2.5 亿美元，其中仅去年就募集了 5 000 万美元。易趣"奉献工程"的总经理克莉丝汀·坎宁安说，易趣的"奉献工程"帮助 8 400 多万易趣用户"支持他们最重要的事业"，并给予 1.5 万个非营利机构"直通主要的赞助商"的机会。

看起来，没有什么物品是不能拍卖的。互联网赌场 GoldenPalace.com 成为野生生物保护协会在玻利维亚新发现的伶猴物种命名权的成功竞标者。赌场出价高于艾伦·德杰尼勒斯，支付 65 万美元购买了命名的权利，取名"callicebus avrei palatti"或"金殿"。其他的奖品也为了一项事业而被拍卖，包括一个 90 英尺长的摩天轮和在一艘 157 英尺长的私人游艇上 5 天的度假。有两项拍卖甚至达到了 7 位数：与沃伦·巴菲特共进午餐的最新机会拍到 211 万美元，由 41 名参议院民主党人签字、要求拉什·利曼葆夫向被其称为"冒牌兵"的反战老兵道歉的一封联名信飙升到 210 万美元。

拍卖主办网站也会从中得到一定份额的回报。希马凯特的拍卖品网站始于 2003 年，通过 4 500 起在线拍卖，为非营利组织筹集了将近 4 600 万美元的资金。与其他举办方类似，希马凯特从每场成功的交易中获得 9% 的提成，接近 4 500 美元，其他部分则直接捐给慈善机构。除了帮助非营利机构省时省钱之外，在线拍卖通常吸引更广泛的观众群——他们随着投标价的上升持续几周营造舆论氛围。最棒的是拍卖所筹措资金的使用不受限制，所以它可以用于营运花销，而直接捐赠人通常青睐特定的项目。

尽管网上拍卖很成功，但大部分的慈善捐助仍然选择离线交易。根据《慈善年鉴》2008 年的调查报告，去年通过网上拍卖所筹措的 11 亿美元只占总筹集资金的 1% 。总的在线筹集的资金包括所有通过慈善网站捐赠的资金，而不仅仅是在线拍卖。而且慈善拍卖

Biddingforgood.com started in 2003 and has raised nearly $ 46 million for nonprofits through 4,500 online auctions. Similar to other hosts, cMarket gets 9% of sold items, up to $ 4,500; the rest goes directly to the charity. Besides helping nonprofits save time and money, online auctions often attract a broader audience —and they can build buzz for weeks as bids rise. Best of all, the money is typically unrestricted, so it can be used for operational costs; direct donors often favor specific programs.

As successful as online auctions are, though, most charitable① giving still happens off-line. The $ 1.1 billion in gifts on the Web last year made up just 1% of overall fund-raising, according to a 2008 survey by the Chronicle② of Philanthropy③. And the online total includes giving through all charity Web sites, not just online auctions. But charity auctions aren't the only new way the Web is being used to raise money. Fund-raisers are increasingly tapping social-media tools and sites such as Facebook, and Presidential candidates Barack Obama and John McCain have sophisticated Web fund-raising operations. This month, Charitybuzz is auctioning a painting of Obama by artist Shepard Fairey with the word "hope" beneath it. Proceeds will benefit the Rush Philanthropic Arts Foundation, a group founded by hip-hop mogul Russell Simmons that exposes disadvantaged urban youth to the arts. The current high bid? $ 108,000 and counting.

(675 words)

---

① charitable [ˈtʃæritəbl] *adj.* 慈善的，仁爱的

② chronicle [ˈkrɔnikl] *n.* 年鉴

③ philanthropy [fiˈlænθrəpi] *n.* 慈善活动，慈善事业

也并不是网络被用来集资的唯一新方式。募捐者正在越来越多地选择社会媒介工具和 Facebook 之类的网站，总统候选人巴拉克·奥巴马和约翰·麦肯锡都有复杂完善的网上募款运营机制。“慈善闲谈”本月正在拍卖艺术家西帕得·法雷绘制的奥巴马画像，画像的下方有“希望”字样。拍卖收益将使“拉什慈善艺术基金会”获利，这是一个由嘻哈派的巨头拉赛尔·西蒙斯建立的组织，使城市的弱势年轻群体能够接触到艺术。目前的最高标价达到了多少呢？108 000美元，并且还在继续上升。

知识链接

eBay “电子湾”是一个可让全球民众上网买/卖物品的线上拍卖/购物网站。每天都有数以百万的家具、收藏品、电脑、车辆在 eBay 上被刊登、贩售、卖出。有些物品稀有且珍贵，然而大部分的物品可能只是个满布灰尘、看起来毫不起眼的小玩意。这些物品常被他人忽略，但如果能在全球性的大市场贩售，那么其身价就有可能水涨船高。只要物品不违反法律或是在 eBay 的禁止贩售清单之内，即可以在 eBay 刊登贩售。服务及虚拟物品也在可贩售物品的范围之内。eBay 推翻了以往那种规模较小的跳蚤市场，将买家与卖家拉在一起，创造了一个永不休息的市场。

Facebook “脸谱网”是一个社交网络服务网站。网站的名字 Facebook 来自传统的纸质“花名册”。通常美国的大学和预科学校把这种印有学校社区所有成员的“花名册”发放给新入学或入职的学生和教职员，协助大家认识学校内其他成员，这就是 Facebook 过去、现在和将来一直要维持的原则和理念。Facebook 于 2004 年 2 月 4 日上线，是美国排名第一的照片分享站点，每天上载 850 万张照片，向用户提供和好友分享与互联的最好工具。Facebook 的用户人数已经覆盖全球各大洲，甚至包括南极洲。

题记

英国人正在转向选择互联网进行便捷地购物，并且在网上寻找更具价值的商品。城市中心的传统零售商将他们的部分市场份额丧失给网络零售竞争对手，因为网络零售商能够根据用户需求提供更为广泛的商品和支持信息。与此同时，网上购物凸显出来的问题也正在不断涌现，本文告诉消费者如何采取简单的步骤保护自己，即使与最大的零售商打交道，也要防止上当受骗或陷入交易往来中的骗局。消费者可以掌握有效的防病毒软件来保护自己、检查销售商的客户评级和使用智能卡付款，使互联网购物朝着有利于消费者的方向发展。

Securing Shopping Online

Shopping online is rapidly becoming the preferred mode of bargain hunting for many. In the last year Britons spent a whopping[1] £55.3 billion via the web—an increase of roughly a third on the previous year—and Britons have already dropped £13 billion into web retailers' tills in the first three months of this year, according to IMRG, the trade body for UK online retailers. The problem is, as spending increases, fraud and the number of online Del Boys trying to relieve us of our cash. Losses from "card not present" fraud, where criminals use stolen credit card details to buy goods online or over the phone, are approaching £300m a year, warns Apacs, the banking payments trade body.

The good news is that there are plenty of simple steps you can take to protect yourself from the scammers or from finding yourself at the sharp end of practices by even the biggest retailers. We'll show you how to enjoy the best of the global bazaar yet steer clear of any infected web pages, pay for goods securely and unearth the best guides to your extensive consumer rights if it does all go wrong.

---

① whopping [ˈwɔpiŋ] *adj.* 巨大的

保护网上购物

网上购物正迅速成为许多人买便宜货的首选方式。 去年，英国人的上网消费达到了553亿英镑的庞大数额，比前一年大约增长了三分之一。 英国在线零售商的一个贸易机构 IMRG 声称，仅在今年的第一个季度，英国人就已经将130亿英镑放进网上零售商的钱柜。 但问题是随着消费的增加，欺诈和试图偷盗我们现金的在线“德尔男孩”现象正在不断涌现。 银行付款贸易机构的雅柏克斯警告说，由“卡不存在”欺诈行为导致的损失一年已达300万英镑之多，这是犯罪分子使用盗窃的信用卡的详细资料在网上或通过电话购物的惯用伎俩。

好消息是你可以采取很多简单的步骤保护自己，即使与最大的零售商打交道，也要防止上当受骗或陷入交易往来中的骗局。 我们会向你展示如何避开受感染的网页，享受最佳的全球市场，即使网络完全出了差错，也要保证安全付款购物，找出最好的方法来维护广泛的消费者权利。

网站看起来是和谐的，但仍然充满秽浊之物，它们总是等待着伏击那些手无寸铁的顾客。 一种正在增长的趋势是骗子利用一个看起来有名的虚假网站引诱你，然后盗取你的信用卡详细信息，这种做法被称为“嫁接”。 其他人则试图让你的计算机在无意中下载躲

Securing Shopping Online

The web can seem benign, but it is full of nastiness lying in wait to ambush[①] the unprotected shopper. A growing trend is for scammers to lure you to a fake website that looks like a well known site and then steal your credit card details — a practice known as "pharming". Others try to get your computer to inadvertently download dodgy software (or "malware") that later steals your personal details. Even legitimate websites have been "injected" with similar malware. So how should you protect yourself? Get Safe Online (www.getsafeonline.org), the government-backed consumer website, is a crucial pit stop. It advises you to always download the latest version of your web browser as these have built-in filters than can spot many fake websites. To be sure of exactly which site you are visiting, download and install SpoofStick (free at www.spoofstick.com), which will then display the real name of the website in the top of your browser window. Antivirus[②] software and a firewall are also must-haves. Yet a YouGov poll for Get Safe Online found more than a fifth of UK internet users didn't employ a firewall and a sixth lacked antivirus software. Many companies sell a bloated suite of internet security software that often slows your computer down. So before you rush to invest, take advice on what you need. The market for one-stop security suites is competitive but ZoneAlarm 7 (£40 from www.zonealarm.com) is hard to beat. Many providers offer free versions of specific software in the hope you will buy their full package later. AVG antivirus from Grisoft (www.grisoft.com) is an excellent program that even

---

① ambush [ˈæmbʊʃ] *vt.* 埋伏

② antivirus [ˌæntiˈvairəs] *n.* 〈计〉反病毒程序

闪软件（或“恶意软件”），后来抢断你的个人信息。即使是合法网站也会被“插入”类似的恶意软件。因此，应该如何保护自己？登陆政府支持的消费网站“在线安全网（www.getsafeonline.org）”，这是一个至关重要的交易场地。它建议你总是下载最新版本的网页浏览器，因为这些浏览器有内置的过滤器可以当场辨认许多虚假网站。为了确保受访网站的准确性，下载并安装 SpoofStick 软件（在 www.spoofstick.com 网站上免费），然后在网站浏览器的窗口顶部将显示真实站名。防病毒软件和防火墙也是必须有的。然而“安全在线”的政府民调显示，超过五分之一的英国互联网用户没有采用防火墙，六分之一的用户缺乏防病毒软件。许多公司销售臃肿的成套互联网安全软件，往往减慢了计算机的速度。所以在仓促投资之前，要征求他人意见，看你到底需要什么。尽管一站式的安全套件市场具有竞争力，但 ZoneAlarm7 程序（花 40 英镑即可从 www.zonealarm.com 网站购买）也很难被击败。许多供应商提供特定的软件的免费版本是希望你以后能购买他们的整套软件。Grisoft（www.grisoft.com）发行的 AVG 防病毒软件是一个卓越的程序，它甚至能自动扫描链接搜索结果，检查他们是否链接到已知的欺骗性网站。“麦卡菲网站顾问”（www.siteadvisor.com）是一个不引人注目的工具，它使用一个交通灯系统，在你点击进入网站之前警告你该网站的合法性。想获得免费的防火墙或间谍软件保护吗？请尝试克魔岛防火墙（tinyurl.com/yuvt5k）或间谍软件终结者（www.spywareterminator.com）吧。

四分之一的网购者不会检查他们访问的网站是不是一个购物安全的地方。如果你使用比价网站淘宝，如价格对比引擎（www.pricerunner.co.uk），购物网站（uk.shopping.com）或购物比较网站

automatically scans links on search results to see if they lead to known scammer sites. McAfee Site Advisor (www. siteadvisor. com) is an unobtrusive① tool that uses a traffic-light system to warn you about the validity of any link before you click on it. Want a free firewall or spyware protection? Try Comodo Firewall Pro (tinyurl.com/yuvt5k) or Spyware Terminator (www.spywareterminator.com).

One in four online shoppers don't check if a website they are visiting is a safe place to shop. If you are out to snaffle② a bargain using a price-comparison website such as Pricerunner (www. pricerunner. co. uk), Shopping.com (uk.shopping.com) or Kelkoo (www.kelkoo.co.uk) you can check an retailer's customer ratings before you hand over any money. It's also worth considering how many reviews a site has received; the more the better. There are also vetting schemes you can consult such as Shopsafe (www. shopsafe. co. uk), which has checked out more than 3, 000 shops and rated them for their range of goods, delivery costs and security. Similarly look for the Internet Shopping Is Safe (ISIS) logo from IMRG (www. imrg. org/isis). IMRG also vets more than 1, 000 accredited retailers for reliability, data protection and security, and excludes any that don't come up to scratch. Always click on any accreditation scheme logos to check they are live links and not pictures put up by dodgy retailers trying to look legitimate. Consumer Direct (www. consumerdirect.gov.uk) warns that just because a website has a uk web address it isn't necessarily based in Britain, so check for a physical

---

① unobtrusive [ˈʌnəbˈtruːsiv] *adj.* 不冒昧的

② snaffle [ˈsnæfl] *vt.* 搜索,寻找

（www.kelkoo.co.uk），你可以先检查销售商的客户评级，然后再付款。网站得到多少评价值得考虑，当然越多越好。你还可以咨询诸如安全购物网（www.shopsafe.co.uk）的数据审查方案，该网站已经检查了3 000多家商店，并为他们的各种商品、运输成本和保障安全定级。同样可在互动媒体零售集团（www.imrg.org / isis）上查找网络购物安全（ISIS）标识。互动媒体零售集团也审查了1 000多个质量合格的零售商的信誉、数据保护和安全措施，并排除了所有不达标的零售商。经常点击认证项目的标识，检查他们的实时链接状态，不要点击奸诈的零售商挂在网上的图片，那些只是看上去似乎合法。消费者指南（www.consumerdirect.gov.uk）警告说，仅仅因为某个网站有一个uk网址并不能说明它的总部一定设在英国，所以要查清楚它是否有实际地址和避免不公开的网站。从国外购物的风险更大，因为英国的消费者保护法不适用，如果出问题很难获得赔偿。

在线付款时应检查该公司是否有安全、加密的链接，在网站地址的浏览器窗口有一个封闭的挂锁标志和https://。最新的网络浏览器现在也变更地址栏的颜色，以表明它是否安全。尽管网上欺诈呈猖獗的上升趋势，但信用卡支付仍然很有意义。根据《消费品信用贷款法》，如果价值在100英镑和30 000英镑之间的商品没有到货或质量低劣，你的损失将得到补偿。作为一个额外的安全等级，注册由万事达信用卡安全码（www.mastercard.com）提供、维萨信用卡（www.visaeurope.com）计划验证的特别个人身份号码或密码安保措施。但是，你必须清楚，美国运通、预付维萨卡和万事达卡的借记卡未被涵盖在这种行为之内。中介服务，如贝宝（www.paypal.

address and avoid sites that don't publish one. Buying from abroad is riskier because UK consumer law doesn't apply and getting redress can be difficult if things go wrong.

When making a payment online, check that the company has a secure, encrypted① connection, indicated by a closed padlock② symbol in the browser window and https:// in the website's address. The latest web browsers now also change the colour of the address bar to indicate whether it is secure. Despite the rampant③ rise of online fraud, paying with a credit card still makes sense. Under the Consumer Credit Act you are covered for your loss if goods valued between £100 and £30, 000 don't show up or are faulty. As an additional level of security, sign up for the extra Pin/password security measures offered by the Mastercard SecureCode (www. mastercard. com) and verified by Visa (www. visaeurope. com) schemes. However, be aware that debit cards, American Express and prepaid Visa and Mastercards are not covered by the act. Middleman services such as PayPal (www. paypal. com) or Moneybookers (www.moneybookers.com) can handle online payments for you so that a retailer never sees your personal details. Though these services are free for customers, once again you lose a whole layer of legal protection compared with paying by credit card.

(925 words)

---

① encrypt [inˈkript] *vt.* 译成密码,编码
② padlock [ˈpædlɔk] *n.* 挂锁,扣锁
③ rampant [ˈræmpənt] *adj.* 猖狂的

com）或 Moneybookers（www.moneybookers.com），可以为你处理在线支付，而零售商绝不会看到你的个人资料。虽然这些服务对顾客都是免费的，但是与信用卡付款相比，你再次失去了整个层面的法律保护。

知识链接

ZoneAlarm 是一款优秀的防火墙软件。只要在安装时填入相关资料，安装完后重新开机，ZoneAlarm 就会自动启动并执行任务。它允许自由设置所有程序连接互联网，也可以设定锁定网络的时间，还可利用它查看开机后使用的网络资源。这些方法锁住网络不让任何程序通过，只有操作者核准的软件才可以通行无阻。

Grisoft 于 1991 年成立，总部在捷克，在德国和美国都有分公司。Grisoft 集中于提供防护免受计算机病毒攻击的软件解决方案。它的主要焦点是在软件市场上提供最全面和最安全的计算机软件系统的保护，其 AVG Anti-Virus System 抗病毒系列产品是欧洲有名的杀毒软件，在功能上相当完整：可即时对任何存取文件侦测，防止电脑病毒感染；可对电子邮件和附加文件进行扫描，防止电脑病毒通过电子邮件和附加文件传播；"病毒资料库"记录电脑病毒的特性和发作日期等相关资讯；"开机保护"可在电脑开机时侦测开机型病毒，防止开机型病毒感染。

题 记

互联网以迅雷不及掩耳之势催生出了无数的新兴产业，而商业应用、商业营销以及商业信息流也随之经历了脱胎换骨的改变。虚拟世界在全球性跨国公司中日益彰显出重要的作用，它缩小了公司众多员工由于地理位置造成的文化和距离差距，大幅提升了遍布全球的员工的工作效率。IBM 已经挤入“第二生命”领域，寻求建立三维互联网和虚拟企业的潜在机会。尽管在了解清楚虚拟世界营销的潜力和局限之前，IBM 尚无法确定这项业务的投资回报率，但它的在线空间已经成功地超越了品牌知名度的范畴，创下“三维网络”虚拟世界营销的奇迹。

The Virtual Global Marketing

Moving beyond Second Life marketing, many companies are infiltrating virtual worlds for employee meetings, mixers, and recruiting. It's not always easy to get new employees to mix well with co-workers—especially when they're scattered across the globe or speak different languages. Few companies know this as well as IBM, the computer services provider that last year alone added 20,000 new staff members, many from Brazil, China, India, and Russia.

But IBM may have found a way to overcome new employees' geographic and cultural barriers. When the Armonk (N.Y.) company can't get recent hires to mingle in person, it has them interact virtually, using the same kind of 3D technology that runs virtual worlds such as Linden Lab's Second Life. "It makes you want to start relationships," says Chuck Hamilton, manager of new media and learning, a division that uses social media to foster collaboration. "People who are farther away—this is especially true of people who are not American-centric—get the feeling that they're not isolated."

Using software from Activeworlds, IBM builds virtual work spaces that let workers in far-flung regions use avatars①, or graphic representations

① avatar [ævəˈtɑː] *n.* 头像

虚拟全球销售

许多公司正在步入虚拟世界，召开员工会议、开展社交活动和招聘员工，进入“第二人生”营销。通常情况下，让新员工和其合作者良好相处并不是件容易的事——尤其是当他们散布在世界各地或者讲着不同语言的时候。很少有公司能够像 IBM 这样清晰地了解这种情况，这位计算机服务提供商仅去年一年就新增了 2 万名员工，其中许多来自巴西、中国、印度和俄罗斯。

但是 IBM 可能已经找到了一种克服新员工地域和文化障碍的方法。当纽约的阿蒙克公司不能确保其新员工亲自参与交往的时候，他们采用菩提树实验室“第二人生”那样运作虚拟世界的三维技术，让员工使用虚拟方式相互交际。新媒体与学习部经理查克·汉密尔顿认为：“它使得你想建立起人际关系。那些遥远地方的人们，尤其是那些非美国主流群体的人们，会有一种不被孤立的感觉。”他的部门主要是利用社交媒体来培养协作。

IBM 利用来自 Activeworlds 的软件，建立了虚拟工作空间，确保远距离的雇员能够借助头像或是他们自己的图像标志处理诸如排练演讲或了解雇员福利等工作。这种试验使 IBM 成为各大公司的先行者，由于已经测试了在“第二人生”这样的网站环境上营销的限度，这种环境正在渗透虚拟世界，并用来应对一系列其他的活动，

of themselves, to handle such tasks as rehearsing① presentations or learning about employee benefits. The experimentation puts IBM in the vanguard② of companies that, having tested the limits of marketing in such online environments as Second Life, are now infiltrating virtual worlds to tackle a range of other activities, from meetings to collaboration, from training to employee recruiting.

First Came Virtual Marketing. At companies like Sun Microsystems, where upwards of 50% of employees may work outside traditional office spaces on any given day, virtual worlds can help scattered colleagues forge closer bonds. "It's difficult to maintain a global corporate culture with people so spread around," says Nicole Yankelovich, principal investigator at Sun Labs, who says the ethos can vary on Sun campuses from Menlo Park, Calif., to Burlington, Mass. "Virtual world technology is a way to bring the company together to build a global corporate culture where people are on equal footing," she says. At least that's the hope. Most big companies, including IBM, Sun, Xerox, Cisco Systems, Unilever, are still in the early stages of using online 3D technology. Many companies embarked③ on virtual world exploration through Second Life marketing campaigns, but some were disappointed with the results. The chances of would-be customers seeing a company's Second Life branding, much less interacting with it, are often slim.

As of the present, there were more than 13.4 million residents of Second Life, but only 340, 623 had logged on in the previous seven days.

---

① rehearse [riˈhəːs] *vt.* 预演,排演

② vanguard [ˈvængɑːd] *n.* 先锋,先驱

③ embark [imˈbɑːk] *vi.* 着手,从事

包括从举办会议到协调合作，从训练技能到员工招聘。

虚拟营销首次来临。在太阳计算机系统这样的公司，任何指定的日子大约会有超过50%的雇员在传统办公室以外的空间工作，虚拟世界能够帮助分散的同事结成紧密关系。太阳实验室的首席调查员尼科尔·洛维奇说，“因为员工分散，很难维系一种全球性的企业文化”。他认为从加利福尼亚州的门洛·帕克到马萨诸塞州的伯灵顿，太阳公司系统内的精神特质可以多样化。她说：“虚拟世界技术是一种方法，它把公司集合起来，建立一种人人拥有平等地位的全球企业文化”。至少这是一种希望。许多大公司，包括IBM、太阳计算机系统、施乐、思科系统、联合利华仍处在使用三维技术的初级阶段。许多公司主要通过“第二人生”营销活动来实现虚拟世界的探究，但是一些公司对其结果感到失望。看到公司“第二人生”品牌的潜在客户的几率通常很渺茫，更不用说与它结合起来了。

截至目前，“第二人生”已经拥有超过1 340万居民，但只有340 623名居民在刚过去的7天内注册。那些使用者依次扩散到6.5万多英亩的范围，所以任何地方的徒步交通——比如说在一个打有品牌烙印的岛屿，都会畅通无阻。虚拟世界咨询公司的创始人兼首席执行官戴夫·厄尔科尼斯说，“当公司开始在‘第二人生’上营销时我们看到泡沫是很正常的，现在公司正在进入内部企业使用没有外部市场营销那么公开的阶段。在‘第二人生’或其他虚拟世界上营销的人数还不是很多”。

建筑师乔恩·布拉库德两年来一直使用“第二人生”帮助他在威斯康星州的小型麦迪逊公司——克里桑多设计公司——的客户处理业务，虚拟他们房屋的原型设计。客户能够使用虚拟模型测试油

Those users in turn are spread out over 65, 000 virtual acres, so foot traffic in any particular place—say, on a company's branded island—tends to be light. "It's fair to say we saw a bubble when companies began to market in Second Life, and now companies are entering less publicly but for internal enterprise use than for external marketing," says Dave Elchoness, founder and CEO of VRWorkplace, a virtual world consulting firm. "There's not a large population for marketing in Second Life or other virtual worlds".

Architect Jon Brouchoud has used Second Life for about two years to help clients of his small Madison (Wis.) firm, Crescendo Design, visualize what their homes might look like. Clients can use the virtual model to test paint colors, material types, furniture layouts, and landscaping options. Brouchoud has also met with builders inside the virtual model for real-time discussions and has collaborated with a British client to design a project he was developing in the U.S. "As the housing market declines, we have stayed very busy with commissions developing virtual architecture for several companies and universities," he says.

But is using virtual world technology cost-effective? Marketing can be expensive: According to a estimate by Parks Associates, companies spent $ 15 million advertising in virtual worlds in the U.S. this year and the figure is expected to rise tenfold by 2012. Other pursuits are less pricey①. The costs of creating a virtual world mainly reflect the time to build and customize an environment, according to Forrester Research (FORR). "Our goal has been to say that for a whole pilot for a year they better be able to do it for $ 10, 000," says Greg Nuyens, CEO of

---

① pricey [ˈpraisi] *adj.* 昂贵的

漆色彩、材料类型、家具布局和园景选择。布拉库德也同虚拟模型中的建筑师见面，举行实时讨论，他已经与一位英国客户合作设计了一项正在美国实施的工程。他说：“当房屋市场不景气时，我们却非常忙，代理了几家公司和大学虚拟建筑的开发。”

但是，使用虚拟世界技术有成本效益吗？营销可能耗资巨大：根据帕克斯公司统计，今年美国公司共花费 1 500 万美元在虚拟世界上做广告，而这个数字到 2012 年有可能增长 10 倍。其他的经营不会有这么昂贵。弗雷斯特研究公司（FORR）认为，创建虚拟世界的成本主要反映在建立和规制用户环境的时间上。Qwaq 公司的总裁雷格·纽恩说，“我们的目标是在一年内，他们能够用 1 万美元完成整个试验任务”。他的公司重点研究较低端的图像以保持低成本。纽恩说，希望更加精心制作的公司可以花更多的资金与其他卖主交易。

许多涉猎在线世界的公司仍在考虑，这种低廉经营的成本和能耗是否物有所值。专家认为，“第二人生”和类似的人造环境无法复制现实世界的交互作用，或者解决拥有分散员工的公司突然出现的大量合作问题。《联合虚拟劳动力》的作者克伦·索贝尔·罗杰斯科说：“虚拟世界能够使共同工作的人略微做得更好一些。”她认为，除去考虑将员工联系在一起的技术，经理主管人员仍然需要发挥重要作用，帮助人们缩小文化、社会和关系差距。

尽管这些新的数字世界可能未被证实，IBM 仍然乐于采用虚拟世界技术。公司已经启动一期指导项目，鼓励已退休或将要退休的员工与新来的员工分享知识。许多该项目的成员利用虚拟世界相互接触、指导和做演讲。从全球范围看，IBM 发现虚拟世界正在开始帮助缩小文化和距离差距。IBM 的汉密尔顿说，虚拟世界真的促使

Qwaq, which focuses on lower-end graphics to keep costs down. Companies that want something more elaborate can spend much more with other vendors, Nuyens says.

Many of the companies dabbling① in these online worlds have yet to determine whether even inexpensive pursuits are worth the cost and energy. Experts say Second Life and similarly artificial environments can't replicate real-world interaction or solve many of the collaboration problems that crop up in companies with geographically scattered employees. "Virtual worlds...can make it somewhat better for people who work together," says Karen Sobel Lojeski, author of Uniting the Virtual Workforce. Executives still need to play a key role in helping people bridge cultural, social, and relationship gaps, regardless of the technologies that connect employees, she says.

As unproven as these new digitized worlds may be, IBM is adopting virtual world technologies with gusto②. The company has begun a mentoring program that encourages people who are retired or are about to retire to share knowledge with newer employees. Many in the program are using virtual worlds to meet, mentor, and make presentations. Globally, IBM is finding that virtual worlds are starting to help bridge culture and distance. IBM's Hamilton says virtual worlds actually make employees want to start working relationships with one another, adding, "Geography doesn't seem to be the barrier it once was."

(941 words)

---

① dabble [ˈdæbl] *v.* 涉猎

② gusto [ˈɡʌstəu] *n.* 爱好,嗜好

员工愿意开始与他人建立工作关系，而且，“曾经是障碍的地理位置似乎再也不存在了”。

知识链接

IBM 国际商业机器公司(International Business Machines Corporation)，总公司在纽约州阿蒙克市，是全球最大的信息技术和业务解决方案公司，业务遍及160多个国家和地区。IBM目前拥有全球雇员30多万人。该公司创立时的主要业务为商用打字机，然后转为文字处理机，并进军计算机领域。IBM为计算机产业长期的领导者，在大型/小型机和便携机(ThinkPad)方面的成就最为瞩目。其创立的个人计算机标准，至今仍被不断地沿用和发展。IBM还在材料、化学、物理等科学领域有很大造诣。硬盘技术即为IBM所发明，扫描隧道显微镜(STM)、铜布线技术、原子蚀刻技术也为IBM研究院发明。在将近一百年的时间里，世界经济不断发展，IBM始终以超前的技术、出色的管理和独树一帜的产品领导着全球信息工业的发展。

Second Life “第二人生”是一个基于互联网的虚拟世界。通过由Linden实验室开发的一个可下载的客户端程序，用户在游戏里叫做“居民”，可以通过可运动的虚拟化身互相交往。这套程序还在一个通常的元宇宙的基础上提供了一个高层次的社交网络服务。居民们可以四处逛逛，会碰到其他的居民，社交，参加个人或集体活动，制造和相互交易虚拟财产和服务。瑞典等国家在“第二人生”中建立了自己的大使馆，IBM在“第二人生”中建立了自己的销售中心，CNN在“第二人生”中建立了自己的游戏报纸以提高自己的影响力……越来越多的公司和个人正在“第二人生”的游戏中创造财富。

题记

新一代运营支撑系统推进了电信运营的战略转型，传统意义上将语音业务、电话业务、视频多媒体业务整合的“三网合一”已经无法满足电信计费系统的需要。在“三网”的基础上融入无线业务，形成“四网合一”已经成为致力于开发新的服务与产品捆绑的移动运营发展方向。无线交易带给广大用户领先全球的产品及服务，它的支付方式就是随身携带收集虚拟钱包，却包容了各种各样的付款机制：现金、信用卡、借记卡、商店的账户卡、航空公司的会员卡以及进入健身房之类的地方需要的卡。纸币和支票作为日常支付的方式将会重蹈黄金和白银的覆辙被时代淘汰，但是无线交易仍然需要技术升级和卖主、商人及金融机构之间的合作来推动行业的发展。

Wireless Transactions

From the race to 3G to spectrum auctions to handset[1] compatibility, wireless providers have very full plates. Yet in that rush for new revenue opportunities, the ability to pay for a small-ticket item such as a ringtone download is fairly high on the list. "I've seen the temperature change," says Cynthia Hswe, senior analyst at the Strategis Group. "In the beginning, people were really hot about mobile payment and m-commerce, because they saw it as one of the few ways in which they'd actually make money off the wireless Internet. They understood that end users wouldn't be happy about paying for access and paying for content, so they perceived m-commerce as a way of driving off some revenue." That attitude has cooled off over the past few months, and now operators are starting to realize that they can make money from m-commerce but that users aren't going to buy big-ticket items. "Mobile payments will be made on goods that are urgent, habitual and small-ticket," she says. "I think even a $20 book is too much."

① handset [ˈhændset] *n.* 手机

无线交易

从随机存取计算机装置到3G到频谱拍卖到手机的兼容性，无限服务提供了非常完整的板块。然而在新的盈利机会涌现的时候，手机铃声下载之类的小额商品支付能力公然高居榜首。策略集团的高级分析师辛西娅·赫斯维说：“我已经看到了温度的变化。一开始，人们十分热衷移动支付和移动商务，因为他们认为这是极少数他们能真正用无线上网服务赚钱的途径之一。他们清楚终端用户对支付路径和内容不会感到高兴，所以他们察觉到移动商务是一种规避税收的方式。”这种态度在过去的几个月中已经开始降温，现在运营商开始意识到，他们可以通过移动商务赚钱，但是用户不会购买大件商品。辛西娅说：“移动支付用于紧迫的、惯常的和小额商品。我认为甚至用20美元买书都太贵了。”

AT&T公司无线网路口袋化服务商业发展部的负责人克里斯·科恩认为，“你需要一个令人信服的理由来购买物品”。科恩说，AT&T公司优先考虑移动商务，AT&T的网路口袋化服务公司目前允许客户通过信用卡交易从Barnes & Noble等公司购买商品。AT&T公司目前正在开发一个无线钱包的产品，但该公司拒绝评论具体细节和何时投入使用。

即使移动服务供应商正在狂热地驾驭移动支付浪潮，终端用户

"You need a compelling reason to buy," says Kris Cone, director of business development for AT&T Wireless' PocketNet service. Cone says that m-commerce has been a priority for AT&T, whose PocketNet service currently allows customers to purchase goods from merchants such as Barnes & Noble through credit card transactions. AT&T is currently developing a wireless wallet product, but the company can't comment on specifics or when it might be available.

Even if mobile service providers are working feverishly① to ride the mobile payment wave, will end users be interested in this new form of payment? The answer seems to be mixed. Many people have yet to make their first purchase through the wired Internet, yet others are already willing to purchase goods through their phones. The Strategis Group surveyed 500 wireless users about how comfortable they would be with purchasing goods and services over their wireless phones. 41 percent said they were extremely, very or somewhat comfortable, while 59 percent said they weren't very or at all comfortable. The Strategis Group also asked the wireless users how they would want to pay for a transaction. 36 percent wanted to charge purchases to a credit card, 35 percent wanted it added to their monthly wireless bills, 20 percent wanted it debited② from a bank account and 9 percent wanted it to be taken from a special online account that the end user had set up. However, it will take time for

① feverishly [ˈfiːvəriʃli] *adv.* 兴奋地

② debit [ˈdebit] *vt.* 记入借方

会对这种新的支付方式感兴趣吗？ 答案似乎好坏参半。 许多人还没有开始通过有线网络购物，而有些人已经乐意通过电话购物。策略集团调查了500名无线用户，询问他们通过无线电话购物和获取服务的舒适度。 41%的人说他们极其、非常或有一些舒服，而59%的人说他们不是非常或完全不舒服。 策略集团也征求了无线用户们的意见，调查他们希望怎样进行交易付款。 36%的人想用信用卡购物，35%的人想将购物款加在每月的无线账单上，20%的人想记入银行账单，还有9%的人希望从终端用户已经建立的一种特殊在线账户上扣款。 但是，用户还需要时间克服安全顾虑和其他的麻烦。 赛论特通讯公司一份题为“无线支付：无处不在”的报告估计，全球范围内移动支付用户的数量将从现在的460万增加到6 100万。 有了这样一个大幅度增长的海市蜃楼，从移动运营商到结算公司到无线钱包卖主等业内人士都非常专注地寻找付款系统的下一步发展。

很多移动运营商甚至提供最基本的无线网络通道，他们拥有自己的团队策划新的付款方案。 今天，移动用户通常可以输入一个信用卡号码，然后进入微型浏览器完成交易，但这并不是最佳方案。开发无线钱包技术的iPIN公司总裁布拉德·罗德说：“如果你考虑一下认证发生的方式，你就不能避免现存系统围绕文件流失构建的事实。 它基于这样的理念，即你必须站在有资格的办事员之前——这些不能使电子交易达到最优化的程度。 新要求越来越难以填补这些现有系统。”

无线钱包的思想将会在很大程度上扩展信用卡号码输入手机的概念，从根本上给予用户选择的权利，与他们习以为常、随身携带

users to get over any security concerns and other tribulations. A report from Celent Communications entitled "Wireless Payments: Into Thin Air," estimates that the number of mobile payment users worldwide will increase from the current 4.6 million to 61 million. With such a substantial increase looming on the horizon, industry players from the mobile operators to billing companies to wireless wallet vendors① are all looking very intently at this next evolution in payment systems.

Most mobile operators that offer even the most rudimentary② of wireless Web access have teams working on these new payment schemes. Today, mobile users generally can type in a credit card number into their microbrowser to complete a transaction, but this is not considered optimal. "You can't escape the fact that the existing systems are structured around paper flow if you look at the way authentication③ occurs," says Brad Rode, CEO of iPIN, which develops wireless wallet technology. "It's predicated on the notion that you'll stand in front of a clerk with credentials—something that's not optimized for electronic transactions. New requirements are growing increasingly difficult to fill with these existing systems."

The idea of wireless wallets would greatly expand on the idea of entering credit card numbers into a cell phone and basically give users

---

① vendor [ˈvendɔː] *n.* 卖主
② rudimentary [ruːdiˈmentəri] *a.* 基本的
③ authentication [ɔːθentiˈkeiʃən] *n.* 证明,鉴定

的钱包几乎不差分毫。Convergys 公司在日内瓦技术分部的无线市场策略经理克里斯·梅里克说:“当你打开钱包时,就会面对各种各样的付款机制,你有现金、信用卡、借记卡、商店的账户卡、航空公司的会员卡,以及进入健身房之类的地方需要的卡。我想选择如何进行付账,虚拟钱包将会包括许多的付款方式。”但是界定交易种类、使用哪种方式付款可能是一个很大的挑战。举例来说,下载一个 25 美分的铃声只需通过每月的电话账单缴费,但是用信用卡买书则更加合适。无论选择什么,有一点很清楚:移动服务供应商是操纵商务决策的关键人士。

iPIN 公司的罗德认为,不管采用何种付款方式,交易都是由类似的过程组成。首先是客户身份的鉴定和证明,将用户名或密码输入手机。其次,交易需要得到授权。罗德说:“交易过程在网上进行,涉及资金来源,既要确保资金的存在,也要能获得有关结算规则的信息。资金来源可以多方面,如银行账户、信用卡、礼品卡或储值账户。”交易的第三步涉及结账和资金清算,第四步是客户支持和服务。

从安全的角度看,处于移动服务供应商控制的中央服务器监控下的存储钱包功能合情合理,但仍然需要寻找移动服务供应商来试验不同的商业模式。梅里克强调,可能有手机付款信息的某些备选方案。“利用通用移动通信系统,你得到一个增强型的 SIM 卡,然后就可以储存授权给你的加密信息,甚至是电子现金。”在短短的几年里,纸币和支票作为日常支付的方式将会重蹈黄金和白银的覆辙。但是无线交易仍然需要技术升级和卖主、商人及金融机构之间的合作来做到这一点。

options that are very similar to those that exist within their regular, physical wallet. "When you open your wallet, you're confronted with a wide variety of payment mechanisms," says Chris Merrick, market strategy manager for wireless at Geneva Technology, a subsidiary of Convergys. "You have cash, credit cards, debit cards, store account cards, loyalty cards for airlines, and cards to gain entry to places like a gym. I want to choose how to pay, and the virtual wallet will encompass a number of methods." But defining which transactions get charged in which manner could be a big challenge. For example, downloading a 25-cent ringtone may be charged simply on the monthly phone bill. But a book purchase makes more sense on a credit card. Whatever the choices, it's fairly clear that the mobile service providers will be the ones driving the business decisions.

Regardless of type of payment, transactions consist of similar processes, according to iPIN's Rode. First, there's the identification and authentication of the customer, which could involve typing a username and/or password into the handset. Second, the transaction needs to be authorized. "This happens online and involves going to the source of funds, guaranteeing it exists, as well as getting information about settlement rules," Rode says. "The source of funds can be many things such as a bank account, credit cards, gift cards, or stored value accounts." The third piece of the transaction involves clearing and settlement of funds, and fourth is customer support and service.

知识链接

AT&T 美国电话电报公司(AT&T)创建于1877年，目前是美国最大的本地和长途电话公司，总部位于得克萨斯州圣安东尼奥。AT&T的前身是由电话发明人贝尔于1877年创建的美国贝尔电话公司。1984年，美国司法部依据《反托拉斯法》拆分AT&T，分拆出一个继承了母公司名称的新AT&T公司(专营长途电话业务)和七个本地电话公司(即“贝尔七兄弟”)，美国电信业从此进入了竞争时代。1995年，又从公司中分离出了从事设备开发制造的朗讯科技和NCR，只保留了通信服务业务。2000年以后，AT&T又先后出售了无线通信、有线电视和宽带通信部门。2005年，原“小贝尔”之一的西南贝尔对AT&T兼并，合并后的企业继承了AT&T的名称。

SIM 卡叫“用户识别卡”，它实际上是一张内含大规模集成电路的智能卡片，用来登记用户的重要数据和信息。SIM卡最重要的一项功能是进行鉴权和加密。当用户移动到新的区域拨打或接听电话时，交换机都要对用户进行鉴权，以确定是否为合法用户。这时，SIM卡和交换机同时利用鉴权算法，对鉴权密钥和8位随机数字进行计算，计算结果相同的，SIM卡被承认，否则SIM卡被拒绝，用户无法进行呼叫。

Convergys 公司（NYSE：CVG）总部设在美国俄亥俄州的辛辛那提，公司在全球设有客户联系中心、数据中心及办公室，拥有约75 000名员工。公司是标准普尔500强、财富1 000强企业，连续7年被《财富》杂志评为“最受尊敬的企业”。Convergys公司整合世界级的资源、软件和经验，帮助在客户和客户的客户间创建高价值的关系。Convergys公司为全球70多个国家的电信、有线电视和宽带服务、技术、金融服务以及下一代服务行业中的

From a security standpoint, storing wallet features at a central server controlled by the mobile service provider makes sense, but look for mobile service providers to experiment with different business models. Merrick adds that there may be some options for putting payment information on the handset. "With UMTS, you have an enhanced SIM card that you will be able to store encrypted[①] information for authorization and even electronic cash." In a few short years paper currency and checkbooks may go the way of gold and silver as forms of everyday payment. But it will take technology upgrades and significant cooperation among vendors, merchants, and financial institutions to make it happen.

(991 words)

① encrypt [inˈkript] *v.* 加密

领先企业提供其屡获殊荣的计费和客户服务产品。目前 Convergys 的软件每天为 1.2 亿多用户生产 150 多万张账单。同时，通过包括客服代表和基于 Web 通信在内的多渠道客户服务中心，Convergys 每天管理的客户活动超过 170 多万。

题 记

有这样一个平台，能够将各种形式的终端包括电脑、手机、商务通、寻呼机、传真机和电话机都可以实时与平台连接，获得任何所需的信息，享受任何相关的服务，真正实现任何时间、任何地点和任何方式的连接。这就是电子商务平台。电子商务语言在这个平台上迅速交换实时信息，世界各地的商贸活动在这个平台上交易流通，实体企业的零售商在这个平台上处理在线付款，特定的网站功能通路在这个平台上保证了客户的安全。电子商务平台就像一个穿越沙漠的旅人，在目标和现实之间设计好路径，保持着顾客的购买力。

The E-Commerce Platform

Doing business on the Web? You better know how to talk to the tech guys. Transacting business seamlessly① over the Internet means having a decent grasp of how things work, and more importantly, why they don't. Put another way, when the e-commerce standard is Amazon.com, small-business owners better bring some serious game.

That's why, with help from the smart folks at technology publisher O'Reilly Media, we've assembled a glossary of e-commerce-related tech terms that every entrepreneur should know. Some of that gobbledygook② is the province of tech jocks. However, if entrepreneurs want to achieve operational excellence while keeping technology investment in check, they have to be able to at least speak the language. And you don't have to know how to get down and dirty with computer code to understand the implications these issues have on strategy and budgeting. Online retailers, for example, are trying to move beyond what has become the conventional, rather static consumer experience. One solution: real-time,

① seamlessly[ˈsiːmlisli] *adv.* 无缝地

② gobbledygook [ˈgɔbəldIˈguːk] *n.* 冗长费解的话

电子商务平台

想要网上交易吗？ 你最好知道如何与技术人员交流。 在互联网上的无缝商务交易意味着必须要合适地掌握交易的进行方式，更重要的是，他们为什么不那么做。 换句话说，当电子商务的标准是亚马逊网站时，小公司企业主最好要慎重对待。

这就是我们在技术发行商奥莱理传媒公司的有识之士的帮助下，汇编与电子商务相关科技术语表的原因，因为这些都是每一位企业家应该知道的。 有些费解啰嗦的语言是技术领域里的行话。但是如果企业家想要在保持技术投资时实现卓越运营，他们至少要能够懂得专业术语。 你不必知道如何开始和处理计算机代码、从而弄明白这些事情对策略和预算编制的暗示。 例如，网上零售商会尽力去超越常规和相当静态的消费经验。 我们可以得出这样一个结论：实时、个性化定价。 尤比公司开发的一个新的系统让商家“意识”到顾客正在他们的网站上寻找哪些商品，还设计了一个建立在库存水平和其他细节基础上的自定义价格。 尤比公司的

individualized pricing. A new system, developed by uBee, allows merchants to "sense" what items a shopper is looking for on their Web sites, and spits out a custom price based on inventory levels and other particulars. "That," says uBee CEO Bill Carpenter, "can give you personalization between buyer and seller."

The e-commerce platform that UBee plans to launch will rely on SOAP, for Simple Object Access Protocol, a technology standard based on using "envelopes" that retailers and uBee use to exchange information quickly enough to make these real-time offers. The "documents" in these envelopes invariably are written in XML, the most common software language in e-commerce, including variants such as XML-RPC and XML Business Reporting Language. Another important building block of e-commerce infrastructure involves activities described by Web Services Description Language, or WSDL. For all the billions of dollars being spent and collected online, the code at the core of e-commerce remains highly fragmented — and that creates communication breakdowns within the overall system.

"The Internet is still the wild, wild west," said Clint Page, chief executive of Dotster, a Vancouver, Wash-based provider of Internet-business services. "It's not like more-developed parts of business and commerce where you get standardized platforms." One programming tactic is called messaging, which involves electronic documents from a

首席执行官比尔·卡朋特说："这可以让你实现买方和卖方之间的个性化。"

尤比公司计划推出的电子商务平台依靠的是简单对象访问协议，它是建立在运用"封袋"基础上的技术标准，零售商和尤比公司利用它来迅速地交换实时协议信息。这些封袋中的"文件"总是使用可扩展标记语言，这种语言是在电子商务中最通用的软件语言，包括 XML-RPC 和 XML-BRL 营业报告语言变体。另一个重要的电子商务基础设施的基本成分是网络服务描述语言，或简称为 WSDL。数十亿美元全在网络上消费和汇集，以代码为核心的电子商务依然高度分散化，这会造成整体系统的崩盘。

Dotster 公司的首席执行官、温哥华人克林特·佩吉是总部位于华盛顿的互联网商业服务提供者，他曾说："互联网仍然是蛮荒的西部，它不像你达到的标准化平台的交易和商务那样更发达的部分。"一种编程策略被称为信息程序，涉及从互联网服务到排列的电子文件，然后对每一信息定期分批处理。佩吉解释说："正是来往信息的流通可以使每个人都能明白正在被发送的信息，并能有效地进行交流。就好像如果我们其中的一个人讲法语，另一个人讲汉语，我们就不能交流了。因此，信息处理可以帮我们双方获得一个如拉丁语的中间语言。"

Web service to a queue that then processes each message in periodic batches①. "It's the flow of information back and forth so that everyone can understand what's being sent and can communicate effectively," explains Page. "It's sort of like, if one of us is speaking French, and the other one is speaking Chinese, we aren't able to communicate. So messaging helps us both get to a middle language like Latin."

Another still-unresolved tension among e-commerce architect is the choice between choreography② and orchestration③, both of which address how information moves around among, different companies. The choreographic process usually relies in part on messaging-oriented programming, and in an ideal world, says Page, choreography would reign: "Everyone would know the rules and play by them and information would just free flow. But we're so far away from that, and we need to crawl before we can walk."

While many of those programming challenges may seem at the subterranean④ level for most entrepreneurs, many other technology decisions demand more tangible, active involvement. Take setting up a merchant account with a bank so that you can accept and process online payments. While bricks-and-mortar⑤ retailers only have to decide

---

① batch [bætʃ] *n.* 程序组

② choreography [ˌkɔ(ː)riˈɔgrəfi] *n.* 舞台舞蹈

③ orchestration [ˌɔːkiˈstreiʃən] 管弦乐编曲

④ subterranean [sʌbtəˈreiniən] *adj.* 地下的,秘密的

⑤ bricks-and-mortar 实体的,具体的

另一个电子商务构建尚未解决的调节装置是舞蹈艺术和管弦乐编曲之间的选择，两者均提出了信息如何在不同公司流通的问题。舞蹈艺术处理通常部分依赖信息导向编程，佩吉认为，在理想的情况下，舞蹈艺术可能占有优势："每个人都应该了解、并遵守规则，而信息则免费流通。但我们离那种状态还很遥远，所以我们可能在行走之前需要学会爬行。"

尽管许多编程挑战对大多数的企业家来说似乎处于未知水平，许多其他的技术决定却需要更加实际地、积极地参与。在银行设立一个商业账户，这样你就可以接受并处理在线付款。实体企业的零售商只需要决定是否接受支票和主要的信用卡，电子商务可以接受所有其他可能的支付方式，包括电子支票、贝宝以及除美元之外的其他货币交易。

你还要了解联营公司项目的一两件事。在这些广告的安排下，公司收取现金，提高网站的交易量，反之亦然。佛罗里达州德拉海滩的美国作家和艺术家的网上营销主管丽贝卡·马特尔说："大约有70% 的在线业务是通过子公司进行的。人们在这里通过第二职业来寻求更好的生活。这些网站的运营像转售我们的计划一样。"她的子公司包括学习策略和南丁格尔·科南特。

然后是安全问题。虽然数以百万计的消费者对登录信用卡信息

whether to accept checks and major credit cards, e-commerce is open to all sorts of other payment possibilities — including e-checks, PayPal and transactions in currencies other than the dollar.

You'll also want to know a thing or two about affiliate① programs. Under these advertising arrangements, companies collect cash for driving traffic to your site, and visa versa. "About 70% of our online business comes through affiliates," said Rebecca Matter, director of online marketing for American Writers and Artists, a Delray Beach, Fla. Her affiliates include Learning Strategies and Nightingale-Conant, "where people go as they're looking to better their lives through a second career. These sites act like resellers of our programs."

Then there's the problem of security. While millions of consumers have grown comfortable with entering credit-card information into a Web site, reports of massive identity theft continue to crimp② online sales. The lines of defense begin with authentication③ programs that determine whether someone signing on under a specific name is actually authorized to use the site via that specific account. Force users to jump through too many hoops, though, and you risk driving them away. Hence the single sign-on approach, in which either the user's computer or the Web site "remembers" passwords. Access control beefs up the barricades by

---

① affiliate [ə'filieit] *n.* 联号,联营公司

② crimp [krimp] *v.* 诱骗

③ authentication [ɔːθenti'keiʃən] *n.* 证明,认证

网站越来越满意，但报告显示大规模的身份窃取仍在继续打击在线销售。该防线开始建立验证程序，以确保使用具体名字签名的某个人得到实际的授权认可使用具体的账户。迫使用户跳过许多陷阱，你也冒着赶走他们的风险。因此，通过单击登录的方式，用户的计算机或网站能够“记住”密码。对进入特定的网站功能通路进行控制加强了路障，如将物品放进购物车。

想确认你的网站真的安全吗？使用用户浏览器窗口增加挂锁图标的软件。位于坦帕的一家名叫 Magnetic 的网络开发公司的信息技术主管帕特·科维奇恩说：“要确保结账过程的安全，更重要的是，当信用卡传递信息时，要保证它们在形式上完全安全可靠，并保证客户的安全。”信用卡公司已经采取紧急措施抵御盗贼，为网上交易提供安全的信息。马萨诸塞州剑桥城的阿克迈技术公司资深业内营销经理比尔·布拉德利说：“全球所有使用信用卡的商家目前已经在遵守网络标准——无一例外。对零售商来说，不遵守网络标准可能意味着罚款，失去公众的信任。这也是人们起初不考虑网上购物的主要原因。”

保持顾客的购买力：这是理解电子商务以及推动电子商务发展的电子技术的全部意义所在。

granting entry only to specific site functions, such as adding an item to a shopping cart.

Want to make it clear that your site is indeed secure? Use software that adds a padlock icon in the user's browser window. "Ensuring that your checkout process and, more important, the credit card forms are well-secured and will guarantee your customers' safety when transmitting their information," says Pat Kaeowichien, director of information technology for Magnetic, a Tampa-based Web-development firm. Credit card firms have taken critical steps to fend off thieves, providing secure communication for transactions over the Internet. "The Internet standard is now in place for all merchants globally who accept credit cards — no exceptions," says Bill Bradley, senior industry marketing manager for Akamai Technologies in Cambridge, Mass. "Non-compliance can mean fines and, for that retailer, a loss of public trust. And that's the main reason people don't buy online in the first place."

Keeping them buying: That's what understanding e-commerce — and the technology that drives it — is all about.

(954 words)

知识链接

Dotster 总部设在温哥华，华盛顿，主要提供域名注册和虚拟主机的服务，是专业的域名注册商，它的域名控制面板功能完善，适合细致管理和域名买卖与经营开发。凭借强有力的市场地位，在域名注册行业，Dotster 已经确立了世界上最大的域名注册、超过 300 万域名持有根据管理和服务的数以十万计的世界各地客户。

***PayPal*(贝宝)** 在中国大陆的品牌为贝宝，是一个总部在美国加利福尼亚州圣荷西市的互联网服务商。它允许在使用电子邮件来标识身份的用户之间转移资金，从而避免了传统的邮寄支票或者汇款的方法。贝宝目前是在线付款解决方案的全球领导者，注册用户数量超过一亿。PayPal 可由易趣买家和卖家、在线零售商和其他商家在 57 个地区以 6 种货币使用加元、欧元、英镑、美元、日元和澳元。贝宝既保证信息的安全，又快捷方便：客户可以在线付款，而不用将银行卡或银行账户的详细信息透露给他人，也可立即向有电子邮件地址的任何人进行付款。2002 年 10 月，全球最大拍卖网站 eBay 以 15 亿美元收购 PayPal，PayPal 便成为了 eBay 的主要付款途径之一。

题　记

随着在线销售“无边界”的出现，互联网化解了地域的藩篱，打破了企业能够根据不同地区的特征来执行价格歧视策略的可能。提升多渠道电子商务的销售转化与重购吸引了越来越多的销售商机支持。多渠道管理的组织架构在操作流程和销售技巧上更加凸显它独特的竞争优势，每一个各具独立性的网站都在快速调整自身的策略，最大程度的服务于可能不同的细分市场。利用易趣业务的影响力，电子邮件营销，购物搜索引擎，创建自己的网站空间等一系列多渠道引导消费者的购物路径，继而实现以消费者为中心的战略制定，同时策划多渠道协同的营销活动。

A Multi-Channel Online Selling

There are several trends in ecommerce that every online seller should be aware of. Ecommerce is continuing to grow at a rapid pace. Most industry analysts peg the growth at 25-30% growth year over year. Today eBay represents about 25% of ecommerce so by selling on eBay you have taken a great first step towards taking advantage of the broader ecommerce opportunity. What this trend means for you if you are exclusively selling on eBay is if you want to grow as fast as ecommerce (or faster) you need to do so by taking share of your category. In other words, if you grow just at the pace of eBay (maintain share), you will be losing ground in the broader market. Taking eBay share sounds like the right way to go, even if it requires some creative pricing. However, as most sellers are painfully aware, as eBay's growth has slowed, in order to achieve their revenue goals, eBay has had to increase fees. This has created a "perfect storm" for many sellers where they want to grow with ecommerce by taking share on eBay, but economically this will probably cause them to actually lose money on the way to that objective. What's a seller to do? The solution for most sellers is to spread their wings, jump out of the eBay nest and

多渠道在线销售

每一个网上卖家应该了解电子商务中的几个趋势。电子商务正在继续快速增长。多数行业分析师认定增长率将比去年同期提高25%~30%。今天的易趣的业务约占电子商务的25%，所以在易趣上卖东西就意味着你已经向着拥有更广泛的电子商务机会迈出了伟大的第一步。如果你专门在易趣上卖东西，这种趋势对于你来说意味着如果你想像电子商务增长速度一样快（或更快），就需要分享你的实物。换句话说，如果你只是保持和易趣同样的增长速度（保持份额），你将失去更广阔的市场。即使需要某些有创意的定价，保持易趣的份额听上去像是正确的选择。然而，大多数卖家正痛苦地注意到，随着易趣增长的放缓，为了实现其收益目标，易趣不得不提高收费。这就为许多卖家催生了一场“完美风暴”，许多卖家想要通过拥有易趣的份额与电子商务一起增长，但从经济上来讲，这可能导致他们实际上在实现这一目标的过程中亏钱。卖方要做什么？对大多数卖家来说解决方案是展开自己

soar into① the broader world of ecommerce. In fact eBay's own published data indicates that 77% of eBay's own top-sellers are now multi-channel.

How to break down the "online channels"? First, expand off-eBay. It's unrealistic to expect you'll be able to start out with an amazon.com kind of buyer-experience with product recommendations, reviews, configurators②, wizards③, eighteen payment methods, etc. Are your products searchable, clearly described, great images and easy to buy? If you invest your dollars into the basic buying experience, and then the rest of your dollars in the channel aspect of off-eBay selling you will do very well. Second, think Multi-channel. As you expand off eBay, you need to think multi-channel. In other words, you want to run your business so that you can add new online channels seamlessly instead of having to do double the work for each channel. This philosophy goes throughout the entire ecommerce operation. For example, think about inventory in a two-channel (eBay and ecommerce) world. There are two ways to handle inventory in a two-channel world. In the first, you take your inventory and enter it into two systems (your eBay and your ecommerce). You then manually move inventory around between the systems trying to make sure you are up to date across both. Alternatively if you think multi-channel you would find a system that allows you to put your inventory in

---

① soar into 上升到
② configurators [kənˌfigiəˈreitə] *n.* 配置
③ wizard [ˈwizəd] *n.* 奇才,高手

的翅膀，跳出易趣的鸟笼飞向更广阔的电子商务世界。事实上，易趣自己公布的数据表明，77% 的易趣顶级卖家现在都是多渠道销售。

如何分解“网上通道”？ 首先，扩展易趣。 希望你可以从亚马逊网站的规模开始，期盼买方经验以及产品建议、评论、配置、向导和18种付款方式等，这些都不现实。 你的产品能否搜索、是否有清楚的说明、是否有极好的形象、是否易于购买？ 如果你把钱投资到基本的购买经验上，然后将其余的钱投到易趣之外的渠道，就会做得很好。 其次，考虑多渠道。 由于你脱离易趣扩展，就需要考虑多渠道。 换句话说，你要经营你的业务，以便可以增加新的无缝在线渠道，而不用为每个渠道做双重工作。 这一理念贯穿于整个电子商务的运作。 例如，库存双通道领域（易趣和电子商务）。 有两种方法在双通道领域处理库存。首先列出库存清单并输入到两个系统（你的易趣和你的电子商务）。 然后手工操作系统之间库存的移动，确保二者交叉更新。 另外，如果考虑多渠道销售，你会找到一个系统，它可以让你马上安置库存，然后把它分配给两者中的任一渠道。 于是，多渠道的系统将为你查明一切。 一旦你使多渠道迅速转换业务量至 3、4、5，甚至 X 个渠道，因为你已经抽象和简化了企业的多渠道，就可以不管渠道，集中精力销售。 总结电子商务

once and then virtually allocate it to either channel. Then the multi-channel system would keep track of everything for you. Once you make the multi-channel leap① your business scales to 3, 4, 5, heck X channels because you have abstracted and simplified the multi-channel aspects of your business and can focus on selling regardless of channel. To summarize the ecommerce platform selection process, that is a balanced approach that takes equally into consideration features, channel-optimization and multi-channel factors.

Once you've selected an ecommerce platform and launched, you need to bring the buyers. The following are some ideas for you to explore from here.

1. Leverage② your eBay business. Think of your eBay business as the wind in your ecommerce sails (or sales!). Just because you are expanding off-eBay doesn't mean you are taking your business off-eBay. In fact your eBay customers can give you a great boost in your off-eBay efforts. Promote your ecommerce site aggressively in every email you send out, your about-me page and even in your packaging. Consider offering coupons③ to eBay buyers for your ecommerce site to get them to make the jump. Also your ecommerce site will give you the ability to offer a much broader selection. Let eBay buyers know this with a simple kind of

---

① leap [liːp] *vt.* 跳,跳跃

② leverage [ˈliːvəridʒ] *v.* 衡量

③ coupon [ˈkuːpɔn] *n.* 赠券

平台的选择程序，就是一个平衡的方法：公平地考虑功能特征、渠道优化和多渠道因素。

一旦选定一个电子商务平台并开始运转，你需要带来买主。你可从下面的想法中获得一些启示。

第一，利用易趣业务的影响力。想象易趣业务是你的电子商务航行（或销售）中的风。你拓展易趣之外的交易并不意味着你的业务脱离了易趣。事实上，你的易趣客户可以大大推进你在易趣外的努力。发送的每一封电子邮件都要积极宣传你的电子商务网站、你的网站介绍以及包装促销。考虑向易趣买家提供你的电子商务网站优惠券，使他们加大购买力度。你的电子商务网站也有能力提供更广泛的选择。让易趣买家明白一个简单的信息："想了解更多？请查看我的网站。"最后，记住给你的易趣买家提供参加网站电邮业务通讯的选择能力。

第二，电子邮件营销。电邮营销是直接电子商务最大的驱动力之一。你需要设定每月、每两周或每周的时间表，向忠实的买家发送简讯。发送慷慨的优惠券和折扣用以建立忠诚的顾客群。有数百种包括智能联系和持续联系在内的服务可以帮助你进行电子邮件营销。

第三，自然搜索。谷歌、雅虎和其他搜索引擎不断在网络寻找

message: "Looking for more? Checkout my website". Finally, remember to offer your eBay buyers the ability to opt-in to your email newsletter for your website.

2. Email Marketing. Email marketing is one of the largest drivers of direct ecommerce. You need to set a monthly, bi-weekly or weekly schedule to send out a newsletter to your loyal followers. Be generous with coupons and discounts to build loyalty. There are hundreds of services that help you with email marketing including IntelliContact and Constant Contact.

3. Natural Search. Google, Yahoo! and the other search engines constantly crawl the web looking for content. Make sure that your items are all indexed① and properly meta-tagged②. Also make sure that you have many related sites linking to you to help with your PageRank (Google's algorithm③ based on link popularity that determines how high you show up in their free or natural/organic/algorithmic results).

4. Paid Search. Google owns 60-80% of this market so start your efforts with Google AdWords. The world of paid-search is very different from eBay. Instead of paying a listing+final-value-fee, you pay a per-click charges for traffic and then it is up to you to turn that traffic into sales. This economic model increases the risk for you (buying lots of traffic that

---

① index [ˈindeks] *vt.* 为……编索引

② meta-tagged 元标记

③ algorithm [ˈælgəriðəm]【数】算法,运算法则

相关内容，确保你的商品编入索引并妥善设置元标记。还要确认你拥有很多相关网站的链接，以丰富你的网页覆盖面（谷歌的算法基于链接人气，这决定了你在他们的自由或天然/有机/演算结果中的排名有多高）。

第四，付费搜索。谷歌拥有 60%~80% 的市场，所以可从谷歌的关键词广告开始搜索。付费搜索领域与易趣有很大的不同。你要支付每次点击流量费，然后就看你能否把这些点击转换成销售量，而不是按照排名+最终价值支付费用。这种经济模式增加了你的风险（购买大量没有转换成销量的流量），但它也给你提供了更多的灵活性。此处成功的关键是拿出一个“尾巴”战略，允许你避开与大公司的竞争，给你足够的关键词和搜索量产生集中效应。一旦你掌握了关键词条，就把雅虎踢开！

第五，需要通过市场数据传送专线将产品加入购物引擎。尽管有 20 多个自定义搜索引擎，重点应放在七个主要网站：Shopping.com，Shopzilla，NextTag，Yahoo，MSN，Froogle，PriceGrabber。如果你觉得这份名单太多，那就考虑利用谷歌的产品 Froogle 一试深浅，这个搜索引擎完全免费。

第六，考虑外区间。创建自己的生存空间并就地出发。人人都是某方面的专家。创建一个博客或维基，发布指南（如果

doesn't convert)， but also gives you more flexibility. The key to success here is coming up with a "tail" strategy that will allow you to avoid competing with the big guys， but give you enough keywords and search volume to generate some mass. Once you've mastered AdWords， then fire up Yahoo!

5. Need to get your products to the shopping engines via a datafeed. While there are over 20 CSEs， focusing on the big seven: Shopping.com， Shopzilla， NextTag， Yahoo! Shopping， MSN Shopping， Froogle， PriceGrabber. If this list overwhelms you， then consider getting your toe in the water via Froogle， Google's offering， which is completely free.

6. Think outside the box. Create your niche and go from there. Everyone is an expert on something. Create a blog or wiki， publish a guide （if you've done these things on eBay， move them off to your website instead）. The search engines will find this content and then buyers will find this content， come to your site and drive sales.

（1,047 words）

您在易趣上做这些事情，把他们吸引到你的网站上来）。搜索引擎会找到这个内容，然后买家会发现这个内容，来到你的网站并推动销售。

知识链接

Froogle 是谷歌2004年推出的对照购物信息网站，主要为顾客提供购物信息和建议，谷歌从每笔在线交易中抽取一定比例的佣金。最初，Froogle网站的商品信息主要依靠代理商索取几百家主要购物中心的存货目录，后来，为了使这项服务更全面，谷歌鼓励所有商场将它们各自精心打造的商品目录提交到新近创建的GoogleBase，这里是一个几乎无所不包的信息交换据点。Froogle会从上述信息库中提取商品信息，可帮助用户透过比价的方式，对数码相机或者苹果电脑出品的iPod音乐播放器等产品分类列出。

PageRank 是搜索引擎使用的一种网页重要性评估方式，PageRank的值决定了网页在搜索结果中的排名。

题　记

家庭网络运营对很多人来说都具有吸引力，因为它看上去能悠闲而快速地赚大钱。其实不然，要想取得家庭网络事业或家庭电子商务的成功，首先就要以一种“全职”的态度对待它，像经营其他任何生意一样精心呵护你的网络运营。在网络发展方面，家庭网络运营商承担着网络营销、广告跟踪、现金流通管理、产品测试、客户服务、网站更新及维护、电邮营销等的控制和管理；在开展业务方面，家庭网络运营商可以进行业务创新，开发一些适用于家庭网络运营的新业务或进行业务捆绑和集成，随时跟踪反馈投入和产出。通过将这些基本的、已被证实成功的策略应用于家庭网络运营，不仅开启了家庭网络运营成功之门的最大机会，而且让更多的人削尖脑袋、想方设法挤入网络运营的激烈竞争之中。

Home Internet Business Strategies

The allure of starting an online business is overwhelming the world. A great many Internet home based business opportunities use lifestyle benefits as their main selling point. Their sales pitch and use of images are very convincing and many people actually do believe that they will be able to quit their job and retire in a matter of months and become a millionaire in one year, drive around in the flashiest[1] of sports cars and own the best piece of real estate in the area. Another attractive sales line of starting an online business is the use of the words "fully automated", which implies that the business owner does not have to do very much work in order to earn a vast income. Unfortunately for us all this is not the case. A great deal of work is required by those seriously intent on building a successful, lasting and profitable home Internet business. It is mainly due to the above that so many people fail in their endeavors to make a success of their Internet business. They have been misled into believing that they can make vast amounts of money from an online business in a short period of time by doing very little work and without having to apply any basic

① flashy [ˈflæʃi] *adj.* 俗丽的,浮华的

家庭网络运营策略

启动网络事业的诱惑正在风靡全球。 大量基于家庭网络的商业机会使用生活方式受益作为主要卖点。 他们的销售定位和使用的产品形象令人心悦诚服，很多人居然就相信他们能够辞掉工作，在几个月内退休，一年内成为百万富翁，开华丽的运动跑车，在本地区拥有最好的房产。 另一个开展网络运营具有吸引力的卖点是“全盘自动化”，它暗示网络运营老板不必做太多的工作即可以赚取巨额收入。 不幸的是，对我们来说这并不是事实。 抱定决心打造成功、持续及盈利的家庭网络运营的人，需要付出大量的艰辛。 由于上述主要原因，很多人开创成功网络运营的努力付之东流。 他们受到误导，认为只要付出极少的努力、不必遵守基本的交易原则、在短期内就可以从网上赚大钱。

像对待其他任何事情那样对待网络运营。 你可能采取的最重要的成功秘诀就是把家庭网络运营当做实体经营来做，而不只是一种业余爱好。 你也可以运用那些完美成功的在线业主日常使用的、已经被证实的成功策略。 大多数人在开始家庭网络运营的同

business principals.

Treat your online business like any other. The first and most important success strategy that you can adopt is to treat your home Internet business like a real business, not a hobby. There are basic proven success strategies that the highly successful online business owners put into practice on a daily basis and you can implement them too. Most people start an Internet home based business while still working a day job in the hope of making some quick and easy money in their spare time. This "part-time" attitude will lead to disappointment and failure. A "full time attitude" is required to build a successful online business in the few hours available. To build a successful and profitable home based Internet business you need to apply basic business principals with a full time attitude to everything related to the business, i.e., Internet marketing, ad tracking, cash flow management, product testing, customer service, website updates and maintenance, email marketing, etc. Be firm with yourself and make the decision to either get into business or get out. When you have decided that you are in business only then can you move forward and accept the challenge and responsibility of building a successful home based Internet business.

Like any other business, time management and cash management are of utmost importance. Decide what is important and what is urgent. Have a daily task list with time limits on each. Diligent cash flow management is a means to allow you to set aside a portion of your profits to invest back into the business. Be sure that you are selling something that has value and

时仍然在做一份全日制工作，希望在闲暇时间快速、轻松地赚钱。这种“休闲时间”态度会导致失望和失败。需要以“全职态度”在尽可能少的时间里创建成功的在线运营。为了建造成功和盈利的家庭网络运营，你需要运用基本的商业原则，以全职的态度来处理任何与运营相关的一切，即网络营销、广告跟踪、现金流通管理、产品测试、客户服务、网站更新及维护、电邮营销等。自己要有主张，决定进入还是退出网络运营。只有在你已经决定从事网络运营之时，你才能前进，并接受挑战和承担成功的家庭网络运营的责任。

像其他的经营项目一样，时间和现金管理是重中之重。应该决定什么是重要的和什么是紧急的。拥有一份每天的任务列表。细心而持续不断的现金流管理是一种允许你留出一部分利润再投资返回到运营中去的手段。要确信你销售的产品具有价值，营销产品的方式要能够吸引合适的潜在消费者进入你的网站。要确信满足潜在顾客的需求和期望，以便将他们转变成实际的消费者。

成为随叫随到的专业人员。重要的是访问网站的潜在客户可以有某种方式联络到你，即通过电话、传真或电邮，这种方式能够建立信任，并给你了解客户的机会。客户能轻松地在你的网站上浏览吗？把客户的需求放在第一位。回答询问要迅速。策划与实体企业一样的专业形象——无须隐藏。在名字旁贴出照片，使

market the product in such a way that you attract the right potential customers to your website. Be sure to meet your potential customer's requirements and expectations in order to turn them into actual customers.

Make Yourself Available and be Professional. It is important that potential customers visiting your website have some way of contacting you, by phone, fax or email-this builds trust and gives you the opportunity to get to know your customers. Can they easily find their way around your website? Put your customers' needs first. Answer queries promptly. Project a professional image of a real business-don't hide away. It is a good idea to personalize your website by putting a face to a name, so if you do add a photograph to your website use a good professional head and shoulders shot as opposed to one of you lounging① under a palm tree with your laptop and cocktail. Be sure that your online business is designed to fulfill a need and you will start making a profit when you put your customers' needs first.

Keep track of what works and what doesn't. Internet marketing requires discipline and hard work and you need to know what is and isn't working and why. Track every possible means that a potential customer has of finding your website. Knowing your conversion rates are important, especially if you are using PPC or other paid advertising. It is vital to constantly monitor and check and adjust where necessary. If you are involved in email marketing, you need to know your opt-in and opt-out

---

① lounge [laundʒ] *vi.* 懒散地斜倚

网站个性化是个好主意，所以，如果你确实要在网站上放一个图片，就用非常职业化的头像，不要用在棕榈树下看着笔记本电脑、喝着鸡尾酒、闲散度日的图片。确信你的网络运营被设计来满足一种需要，并把客户的需求放在首位的时候，你就开始盈利了。

持续跟踪行得通和行不通的地方。网络营销需要规则和努力工作，你需要知道什么行得通、什么行不通以及为什么。跟踪每一位潜在的客户可以找到你的网站的手段。了解转换率很重要，使用点击付费广告或其他付费广告时尤其如此。实时监控、检查和必要的调整至关重要。如果你使用电邮营销，需要了解客户参与和退出的统计数据，包括达到什么等级时客户选择退出？找到原因并做出调整。你知道什么交易资源生成最高参与率吗？跟踪、测试、监控你做的任何事情。对网站做改变时，一次只改一个地方，当你得到不同的结果时，你就会确切地知道是什么导致了新的结果。要知道什么是你的顶级运行关键词和关键词组，在搜索引擎的哪个部位他们表现最好。了解你的点击率和销售转换率之间的关系。在网络变化如此迅速的环境中，你需要分解网络营销链的每一单个程序，并准确地了解正在发生的事，以便迅速做出调整，跟上潮流。网络令人惊异的一面是你可以跟踪一切，成功就是不要玩猜谜游戏，而是遵守纪律。

虽然这是些非常基本的经营原则和在线运营成功的秘诀，但它

statistics, including at what stage prospects are opting out? Find out why and make a change. Do you know what traffic sources generate the highest opt-ins? Track, test and monitor everything you do. When making changes to your website, make one change at a time and when you get different results you will then know exactly what caused the new result. You need to know what your top performing keywords and keyword phrases are and at what position in the search engines they perform best. Know your click-through rate to sales conversion rate. With the Internet being such a fast changing environment you need to break down every single process in your Internet marketing chain and know exactly what is happening so that you are in a position to quickly make adjustments to keep up with the trends. The amazing thing about the Internet is that you can track everything; success is just a matter of avoiding the guessing game and being disciplined.

Although these are the very basic business principals and online business success strategies they will form a very solid foundation to an online business. Combine these with your decision to "get into business" with a "full time attitude" and you are on the road to building a highly profitable and successful home based Internet business.

(966 words)

们构成了在线运营非常坚实的基础。 把这些基本原则和你以“全职态度”“进入在线运营”的决心相结合，那你就走上了高回报和成功的家庭网络运营之路。

知识链接

***PPC*（*Pay-Per-Click*）** 点击付费广告，即根据点击广告或者电子邮件信息的用户数量来付费的一种网络广告定价模式。

题记

美国是个商品化高度发达的国家，不仅刚研制出来的新产品充斥市场，琳琅满目，而且过时的、陈旧的、闲置的以及多余的商品也大有去处，尽可供卖方出手，供需方挑选。而互联网的普及，促使一种新型的网上跳蚤市场迅速崛起，而且很少受到互联网泡沫破灭的影响。面对高债务、高物价和20世纪90年代以来最艰难的日子，互联网上拍卖和跳蚤市场生意出现惊人的增长。人们为了筹集现金应付日常生活开支，将珍贵的物品、甚至是家传之宝低价拿到网站上拍卖。在线交易的新产品有人抢着要，而旧东西同样有广阔的市场空间。

Online Flea Markets

The for-sale listings on the online hub Craigslist come with plaintive[1] notices, like the one from the teenager in Georgia who said her mother lost her job and pleaded, "Please buy anything you can to help out." Or the seller in Milwaukee who wrote in one post of needing to pay bills, and put a diamond engagement ring up for bids to do it. Struggling with mounting debt and rising prices, faced with the toughest economic times since the early 1990s, Americans are selling prized possessions online and at flea markets at alarming rates. To meet higher gas, food and prescription drug bills, they are selling off grandmother's dishes and their own belongings. Some of the household purging[2] has been extremely painful-families forced to part with heirlooms[3]. "This is not about downsizing. It's about needing gas money," said Nancy Baughman, founder of eBizAuctions, an online auction service she runs out of her garage in Raleigh, N.C. One former affluent customer is now unemployed and had to unload Hermes leather jackets and Versace jeans and silk shirts.

---

① plaintive [ˈpleintiv] *adj.* 悲哀的,哀伤的
② purging [ˈpəːdʒiŋ] *n.* 清洗,清除
③ heirloom [ˈeəluːm] *n.* 传家宝

网络跳蚤市场

Craigslist 网络中心的待售清单里最近有很多让人觉得悲哀的出售通知，如乔治亚州的一位十几岁的女孩说，她母亲丢掉了工作，她恳求“请买任何东西帮帮忙”，还有密尔沃基的卖家标价拍卖一枚钻石订婚戒指，网上发帖子说要支付账单。美国人在堆积如山的债务和飞速增长的物价中挣扎，面对 20 世纪 90 年代以来最困难的经济形势，他们以令人惊讶的低价在网上或者跳蚤市场出售珍贵物品。为了支付高额的煤气、食品和处方医药账单，他们出售祖母传下来的碗碟和他们自己的财物。有些家庭的拍卖举步维艰，尤其是被迫出售传家宝的家庭。eBizAuctions 的创始人南希·鲍曼说，“这与减少规模无关。这是为了支付煤气费”。这家网上拍卖服务是从她在北卡罗来纳州雷利市的车库开始做起的。昔日生活富裕的顾客现在失业了，被迫出售爱马仕夹克、凡萨奇牛仔裤和丝绸衬衫。

Craigslist 已经成为一个全世界的网上跳蚤市场，待售清单从去年 7 月起已经上涨 70%。3 月份，清单上的待售量与去年同期相比增加了一倍多，增长到 1 500 万。Craigslist 的首席执行官杰夫·巴克马斯特承认了正在上涨的各式网上销售物品，但表示增长率“正

At Craigslist, which has become a kind of online flea market for the world, the number of for-sale listings has soared 70 percent since last July. In March, the number of listings more than doubled to almost 15 million from the year-ago period. Craigslist CEO Jeff Buckmaster acknowledged the increasing popularity of selling all sort of items on the Web, but said the rate of growth is "moving above the usual trend line." He said he was amazed at the desperate tone in some ads. In Daleville, Ala., Ellona Bateman-Lee has turned to eBay and flea markets to empty her three-bedroom mobile home of DVDs, VCRs, stereos and televisions. She said she needs the cash to help pay for soaring food and utility bills and mounting health care expenses since her husband, Bob, suffered an electric shock on the job as a dump truck driver last year and is now disabled. Among her most painful sales: her grandmother's teakettle. She sold it for $6 on eBay. "My grandmother raised me, so it hurt," she said. "We've had bouts① here and there, but we always got by. This time it's different."

Economists say it is difficult to compare the selling trend with other tough times because the Internet, only in wide use since the mid-1990s, has made it much easier to unload goods than, say, at pawn shops. But clearly, cash-strapped people are selling their belongings at bargain prices, with a flood of listings for secondhand cars, clothing and furniture hitting the market in recent months, particularly since January. Earlier, people tapped their inflated home equity and credit cards to fuel a

---

① bout [baut] *n.* 一回,一场

在超过正常成长趋势”，他说他很惊讶一些广告里令人绝望的腔调。在阿拉巴马州的德勒维尔市，依洛娜·贝特曼·李求助易趣和跳蚤市场变卖装满三间活动房屋的DVD、VCR、音响和电视机。她说自从去年还是自动倾卸卡车司机的丈夫鲍勃工作时遭受电击、现已残疾之后，她就急需现金来支付飞速上扬的食品、电费账单和堆积如山的卫生保健开支。她最痛心的拍卖是老祖母留下的茶壶，她在易趣网上仅仅卖了6美元。她说：“祖母把我养大，因此很伤心。我们过去碰到过这样那样的困难，但总能克服。这次真的不一样。”

经济学家说，现在很难和其他经济困难的时期比较出售趋势，因为20世纪90年代中期开始广泛使用的互联网比典当行更容易出手物品。但是很明显，身无分文的人正在廉价出售值钱物品，近几个月，尤其是自1月份以来，网上拍卖物品洪水般涌出，包括二手车、衣服和家具。早些时候，人们选择膨胀的家庭资产净值和信用卡放纵消费，如今，缓慢增长的家庭价值和信用危机切断了现金来源。与此同时，煤气和食品开支比微薄的工资增长快得多。有些地区的煤气价格已经涨到了4美元1加仑，今年暑假这个价格可能分布更广。正在萎缩的劳动力市场是另一件令人担忧的事情。克里斯廷·哈德利是宾夕法尼亚州雷丁市有执业资格的53岁护士，她说她过去是“一个购物狂”，挥霍金钱购买昂贵的Dooney & Bourke手提包。但是和她同居的男友去年走了，她现在找工作都有困难。成堆未支付的账单迫使她出售了80多件物品，包括她在AuctionPal.com网站上花1 000多美元购买的手提包。现在哈德利的房子看上

buying binge①. Now, slumping② home values and a credit crisis have sapped③ sources of cash. Meanwhile, soaring gas and food prices haven't kept pace with meager④ wage growth. Gas prices have already hit $4 per gallon in some places, and that could become more widespread this summer. The weakening job market is another big worry. Christine Hadley, a 53-year-old registered nurse from Reading, Pa., says she used to be "a clotheshorse," splurging on⑤ pricey Dooney & Bourke handbags. But her live-in boyfriend left last year, and she has had trouble finding a job. Piles of unpaid bills forced her to sell more than 80 items, including the handbags, which went for more than $1,000 on a site called AuctionPal.com. Now, except for some artwork and threadbare⑥ furniture, her house is looking sparse. "I need the money for essentials-to pay my bills and to eat," Hadley said.

At AuctionPal.com, which helps novices sell things online, for-sale listings rose 66 percent from February to March, much faster than the 25 percent to 30 percent average monthly pace since the company was formed in September, CEO Maureen Ellenberger said. She said she was surprised to see that most of her clients desperately needed to sell items to raise cash. For LiveDeal.com, a classifieds and business directory site, for-sale listings for January through March rose 10 percent from the previous year.

---

① binge [bindʒ] *n.* 狂闹,狂欢
② slump [slʌmp] *vt.* 使降低,使衰落
③ sap [sæp] *vt.* 使衰竭,逐渐侵蚀
④ meager [ˈmiːgə] *n.* 兆
⑤ splurging on *v.* 挥霍,浪费
⑥ threadbare [ˈθredbeə] *adj.* 穿破旧衣服的,俗套的

去空空如也，只剩下稀稀落落的几件艺术品和一些破旧家具。哈德利说："我需要钱维持基本生活：付账单和吃饭。"

首席执行官莫林·官埃伦伯格说，在帮助新手网上出售物品的 AuctionPal.com 上，从 2 月份到 3 月份待售标签增加了 66%，较这个公司 9 月份成立以来平均每月 25% 到 30% 的增长速度要快得多。她说看到多数客户不顾一切地出售物品以筹集现金，让她感到惊讶。在分类和企业行名录网站 LiveDeal.com 上，待售标签从 1 月份到 3 月份较去年增长了 10%。网站首席运营官瑞文说："我们能肯定地察觉，部分顾客有经济压力。"

Craigslist 的巴克·马斯特说，每四个迅速增长的待售种类就有三个与汽油相联——休闲的交通工具，如帐篷车和拖车，汽车和卡车以及船只等。瑞文指出，越来越多的清单提供家具，尤其是迈阿密和拉斯维加斯周边地区，以及其他受住房危机严重影响的地区。

掌管 eBizAuctions 公司的鲍曼说，在过去 4 个月里，她主要和绝望的卖家打交道，而不是以临时的卖家为主。她说，顾客主要是无法付账单的中产阶级人士，现在他们希望向买家提前支付，而不需要等到物品卖出之后，这种趋势也可能伤害二手商店。对基督教救世军的捐助从 1 月到 3 月期间也下降了 20%，这个慈善机构主持全国公共关系和发展工作的秘书佐治·胡德说，部分原因可能是他们的财产正在被售。

二手物品的买家现在也希望更合理的交易，使价格降低。塔楼集团咨询公司的高级分析师布赖恩·赖利估计，网上二手商品的出

"We can definitely detect economic stress on the part of the consumer," said John Raven, the site's chief operating officer.

On Craigslist, Buck master said, three of the four fastest-growing for-sale categories are tied to gas — recreational vehicles like campers and trailers, cars and trucks, and boats. Raven noted more and more listings for furniture, particularly in areas around Miami and Las Vegas and other regions hardest hit by the housing crisis.

Baughman, who runs eBizAuctions, said that over the past four months she's been working with mostly desperate sellers instead of mainly casual ones. Most are middle-class customers who can't pay their bills and now want to be paid up front for the items instead of waiting until they are sold, she said. The trend may be hurting secondhand stores too. Donations to the Salvation Army were down 20 percent in the January-to-March period. George Hood, the charity's national community relations and development secretary, said that was probably partly because people were selling their belongings instead.

And secondhand buyers want better deals now as well, driving prices down. Secondhand merchandise online is going for 25 to 35 percent below what it commanded a year ago, estimated Brian Riley, senior analyst at research firm The TowerGroup. "It won't hit the saturation point until the (economy) hits the bottom and right now, we don't know when that is," he said. In Alabama, Bateman-Lee said that she only received \$ 30 for her TV and \$ 45 for her DVD player at a local flea market. She doesn't have too much left to sell, but she's going back to "sort through more things." Her \$ 30 water bill is due this week.

(965 words)

售价格会较一年前下降 25% 到 35%。他说，“这种情况直到经济恶化见底时才会达到饱和，现在我们还不知道那会是何时”。贝特曼·李说，在阿拉巴马州当地跳蚤市场上她能接受的电视机最低价是 30 美元，DVD 播放器是 45 美元。她已经没有太多剩下的物品可卖了，但是她打算回去“整理更多商品”。她的水费账单 30 美元本周到期。

知识链接

Craigslist 是一个网上大型免费分类广告网站。该网站于 1995 年由 Craig Newmark 于美国旧金山湾区创办。目前，Craigslist 已在 50 个国家共 450 城市提供服务，其唯一的收入来源是支付招聘广告。

Dooney & Bourke 从 1975 年公司创立之初生产的首个男士古典系列产品，到现在的提包、露营用具等多个系列产品，Dooney & Bourke 确立了其在配饰产品领域的领先地位。Dooney & Bourke 的独到之处在于经典的剪裁、跳跃的色彩和耐久性。

题记

稻草编成金条的时代一去不复返，营销开始走向理性。今天，更多的人意识到真正的竞争力必定来自企业的综合实力，既包括狭义营销动作，也包括产品力、品牌力提升，甚至更靠后端的企业发展战略规划和组织保障、团队文化水平等。后端产品意味着消费者购买某一项产品之后，营销者可以立即向他们推荐他们可能需要的另一种商品，比如买了电脑，就可能要买杀毒软件这样一种后端产品。价格折扣、预订付费、分步提供产品、出售升级产品、制作营销视频或宣传书以及销售他人的产品都是后端营销模式的最佳选择。营销网络绝不能做那个在树荫下苦苦等待第二只兔子的人。

Marketing Online Backend Products

Don't just bank on one product. Learn how to generate even more sales by adding backend items. People are always coming up to me and asking, "What can you tell me to help increase my internet sales?" And all too often, when I ask them to tell me about their business model, I discover they're selling only one product. So I ask them, "Have you ever considered selling backend products to your customers?"

Backend products are simply other products you can offer to your existing customers after they've made their initial purchase. Because you know what they've already bought from you, you should have a good idea of other things your customers would likely buy. And that should make it easy for you to think of new things they'd want to purchase. In fact, by adding just one more product to your site, you can increase the lifetime value of your customers — and increase your revenue — by 30 to 50 percent. Here's an example: The other day, I got an e-mail from Amazon.com telling me about a new internet marketing book they just got in stock. They knew I might be interested in it because I'd bought other internet marketing books from them before. And I was interested in that new one, too. In fact, as soon as I got the e-mail, I immediately clicked through to

营销网络后端产品

不要只在一种产品上孤注一掷。学会怎样通过增加后端产品来产出更多的销售业绩。人们经常来问我："你能告诉我怎样才能增大我的网络销售？"当我询问他们的营销模式时，往往发现他们只销售一种产品。于是我会提醒他们："你有没有尝试对顾客销售后端产品？"

后端产品只不过是现有顾客购买前端产品之后，你可以为他们提供的其他产品。因为你知道他们已经从你这里买走了什么，你就应该完全了解你的顾客还可能购买的其他商品。这有助你容易思考他们要买的新产品。事实上，你只要在网站再增加一种产品，就可以提高顾客30%到50%的终身价值，还会增加你的收益。这里有个例子：有一天，我收到一封来自亚马逊的邮件，告诉我他们有一本网络营销的新书在售。他们知道我可能对这本书感兴趣，因为我以前从他们那里买过其他网络营销的书。我也会对这本新书感兴趣。事实上，我一收到邮件，就马上点击进入网站，查看了那本书并把它买下。这种行为使我在亚马逊网站的终身价值增加了20美元。

简单地说，终身价值指一个顾客在与你交易的过程中给你带来的收益。如果你只经营一种产品，而这种产品很可能不会再被订

the site, checked out the book and bought it. And in doing so, I boosted my lifetime value to Amazon by another 20 bucks.

Lifetime value is simply the income generated by a single customer over the course of your relationship with them. If you sell only one product — and if it's something that doesn't need to be reordered — then your customers' lifetime value will be limited to the net income that comes from a single sale of your product. But if you sell a wide range of products, your income can grow exponentially①. In fact, I've bought maybe one book a month from Amazon over the past five years at an average cost of $ 20 each — meaning my lifetime value to them so far is about $ 1,200. And selling to existing customers is easier and cheaper than selling to strangers because you've already cultivated a relationship with them. You've put in the time and money to: get their attention; establish your credibility; build their trust in you; overcome any resistance they may have to buying online; close that first sale.

On top of that, you now know what your customers like. The important thing to remember is the backend products you offer have to be things your target market is going to be interested in. So how do you find the killer products that make this strategy so profitable? It's a lot easier than you think. For example, you can: Offer products that complement your initial product. For instance, if you sell golf clubs, offer your customers a golf club bag to carry them in. Or you could sell golf balls,

---

① exponential [ˌekspəuˈnenʃəl] *a.* 指数的,幂数的

购，那么你的顾客的终身价值就局限于产品单次交易的净收入。但是，如果你经营一系列各种各样的产品，你的收益就会成指数增加。事实上，在过去的5年里，我基本上每个月都要从亚马逊网上购买一本平均价值20元的书，这就意味着我的终身价值对他们而言到目前为止已经差不多1 200美元了。与和陌生人做生意相比，和你现有的顾客做生意会容易而且便宜得多，因为你已经和他们建立了关系，你已经投入时间和金钱：引起他们的注意；建立你的诚信；取得他们的信任；克服他们网络购物的阻力；完成第一次交易。

另外，你现在了解顾客的喜好。重要的是记住：你提供的后端产品一定要是你的目标市场兴趣所在。所以，你如何找到匹配的产品使这个策略有利可图呢？可能比你想象的要容易得多。打个比方，你可以提供与前端产品互补的产品。例如，如果你经营高尔夫球杆，给你的顾客提供一个高尔夫球杆袋，以供他们把球杆装在里面。或者说你还可以卖高尔夫球、高尔夫球座、高尔夫鞋、高尔夫训练录像等，这份清单可以无穷无尽。

购买更多的同类商品可以给予价格折扣。如果你的产品适于再填充或需要有规则地替换，这种策略特别奏效，例如，你经营打印机墨盒或电池之类的产品，这种策略就有成功的把握。但是，即使你的产品不需要经常更换，你可以给顾客提供他们已购产品的特殊折扣，表示你对他们的感谢。用这种方式，如果他们喜欢这个产品，他们就可以买下来作为礼物送给家人和朋友。

使用预订付费作为后端产品。如果你已经确立自己是行业专

golf tees[1], golf shoes, golf training videos—the list is endless.

Sell more of the same product at a discounted price. If your product is refillable[2] or needs to be regularly replaced, this strategy works especially well. For example, if you sell things like printer cartridges[3] or batteries, you've got it made. But even if your product isn't refillable, you can show your customers you appreciate them by offering them a special discount on the product they've already bought. That way, if they like the product, they can buy it as a gift for family and friends.

Use paid subscriptions[4] as backend products. If you've established yourself as an expert in your industry, you can build on your reputation by offering a subscription to premium information, available only to members. For example, if your main product is a fly fishing kit, you could sell a subscription to an exclusive course on advanced fly fishing techniques as a backend product. You could deliver this paid-for content through a members-only website or by e-mail.

Try splitting up your current product. For example, if you were selling a book on how to organize your home, you could offer a basic version for $9.95 to generate a large volume of sales at a low price. Then, 30 days later, you could offer your customers an advanced, expanded version that includes home office management and scheduling software for $29.95 or even $39.95 — and increase your profits

---

① tee [tiː] *n.* 球座,发球处

② refillable [ˌriːfiləbl] *adj.* 可再装满的,再灌满

③ cartridge [ˈkɑːtridʒ] *n.* 弹药筒

④ subscription [sʌbˈskripʃən] *n.* 订购

家，可以通过提供额外信息的预订费建立信誉。而且这些信息只提供给会员。例如，如果你的主打产品是飞钓行李箱，就可以销售预订金，提供独家高级飞钓技术课程作为后端产品。你可以通过只对会员的网站或电子邮件发布这种付费信息。

分步提供当前的产品。例如，如果你正在销售一本如何管理家庭的书，初级版本可以卖 9.95 美元，以低价赚取大量的销售额。那么，30 天后再给顾客提供一个先进的升级版，包括 29.95 美元、甚至 39.95 美元的家庭办公管理和日程安排软件，极大地增加了你的盈利。

向你的顾客出售升级产品。如果顾客已经使用并喜欢你的基础产品，他们很容易接受你的升级版本。例如，你出售教人如何使用某种特殊软件的电子书，当这种正在讨论的软件包升级后，你可以对以前的顾客出售升级软件版的电子书。

写一本书或者制作一段视频。电子书是有高额利润率的强大的后端产品。可以考虑写一本关于产品和服务的小型电子书。例如，如果你经营美味的狗食，可以考虑写一本名为《训练秘诀：一周之内让每只狗训练有素、学会基本服从》。你甚至可以提供一段特殊视频，配合你的产品和服务。如果你经营烧烤器材，你可以提供一段视频，教人如何完善烧烤技术。

销售他人的产品。也许最快、最容易在网站增加新产品的方法是加入另外的商业联盟项目，推荐他人的产品，赚取每一相应销售额的利润提成。销售分支机构产品是一个利润非常可观的方法，增

dramatically.

Try selling your customers an upgrade to their product. If they've used and liked your basic model, your customers will be open to receiving offers for an upgraded version. For example, if you sell e-books that teach people how to use a particular piece of software, you can sell updated versions to previous buyers when the software package in question is upgraded.

Write a book or create a video. E-books are great backend products with high profit margins. Consider writing a short book on a topic related to your product or service. For instance, if you sell gourmet puppy food, you might consider writing a book titled "Training Secrets That Will Have Every Puppy Housebroken and Learning Basic Obedience in Less Than One Week." You could even offer a special video that complements your product or service. If you sell barbecue equipment, you might offer a video that teaches people how to perfect their barbecuing techniques.

Offer someone else's product. Probably the fastest and easiest way to add new products to your site is to join another business's affiliate program and recommend their products in exchange for a percentage of each resulting sale. Selling affiliate products can be a very lucrative way to increase your sales, especially since you don't have to spend any time or money developing a new product of your own.

The bottom line is, if you're not offering backend products to your customers, you're losing out on a lot of potential income.

(996 words)

加了你的销售量，尤其是因为你不必花费任何时间或金钱开发自己的新产品。

归根结底一句话：如果你不对顾客提供后端产品，你将失去很多潜在的利润。

知识链接

***Customer Life-cycle Value*(*CLV*)**　“客户终生价值”是指在维持客户的条件下，企业从该客户持续购买中所获得的利润流的现值。客户终生价值包括三个部分：一是客户直接购买企业的产品或服务而给企业带来的收益，指潜在客户价值、现有客户价值和忠诚客户价值。二是客户间接购买价值，指客户因对企业的产品或服务感到满意，进而向其他客户推荐购买本企业的产品或服务带来的价值。三是客户因交互满意而降低企业营销成本带来的收益，即满意客户不斤斤计较短暂的得失，对价格和包装设计不敏感；满意客户不会提出苛刻的交易条件，企业的维系成本较低并且流失率低。

题 记

网络营销采取新的营销管理模式，它通过互联网改造了传统的企业营销管理组织结构与运作模式。网络广告的传播不受时间和空间的限制，信息在厂商和客户之间互动传播，网络广告可以直接命中最有可能的潜在用户，消费者能亲身体验产品、服务与品牌。这种以图、文、声、像的形式，传送多感官的信息，让顾客如身临其境般感受商品和服务，并能在网上预订、交易与结算，顺应了经济时代实时、灵活、低成本的特征。网络营销为美国各行各业的公司企业创造了更多新的市场机会。

Setting up Shop Online to Tap Consumers

When sales at his wholesale business started to wane, Eli Mechlovitz decided to take a direct approach. Mr. Mechlovitz and his family had been selling glass and tiles① wholesale in the New York area for more than 20 years. But as the real-estate bubble began to burst, the company's retail clients started losing shoppers and slashing orders. So last September, the co-owner launched a specialty Web site, GlassTileStore.com, to sell custom tiles and mosaics② directly to consumers. The site allows customers to see close-up③ images of tile and mosaic designs. And they can call in for a design consultation. "People always want to redo their kitchens," Mr. Mechlovitz says, but with the economic slowdown, they "aren't willing to go out and spend a lot in a store. They are looking online for deals." Some of the products they sell online cost as much as 50% less than what they would at a retail store. The move seems to be

---

① tile [tail] *n.* 磁砖

② mosaic [mɔ'zeik] *n.* 镶嵌细工,镶木细工

③ close-up ['kləuzʌp] *n.* 特写镜头

拓展客源开网店

当伊莱·麦克洛维兹的批发业务销售量开始减少时，他决定采用一种直接的方式。麦克洛维兹先生和家人在纽约地区做玻璃和瓷砖批发生意已经20多年了。但随着房地产泡沫的破裂，公司的零售商开始失去顾客并削减订单。于是去年9月，合伙人启动专业网站GlassTileStore.com，直接对顾客出售瓷砖和马赛克。网站可以让顾客查看瓷砖和马赛克图案的特写镜头。客户可以电话咨询设计方案。麦克洛维兹先生说："人们总是想改装厨房"，但是随着经济的衰退，他们"不愿意出门，在商店多花钱。他们开始在网上寻找交易"。他说，他们在网上销售产品的成本有些比零售商店少一半以上。迄今为止，这一策略似乎取得了成功。8月份，网站销售了20 000平方英尺用玻璃和石头做成的马赛克，和批发商的旺季销售量一样多。

随着存货的增加和零售商销售的持续萎缩，越来越多的批发公司在一定程度上减少了中间商，转向网络产品销售，以批发的价格将产品直接卖给顾客。他们希望引诱在家居装饰店购买新瓷砖时犹

paying off so far. In August, the Web site sold 20,000 square feet of mosaics made of glass and stone, as much as the wholesale business typically sold in a busy month.

With inventories growing and sales at retailers continuing to shrink, an increasing number of wholesale companies are cutting out the middleman to some extent and turning to the Web to hawk their products—at wholesale prices-directly to consumers. The hope is that consumers who are hesitating to buy that new tile in the home-improvement store will be enticed to do so when they see it for substantially less online. But shifting gears from wholesaler to Web retailer isn't seamless. The biggest obstacle: Wholesalers are generally not accustomed to dealing directly with consumers. So they are being forced to learn about customer service—how to answer questions, for instance, and ease consumers' concerns, offer advice and fix problems. And they are getting a crash course① in consumer advertising to get themselves noticed online. "Web sites need development, Web marketing search engines need to recognize your site," says Bruce Clay, an Internet business consultant in Moorpark, Calif. "In an e-commerce world, this is something a wholesaler may be ill prepared to handle."

Mr. Mechlovitz admits that selling online is definitely "more work." Before, he says, interacting with customers mainly meant receiving orders from repeat retail clients and setting up delivery. Now, workers must interact daily with individual consumers, helping them with tile

---

① crash course 速成班

豫不决的顾客看到网上价格便宜很多时购买产品。但是，从批发商转为网上零售商并不是无缝链接。最大的障碍是：批发商通常不习惯直接和顾客打交道，所以他们正在被迫学习客服知识，例如，如何回答问题，缓解客户的紧张，提供建议和解决问题。他们参加消费者广告速成班，以使他们在网上得到关注。加利福尼亚州墨尔帕克市的互联网业务咨询师布鲁斯说，“网站需要发展，网络营销搜索引擎需要识别你的网站。在一个电子商务的世界里，这就是一个批发商可能会难以驾驭的领域”。

麦克洛维兹先生承认，网上销售确实意味着“更多的工作”。他认为，以前与顾客打交道主要指零售商客户再定货和配送。现在工人必须每天和个体消费者打交道，帮助他们选择瓷砖和回答设计问题，这些工作过去是和顾客打交道的零售商的任务。公司的网上业务每天要接 50~100 个顾客电话。网站每天接 50 个订单，平均每个订单价值 300 到 500 美元。这是批发经营的巨大转变，批发商一般每月只处理少量的价值数千美元的大宗订单。去年网上交易成交额价值 70 万美元，而批发业务成交额大约 60 万美元。为了让品牌在网上拥有人气，GlassTileStore.com 网站交钱申请了专营点击付费广告、搜索引擎优化和网络图像的公司服务。麦克洛维兹先生说，他每月花费 5 000 美元用以支付网址和在线广

selection and answering design questions—tasks that used to fall to the retail clients who dealt with the customers. With the online business, the company answers about 50 to 100 customer phone calls a day. The site receives about 50 orders daily, with the average order going for \$300 to \$500. That's a big change from the wholesale operation, which typically processed a handful of bulk orders per month worth thousands of dollars each. The online business generated about \$700,000 in sales last year, while the wholesale business had sales of about \$600,000. To get its name out there, GlassTileStore.com pays for services from companies that specialize in pay-per-click ads, search-engine optimization and Web graphics. Mr. Mechlovitz says he spends about \$5,000 monthly on maintaining the Web site and online advertising. "Wholesalers new to the e-commerce world need to make a strong investment in infrastructure that supports all aspects of customer service, technical support, product support, returns," says John Metzger, chief executive of Metzger Associates, a Boulder, Colo., communications firm that helps companies create online business strategies. Whereas retailers wouldn't typically fuss over① one or two broken items in a large shipment, "if something is broken, the consumer expects it to be fixed right away and they want someone to help them fix it."

Customer service has been the key for the online business. When Yomesh Shah saw sales from his family's 30-year-old New York business

---

① fuss over 过分关心或体贴

告。为公司提供网上业务策略的科罗拉多州博尔德市梅斯格通信公司的主管约翰·梅斯格说："对电子商务陌生的批发商需要在支持顾客服务的各方基础设施上加大投资力度，如技术支持、产品支持和退货。"尽管零售商在大宗出货时对一两个损坏的产品一般不会大惊小怪，"如果有坏掉的产品，顾客希望马上修好，他们希望有人帮助他们修理"。

顾客服务一直是网上营销的关键。当约迈西·萨克先生发现家族经营了30年的纽约买卖滞销时，他启动了B2Cjewels.com网站，以赢得更广泛的顾客。但是由于大部分人不习惯在互联网上购买高价位的个人物品——如订婚戒指，公司的主要挑战就是保持顾客对网站和产品的信任度和安全感。一开始，萨克先生谨慎地选择在网上提供的产品。网站根据预算和品位使商品个性化，允许顾客制作自己的戒指、耳环和手镯，一步一步地引导他们挑选金属、框架和石头。萨克先生是一位受过训练的宝石学家，为了让顾客在网站上感到更舒适，制作了一个术语表——如合金和海蓝宝石——还有一系列的指南，帮助顾客了解更多的钻石、珍珠、黄金和宝石。今年，公司从网上获得的销售额达到50多万美元。萨克先生说，达到这些销售额的关键是很快意识到"仅仅做好优秀的产品或网站还不能真正起作用，最

stagnate[1], he launched an online site, B2Cjewels.com, to reach a wider audience. But because most people were unaccustomed to shopping for big-ticket[2], personal items such as engagement rings over the Internet, the company's main challenge was to make customers feel confident and secure about the site and the products. First, Mr. Shah carefully selected the products offered online. To personalize the items for budget and taste, the site allows customers to create their own rings, earrings and bracelets—leading them through a step-by-step process of picking a metal, setting and stone. To make the customer feel more comfortable with the Web site, Mr. Shah, a gemologist[3] by training, created a glossary of terms—such as alloy and aquamarine—as well as a number of tutorials to help customers learn more about diamonds, pearls, gold and gemstones. This year, the company has had more than $500,000 in sales from the site. Mr. Shah says the key to getting those sales was quickly realizing "that just making a great product or site wouldn't really help. The most important thing is to get the word out there about our business." So B2Cjewels.com explores every possible advertising channel, including posting on blogs about the jewelry industry and buying pay-per-click ads.

Indeed, getting noticed is one of the biggest issues for the wholesalers expanding to online retailing. With the wholesale business, advertising often means simply supplying a retailer with catchy displays for

---

① stagnate [ˈstægneit] *v.* 停止,停滞

② big-ticket 高价的,昂贵的

③ gemologist [dʒeˈmɔlədʒist] *n.* 宝石学家

重要的是把我们的业务从网站上发布出去”。所以，B2Cjewels.com探索每个可能的广告渠道，包括在博客上发布珠宝行业的帖子和购买点击支付广告。

得到关注对拓展网络零售业务的批发商的确是一件大事。在批发行业中，广告通常意味着给只供商店的零售商提供引人注目的夸张广告。床垫和寝具批发商迈克·吉佩利说：“网站就像是森林里的一个商店。如果没人光临，产品的优劣和价格的高低就都不重要了。”他是经典睡眠产品公司的主管，其网上商店是Abed.com。吉佩利先生的业务受到国内销售额下降以及顾客消费减少的影响，他尝试通过拓展品牌形象来弥补零售顾客下降的床垫销售额，于6个月前启动了一个网上商店。公司还利用网站以折扣价销售停产的产品。由于之前没有开办网上商店和与个体消费者交流的经验，公司雇佣了两名全职员工来关注客户服务，还雇了两个网站设计和广告的员工。吉佩利先生说，雇员花了几个月的时间试验不同的网页设计和点击支付广告，看哪种页面能得到网络用户最多的点击率。他们还在各种各样的博客上发布评论和公司网站链接，甚至将某几种产品放到易趣拍卖网站，将交易拉回到Abed.com。今年网站在广告花费上投入达35万美元。床垫公司的网络销售额一年大约200万美元，仍然

a store. "It's like being a store out in the woods," says Mike Zippelli, chief executive of mattress① and bedding wholesaler Classic Sleep Products Inc. and its online store Abed.com. "If no one visits it, it doesn't matter how good your products and prices are." Mr. Zippelli's business, stung by the decline in home sales and a slowdown in consumer spending, tried to make up for declining mattress sales at retail clients and expand its brand recognition by launching an online store about six months ago. It also uses the site to sell discontinued products at a discounted price. Because it didn't have previous knowledge of running an online site and interacting with individual customers, the company hired two full-time employees to focus on customer service and two others to work on Web-site design and advertising. Mr. Zippelli says the employees spent months experimenting with different page designs and pay-per-click advertising to see which pages received the most clicks from Web users. They also post comments and links to the company's Web site on various blogs and even place certain products on auction site eBay to drive traffic back to Abed.com. The site spent $350,000 on advertising this year. The mattress company's online sales are at about $2 million a year, which is still a small percentage of its wholesale sales. Last year, the company had total sales of $30 million. But "our big goal is to extend our brand image and strengthen the recognition of our company," Mr. Zippelli says, "and that has definitely worked."

(1,144 words)

---

① mattress [ˈmætris] *n.* 床垫

只占少量的批发销售额。公司去年的总销售额达 3 000 万美元。但是吉佩利先生说，“我们的大目标是拓展品牌形象和加强公司的认知度，这个目标已经如愿以偿”。

知识链接

GlassTileStore. com 是美国著名的销售厨房、浴室及游泳池瓷砖和马赛克的网络消费目标地。网站有超过 300 种风格时尚、设计独特的瓷砖和马赛克款式。作为网络零售商，公司取消了中介，产品直接批发给顾客。瓷砖和马赛克的价格一般比商店零售低 40%~60%。

B2Cjewels. com 是美国著名的珠宝采购网站，出售精致的戒指、耳环、手镯和宝石。你可以在网上查看所有的产品并了解价位。为了便利网上购买，首先建银行卡，然后提供个人信息，选择产品，点击购物车。发货信息在付账后提供，也可以在电子邮件中注册“单独发盘”。

题　记

当城镇中最繁华的商业区退出消费者时尚行列之时，网络零售商能够根据用户需求提供更为广泛的商品和支持信息，聪明的英国人不失时机地转向选择互联网便捷购物，随之而来的则是网上购物逆市暴增的业绩：虽然 NEXT 和 M&S 的实体商店销售额下滑，但它的在线业务却在增长；ASOS 一直以大幅增长的销售额成为英国的头号时尚网站；Net-A-Porter 是在线奢侈品零售的典型代表，在奢侈品的寒冬中创造了惊人的业绩。运营思路的转变给时尚品牌的销售带来新的生机，虚拟的网上商铺已经八面风光地涉猎时尚业的网络零售。专家们预测，城市中心的传统零售商在不久的将来可能会将他们 15%的市场份额丧失给网络零售竞争对手。在线销售仍有极大的成长空间。

Online Fashion Retailers

As the capital gears up for London Fashion Week, the bosses of the nation's biggest clothing chains are more likely to be found drowning their sorrows than cracking open the champagne. But online sellers should be easy to spot on the party circuit: they will be the ones smiling.

For while the High Street is falling out of fashion with consumers, online shopping is in vogue, and the migration to the net is expected to accelerate as the economy deteriorates①. In recent months, bad news has poured out of the clothing sector. A string of profits warnings from some of retail's biggest names, alongside high-profile credit-crunch casualties such as shoe chain Dolcis, has revealed the extent to which discretionary spending is under pressure. This week saw Next chief executive Simon Wolfson deliver a miserable verdict on the sector: there is little hope of recovery until 2010. So the last thing retailers need is to have market share snatched away by internet upstarts.

Just eight years ago, with the ignominious collapse of early fashion site Boo.com, online stores were already looking passé. But the dark days

① deteriorate [di'tiəriəreit] *vi.* 恶化,变坏

时尚品在线零售

随着资本为伦敦时装周加速运转，英国最大型服装连锁店的老板们没有开香槟庆祝，差不多都沉浸在悲伤之中。但人们却很容易在社交圈发现网络销售商：他们才有可能是微笑的人群。

当城镇中最繁华的商业区退出消费者时尚行列之时，网上购物便开始盛行，随着经济的恶化，人们期待网络移民加速增长。在最近的几个月里，坏消息已经充斥着服装行业。伴随着高姿态的信贷紧缩危机，一连串来自最大零售商的利润警告，如Dolcis鞋链，已经显示可自由支配的个人开支范围处于压力之下。本周见证了下一任首席执行官西蒙·沃尔夫森发布了一份悲惨的判决：到2010年都几乎没有希望恢复。所以，零售商需要做的最后一件事是分享互联网暴发户已经抢走的市场份额。

就在8年前，随着早期时尚网站boo.com不光彩的倒闭，网上商店已经看上去过时了。但是，网络泡沫崩溃的黑暗日子已经过去了很久。网络空间的服装消费今年在英国预计将达到30亿英镑，占市场总额的6%，敏特公司预测这种情况将在今后5年增加一倍以上。城镇中最繁华的商业区和在线商店财富的鲜明对照已经清晰可见。6月份服装和鞋的店面销售尽管普遍打折，还是创下了历史的最低纪录，但这时却是互联网的销售膨胀期，服装销售收入增长

of the dot-com crash are long past. Clothes spending in cyberspace is expected to reach £3bn this year in the UK, 6% of the total market, and Mintel forecasts this will more than double in the next five years. The contrasting fortunes of the High Street and online stores are clear to see. Clothing and shoes sales in stores plunged at a record rate in June despite widespread discounting, but it was a boom month for the internet, with clothes sales rising 32% and footwear up 38%.

Convenience, access to a bigger product range, the spread of broadband① and increased trust in the internet as a sales medium are all major drivers of growth. A study by Capgemini and the Interactive Media in Retail Group concluded last year was the first year that soaring online sales really started to affect traditional bricks-and-mortar retailers. But worse is to come for those yet to enter cyberspace: as the consumer spending squeeze continues, the bricks-to-clicks transition will accelerate as the soaring cost of a trip to town forces shoppers to opt for the mouse over the mall. "We are bullish about the scope for fashion sales online," says Kaupthing retail analyst Matthew McEachran. "The high cost of petrol and economic downturn will drive more and more customers away from the High Street and on to the internet." With disposable incomes plunging, Capgemini and IMRG expect consumers to develop smarter shopping habits, another driver of online sales growth, boosted by the perception that goods are cheaper on the internet.

---

① broadband [ˈbrɔːdbænd] *n.* 宽带

32% ，鞋类销售增长 38% 。

互联网作为销售媒介的方便、易获得更大的产品范围、宽带传播和增强的信任度都是在线零售增长的主要驱动力。一份凯捷和互动媒体零售集团的研究报告断定，去年是在线销售飙升的第一年，并真正开始影响传统的零售商。但是更糟糕的是那些有待进入网络空间的厂商：随着消费支出的降低，网络销售运转将加速，因为进城往返旅行费用的上扬迫使购物者选择鼠标而不是大超市。酷普亭零售分析师马休·麦克瑞恩说：“我们看好时装在线销售的机会。汽油的高成本和经济衰退将驱使越来越多的消费者远离城镇中最繁华的商业区，进入互联网。”随着可支配收入的下降，凯捷公司和 IMRG 预期消费者养成更加理性的购物习惯，互联网上的商品较便宜的价格刺激了另一个在线销售增长的驱动力。

许多零售商早已意识到建设强大的互联网站的需要，并已对在线服务投入巨资。这些公司企业结合在线电子商务和传统零售渠道的营运策略——如 NEXT 和 M&S——据报道即使商店销售额下滑，在线业务也在增长。NEXT 的沃尔夫森说：“我们没有看到消费放缓影响在线销售的任何迹象。网上有超过 60% 的目录销售，而且销售额也增加了 2.2% 。”但其他人依然在徘徊观望。牛津街、毗邻马克、扎拉、H&M 和玛塔蓝仍在等待互联网推出完全的交易网站。

那么，谁是完美的在线大赢家呢？较便宜的终端区域是 ASOS，受到 20 岁左右的青少年时尚女皇们的追捧。根据仲裁监督研究公司的高级零售分析师马尔科姆·平克顿的预测，该公司正在偷窃 NXET，Topshop，甚至 Primark 的市场份额。ASOS 一直以大幅增长的数字在城市中取得了巨大的成功——今年的销量已上升了

Many retailers have long been aware of the need for a strong internet site, and have invested heavily in their online offering. These hybrid clicks-and-mortar businesses — NEXT and M&S being prime examples - are reporting growth online even as store sales slide. "We are not seeing any sign of the consumer slowdown affecting online sales," says NEXT's Wolfson. "Over 60% of the Directory's sales are online, and there sales are up 2.2%." But others still linger on the sidelines. Selfridges, Primark, Zara, H&M and Matalan are yet to embrace the internet with the launch of fully transactional sites.

So who are the big pure-play online winners? At the cheaper end of the sector is ASOS, adored by teen and twenty something fashion queens. According to Verdict Research's senior retail analyst Malcolm Pinkerton, the company is stealing market share from Next, Topshop and even Primark. ASOS consistently wows the City with bumper① figures—sales have been up 90% this year — and it is ready to overtake Next as the number one fashion website in the UK next year. Brokers are widely calling ASOS stock as a buy: shares in the company are as much a must-have as the latest Roland Mouret dress.

Meanwhile, Net-A-Porter is the poster child for online luxury retailing, delivering staggering sales and profits growth. The well-heeled increasingly turn to the boutique for their fashion fix, showing internet shoppers now trust the medium enough to fork out £6000 on an Oscar

① bumper[ˈbʌmpə] *adj.* 丰盛的,丰富的

90% ——作为英国明年的头号时尚网站，它已准备取代 Next 公司。经纪人正在广泛呼吁购买 ASOS 股票：该公司的股份就像你必须拥有最新的罗兰莫特礼服一样。

与此同时，Net-A-Porter 是在线奢侈品零售的典型代表，提供惊人的销售额和利润的增长。穿着考究的人根据他们的时尚定位越来越青睐专卖精品的小商店，这表明现在的互联网购物者对媒介的信任，足以交易 6 000 万英镑的奥斯卡德拉伦塔礼服。网络销售增长得如此之快，以至于去年的销售额超过了迄今为止的最初 6 年的总和。分析人士认为，它能够及时证明它对百货公司有相当大的威胁。那么，还有在线拍卖网站如易趣，供现金拮据的消费者寻找便宜货从中受益。

但是毫无疑问，宽带技术的广泛应用——主要的增长动力——将会放慢速度，它阻碍了网络服装销售的扩张吗？道德网络商店阿迪利的首席执行官亚当·斯密认为，这有很长的路要走：宽带市场的渗透将萎缩，但消费者接受网上购衣仍然会滞后，所以仍然存在大量的潜在客户，他们尚未初试牛刀。网上购物是一种趋势，而且不会在下一季被淘汰，但应该证明它作为永恒的小黑装。随着零售前景的快速变化，担心经济衰退的出现，强大的互联网出售物可能是城镇中最繁华的商业区生存机会的一个主要因素。

知识链接

Mintel International Group Ltd 英敏特信息咨询有限公司是消费、媒介和市场研究的全球供应商，也是英国商务交易的超级品牌。30 多年来，他们广

de la Renta gown. It is growing so fast that last year's sales outstripped the total for the first six years of its existence. Analysts believe in time it could prove a considerable threat to department stores. And then there are online auctioneers such as eBay, benefiting as cash-strapped consumers search out bargains.

But surely, the spread of broadband technology—a major driver of growth—will slow, hitting the expansion of online clothing sales? Adam Smith, chief executive of ethical online store Adili, believes this is a long way off: Market penetration of broadband will tail off, but the consumer is still lagging in terms of acceptance of buying clothes online, so there is a big pool of potential customers who haven't yet dipped their toe in the water. Online shopping is a trend that won't be going out of fashion next season, but should prove as timeless as the little black dress. With the retail landscape changing rapidly and fears of a looming recession, strong internet offerings could be a major factor in High Street stores' chances of survival.

(876 words)

泛的产品提供了独特的视野，可靠而有价值的原始市场信息，对客户的成功产生了直接的影响。英敏特帮助客户发现机会，监控竞争对手，开发产品和服务，占领营销和广告市场。英敏特坚持不懈地创造新产品和改善现有产品的质量，保证与市场研究的一致性和综合性。

IMRG 英国互动媒体零售集团是电子零售行业全球领先的网络零售组织，其成员由数百家提供网络零售技术和服务的零售商和企业组成。IMRG 的目标是最大化地挖掘在线购物的商业潜力。IMRG 集团的网络销售额随着电子商务市场的快速发展逐年递增，集团帮助其成员最大限度地把握商机，与零售市场现代化的发展同步。

Capgemini 凯捷咨询顾问公司创建于 1967 年，是全球最著名的管理咨询、技术和外包服务的供应商之一。凯捷以自己独特的方式与客户进行协作，称之为协同管理关系。基于对互利双赢和由此产生的企业价值增长的郑重承诺，凯捷帮助企业制定发展战略，并提供相应的技术支持。凯捷在 34 个国家拥有员工，在专业服务领域中位居世界前三名。

NEXT 公司是英国领先的服装零售集团，经营着规模庞大的多品种、小批量的服装零售及邮购订单业务。NEXT 品牌价格中下、品质中上，非常适合上班族，英国办公室里的男性职员 10 个有 9 个穿 NEXT 品牌的衬衫。

ASOS 英国时尚网店。英国在线时装零售商 ASOS 办公地位于伦敦北部一座吸引人的装饰艺术风格建筑的二楼，它的大门部分与 NHS 保险公司共用。ASOS. com2000 年 6 月上线，现在是英国最大的独立在线时尚品零售商。ASOS. com 有 19 400 品牌和标签产品，每周有 1 000 种新款上市，网站已快速成为英国在线时尚领域的市场领袖。ASOS. com 瞄准的目标顾客是 16~34 岁的时尚奢侈品消费主流人群，网站每月的访问人流超过 6 300 万人，有 280 万注册使用人。

题 记

从诞生的第一天起，电子游戏就伴随着各种各样的商业盈利活动—游戏机、游戏卡、游戏相关产品等。随着全球游戏产业快速地向在线化、网络化方向发展，电子游戏已经呈现出多元化的发展特征，电子游戏的盈利模式也就更加不顺从单一模式的路线，向着发散路线而发展了。游戏公司让用户免费注册，但强迫用户购买游戏装备，登录游戏时浏览30秒的广告，用真实的现金购买虚拟金币，向用户销售虚拟的盔甲、枪和攻击行动。电子商务平台的优势孵化了消费流量，并且有效提升了游戏用户体验和服务品质，用金币在网络游戏的一池碧波水中激起微澜。

How Free Games Make Money

When a game's not working, some people quit. Others change the rules. Three years ago, Howard Marks, best known for resurrecting① the financially flailing② game maker Activision in the early 1990s, snapped③ up the remaining assets of bankrupt Acclaim Entertainment for $100,000. Now Acclaim is releasing games—charging players nothing to play—and aiming to be profitable within the next 12 months. Instead of monthly fees, Marks is betting that he can create a profitable business entirely supported by posting in-game advertisements and selling virtual tchotchkes. "We believe that consumers would prefer to play high-quality games for free rather than pay $60 for a game in a retail store," says Marks. It's a gutsy—but not entirely irrational strategy. The U.S. gaming market sells about $18.8 billion a year—about half of which is sales of software for PCs and other devices, according to analyst NPD Group. Subscription gaming revenues in the U.S. last year amounted to about

---

① resurrect [ˌrezəˈrekt] *vt.* 复兴
② flail [fleil] *n.* 联机
③ snap [snæp] *vi.* 猛地吸住,猛咬

免费游戏赚钱有道

当一个游戏不能正常运作时，有些人就会退出，另一些人会改变规则。3年前，使联机游戏制造商Activision公司在20世纪90年代初期起死回生的霍华德·马克斯，用10万美元收购了已告破产的喝彩娱乐公司的剩余资产。现在，喝彩娱乐公司推出了一款游戏——对玩家免费开放——目标是在未来12个月内获利。马克斯没有收取月费，打赌说他可以完全靠置入游戏广告和出售虚拟游戏币创造营销利润。马克斯说："我们相信顾客偏好高品质的免费游戏，而不是付60美元在零售店买一个游戏。"这是一个勇敢、但并非完全无理智的策略。根据NPD咨询公司的分析，美国游戏市场年销售额是188亿美元，其中一半的软件销售额流向个人电脑和其他设备。圣地亚哥市场调查公司DFC智能部门主席大卫·科勒说，去年美国订购游戏的收入达到600万美元。他补充说，售货清单并没有登记注册。

然而，亚洲的销售业绩并非如此。在过去7年多来，韩国及

$ 600 million, says David Cole, president of DFC Intelligence, a market research firm in San Diego. Item sales barely register, he adds.

That's not true in Asia, however. Over the past seven or so years, gaming companies in Korea, and more recently, China, have built gaming empires by letting people play for free and selling them anything from virtual weapons to fashionable boots. San Francisco-based Pearl Research estimates that as much as 75% of the $ 1.7 billion Chinese gaming market is built on virtual item sales. Now Marks, and a small but growing number of U.S. gaming companies, are venturing down the same path. Marks sold on free-to-play games soon after buying Acclaim. Two weeks after the deal, Marks headed to Korea to tour 30 developers. Their stories were compelling: Company after company recited how it increased revenues several-fold by dropping subscription fees and making games free. With no entry fee, players turned out to be willing to spend money to accessorize① and augment② their characters. Seoul-based game maker Nexon collected $ 230 million from its library of free-to-play, item-supported games. At least in Korea, the subscription model of games seemed a dead end. "I instantly had an epiphany③," Marks recalls. He would follow Korea's lead—both by rebuilding top-selling Korean games for the U.S. market and by relying on advertising and in-game sales to

① accessorize [æk'sesəˌraiz] *vt.* 装饰,补充
② augment [ɔːg'ment] *v.* 增加,增大
③ epiphany [i'pifəni] *n.* 灵感出现

免费游戏赚钱有道

近来的中国游戏公司已经建立了游戏帝国，他们给玩家提供免费的游戏，对他们出售从虚拟武器到流行靴子之类的任何商品。总部位于旧金山的Pearl市场研究公司估计，多达17亿美元的中国游戏市场的75%建立在虚拟商品的销售上。现在，马克斯和越来越多的小游戏公司正在冒着重蹈覆辙的风险。马克斯一买下喝彩娱乐公司，马上开始经营免费游戏。交易两周之后，马克斯走访了韩国的30家开发商。他们的业绩令人瞩目：一家又一家的公司讲述着他们是如何通过降低订购费用和使用免费游戏使收入成倍增长。由于取消了入场费，玩家开始愿意花钱装饰和突出自己的角色个性。总部位于首尔的游戏开发商Nexon从免费和产品支持游戏库中获利2.3亿美元。至少在韩国，游戏订阅模式似乎是死路一条。马克斯回忆说，“我立刻顿悟了”。他应该遵从韩国的领先模式：既在美国市场重建最畅销的韩国游戏，又依赖对玩家的广告和游戏内销。马克斯说，“我相信，这是人们在不久的将来玩游戏的唯一方式”。

在大游戏开发商日益占主导地位的游戏业，游戏免费是较小的游戏开发商能够为自己开拓一片天地的方式。例如，在全球有1 000万玩家的《魔兽世界》已经成为艾尔文公司的利润喷泉，艾尔文公司是位于加州的暴雪娱乐公司维旺迪游戏程序的一个部门。但

players, rather than subscription fees. "I decided this is the way people will play games in the near future," says Marks.

Going free is one way smaller game publishers can carve out a space for themselves in an industry increasingly dominated by enormous game distributors. World of Warcraft, for instance, which commands the attention of 10 million players worldwide, has become a profit geyser for Irvine, Calif.-based Blizzard Entertainment, a division of Vivendi Games. But getting into such multi-player, role-playing games is a big commitment, involving fees of $15 a month and often soaking up 20 hours a week as players inch their way up competitive rankings. By contrast, anyone with a computer and Internet connection can drop in to play a free-to-play game. Instead of spending hours advancing their characters, players can shore up their inexperience by buying better swords, more potent potions or protective garments. Acclaim's gratis[1] games offer players a variety of ways to play for free. In "Bots!!," a robot arena game, players buy "Acclaim Coins" they can spend on virtual armor, guns or attack moves. In the adults-only "2Moons," gamers can opt in to watching video ads in exchange for boosting their characters' experience level. The Kung Fu-themed "9Dragons" rewards players who click through to video advertisements with in-game currency and special items.

Other small game companies began catching free-to-play fever, too.

---

① gratis [ˈgreitis] *adj.* 免费的

是，进入这样一个多人、角色分工游戏是一个大工程，玩家逐步获得有竞争力的排名需要每月花费 15 美元、每周在线游戏 20 小时。相比之下，有电脑并能联网的任何人都可以顺便玩免费游戏。 玩家并没有花时间推进自己的角色，他们通过购买更好的剑、更有效的药剂或防护服支持经验缺损。 喝彩娱乐公司的免费游戏向玩家提供各种免费的游戏方式。 在机器人游戏《僵尸》中，玩家需要先购买“喝彩币”，然后用它购买虚拟的盔甲、枪和攻击行动。 在只对成年人的“2Monns”游戏中，玩家可以选择观看视频广告来提高角色的经验等级。 以功夫为主题的“9Dragons”游戏使用游戏币和特殊产品奖励点击视频广告的玩家。

其他一些小的游戏公司也开始迷恋免费游戏狂潮。 总部位于旧金山的三环公司首席执行官丹尼尔·詹姆斯说，获得巨大利润的秘诀是在玩家面前吊一根正确的胡萝卜。 推出《海盗之谜》的多人休闲游戏不久后，詹姆斯计算出，在游戏中增加一个玩家的成本是微不足道的。 于是，詹姆斯取消了公司指定的收费点，反过来让玩家用真实的现金购买虚拟金币，他们转而又可以用来装饰战利品海盗或购买其他的身份象征物。 一年多来，《海盗之谜》通过出售虚拟货币从每月获利 50 000 美元到利润翻番。 尽管只有 15% ~20% 的《海盗之谜》玩家会购买金币，但凡买者就会购买很多。 虚拟货币的购买量占

The secret to winning big revenue is to dangle① the right carrot in front of players, says Daniel James, chief executive of San Francisco-based Three Rings. Soon after launching its casual multiplayer game "Puzzle Pirates," James calculated the cost of adding additional players to the game was negligible. So James broke down the toll booth-instead, players could use real cash to buy virtual doubloons—which, in turn, they could use to bedeck their pirates in loot or purchase other status symbols. Over a year, "Puzzle Pirates" went from collecting $ 50,000 a month in subscriptions to raking in twice that by selling virtual doubloons. Only 15% to 20% of "Puzzle Pirates" players ever buy doubloons—but those who do buy a lot. Virtual currency purchases accounted for roughly 75% of Puzzle Pirates $ 4 million revenue. It's a lot like letting crowds into a movie theater for free, then collecting serious coinage from those who crave popcorn and Jolly Ranchers.

Inspired by such success, big gaming companies are now entering the free fray②, too. "We knew which direction the world would go," says Sony, Online Entertainment President John Smedley. "We're going to be right on that wave." Sony's next game, "Free Realms," slated to launch later this year, will rely primarily on in-game advertising and item sales. Players who don't want to sit through a 30-second ad at login but do want "velvet rope" benefits can choose to subscribe. "My gut tells me

① dangle [ˈdæŋgl] *v.* 摇摆

② fray [frei] *n.* 竞争

《海盗之谜》400 万美元收入的大约 75%。这就像让观众进入电影院免费看电影，然后从那些喜欢吃爆米花和棒棒糖的人身上赚大钱。

大公司从这种成功中获得灵感，现在也进入了自由竞争。索尼公司在线娱乐部门主席约翰·斯梅德利说，“我们知道游戏领域将向哪个方向发展，在这一浪潮中我们将会成功”。索尼的下一个将在今年晚些时候推出的游戏《自由王国》，主要依靠游戏中的广告和产品销售盈利。不想在登录时浏览 30 秒的广告、但又确实想得益于《华丽冒险》的玩家可以选择订购。斯梅德利说，“我的直觉告诉我这样可行。我们现在是在数百万人中寻找数十个用户，不是在数千人中寻找数百个用户”。如果《自由王国》盈利，索尼未来所有的大型多人联机游戏都可以免费。甚至电子艺界游戏公司也正在开发即将命名为《战场英雄》的免费游戏——一个流行的单机版射击游戏的随机分支。指定在 9 月份推出的《战场英雄》将按照玩家等级销售物品，并从官方网站的赞助商那里获得广告收入。电子艺界游戏公司的首席执行官约翰·里奇蒂耶洛更是宣布，60 美元一个的零售游戏将在未来 10 年内过时。

马克斯说：“很多游戏发行商不可能投注是因为他们想维持现有的商业模式。他们可能在向免费游戏模式转换的过程中无法生存。对我们而言，我们已经开始朝着那个方向转变。”

this will work," says Smedley. "We're now looking at tens of millions of people, not hundreds of thousands." And if "Free Realms" turns a profit, all of Sony's future, massively multiplayer gaming titles could go free, too. Even Electronic Arts is testing out free-to-play with an upcoming title, "Battlefield Heroes"—a casual offshoot of its popular PC-and-console shooter game. Slated to launch in September, "Battlefield Heroes" will sell items to pump up players' rankings as well as collect ad revenue from banners hosted on the official site, which players must visit to launch the game. EA Chief Executive John Riccitiello has gone so far as to declare that the $60 retail game will be obsolete within the next 10 years.

"Many publishers will not be able to jump in because they want to protect their existing business model," says Marks. "They may not survive a transition to the free-to-play model. In our case, we started there."

(1,018 words)

知识链接

Activision 是一家电子游戏和电脑游戏的发行商，也是全球顶级的互动娱乐软件出版商之一，成立于1979年，现在排在电子艺界公司之后位列第二。美国动视同时拥有针对不同目标市场、各种类型的娱乐软件，遍及目前流行的所有硬件平台和操作系统。对应持续增长的各类消费群体，美国动视创建、认证、获得了许多具有很高知名度的娱乐软件品牌，包括——《使命召唤》(Call of Duty)、《毁灭战士》(DOOM)、《雷神之锤》(Quake)等，其产品囊括了动作、冒险、运动、竞速、角色扮演、模拟、战略等多种类型。

NEXON 是韩国的电脑游戏公司，1995年5月成立，总部位于韩国首尔，擅长开发休闲类的网络游戏，目前主要的作品有《疯狂泡泡堂》、《弹水阿给》、《爆爆王》、《跑跑卡丁车》、《神之领域》、《枫之谷》和《玛奇》等。

题　记

网络招聘也称在线招聘或者电子招聘(E-Recruiting)，指利用互联网技术进行的招聘活动，包括信息的发布、简历的搜集整理、电子面试以及在线测评等。网络招聘是网络技术在人力资源管理中应用最快的领域。据统计全球每天约发布2 000万条就业信息，3 000多万人在互联网上发出求职简历。在互联网的发源地美国，平均每年有50%以上的人通过互联网更换工作，全球500强公司中有88%使用网络招聘员工。中国的网络招聘存在巨大的发展潜力，每年毕业的7 000万大学生，以摧枯拉朽之势激活了网络招聘市场，并吸引了全球最大的专业招聘网站怪兽公司注资进入中国网络行业。

Online Recruiting: Monster's Big China Move

As it takes full control of ChinaHR, Monster thinks it can avoid the struggles other U.S. Internet companies have experienced in the country. There's no shortage of U.S. Internet companies that have failed to replicate their successes at home in Chinese cyberspace. Despite throwing considerable resources at its Chinese-language operation, for instance, Google is a distant No. 2 in online search behind local champion Baidu. com. In online auctions, eBay threw in the towel after failing to dislodge① the market leader, Hangzhou-based Taobao, and joined forces with Hong Kong billionaire Li Ka-shing's TOM Online. In instant messaging, Microsoft lags far behind local rival Tencent. Most recently, News Corp.'s MySpace has had a disappointing performance in its attempt to export its social-networking model to China.

Edward Lo, the top China executive for online recruitment company Monster Worldwide knows all about this sorry track record, but he says

---

① dislodge [disˈlɔdʒ] *vt.* 逐出,驱逐

怪兽网络招聘大步迈进中国

随着对中华英才网的全面收购，怪兽公司认为自己能避免其他美国网络公司在这个国家经历过的种种艰难竞争。未能将本土的成功经验复制到中国信息空间的美国网络公司不胜枚举。例如，尽管谷歌对中国语言运营系统投入了相当多的资源，其网络引擎远远落后于中国本土冠军百度，只能位列第二。在网络拍卖方面，易趣未能驱赶市场的领先者，已经向位于杭州的淘宝认输，与香港亿万富翁李嘉诚的 TOM 在线联合经营。在即时通信服务方面，微软远远落后于本土竞争者腾讯。就最近来看，澳大利亚新闻公司的聚友网在尝试向中国输入其社会网络模式的行动中，表现得也不尽如人意。

作为怪兽全球网络招聘公司的大中华区首席执行官，爱德华·罗对所有这些令人惋惜的记录了如指掌，但是他说那些失败的案例并不会妨碍他和他的同事。怪兽公司已经宣布全资收购中国顶尖的网络招聘公司之一——中华英才网，而这也表明了罗和同事们的自信。怪兽公司此前已经拥有该公司的小部分股权，此次花费 17 400

those failures won't deter him and his colleagues. In a sign of their confidence, Monster announced it was taking 100% control of ChinaHR, one of the top online recruiting companies in the country. Monster, which already owned a minority stake in the company, is paying $ 174 million for the remaining 55% of the Beijing-based ChinaHR. Why is Lo so confident that Monster can avoid the traps① other U.S. e-commerce powerhouses faced in China? Demographics②. With some 7 million college graduates a year, China has a strong demand for online recruitment, he argues, and Monster can capitalize on that. "The key thing is, we are in the right space," says Lo, a former executive at AIG who joined Monster later.

Net-savvy job seekers are endless. Another plus: China's young people are extremely savvy about using the Net, he says. Chinese college students spend a lot of their time playing online games, sending instant messages, and participating in social networks. So it's only natural that young Chinese will turn to the Internet to find their first jobs out of school. "You have a young generation. When they start thinking of careers and jobs, obviously they go to the Internet," says Lo. And while China already has more Internet users than any other country, with 260 million Chinese online, the potential for growth is large, since only 15% of the country's population is connected. "This is the generation that's growing

---

① trap [træp] *n.* 陷阱

② demographics [demə'græfɪks] *n.* 人口统计特征

万美元获得了总部位于北京的中华英才网余下的55%的股份。为何罗能如此自信怪兽公司能避免其他美国电子商务巨头在中国面临的陷阱呢？答案是人口特征。罗说中国每年有7 000万大学毕业生，因此中国对于网络招聘有着强烈的需求，所以怪兽公司能在这方面投资。作为曾经的美国国际集团的首席执行官、而后加入怪兽公司的罗说道："关键在于，我们处在正确的空间。"

熟谙网络的求职者应接不暇。罗提出的另一个理由是：中国的年轻人在使用网络方面表现出极大的悟性。中国的大学生花很多时间玩网络游戏、发短信、参与社会网络活动。所以自然而然地，中国的年轻人将求助于网络、寻求他们在校外的第一份工作。罗说，"这是年轻的一代。当他们开始考虑职业生涯和工作的时候，他们显然会走向网络"。尽管中国已经拥有比其他国家更多的网络用户——2 600万中国网民，但这也只占中国人口的15%，网络仍然存在巨大的发展潜力。罗认为"这是正在飞跃成长的一代"。

然而也存在足够理由让我们保持谨慎。总部位于北京的市场调查公司——博达中国公司董事长特德·迪安认为，大型美国网络企业在中国投资过程中有着"多变的经历"，并总是试图将他们在国内取得的成功复制到中国市场。他说，"很难提出一个与已经完成的美国网络企业成功相媲美的案例"。迪安认为，

by leaps and bounds," Lo says.

Still, there's good reason for caution. Ted Dean, president of Beijing-based market research firm BDA China, says big U. S. Internet companies have a "checkered past" investing in China and trying to replicate in the Chinese market the success they had at home. "It's hard to come up with a successful example of an American Internet company that has pulled that off yet," he says. The problem, says Dean, is often an inability for U.S. executives to understand how to connect with Chinese consumers. "A lot of these things are thought of as technology companies because they are on the Internet, but in many ways the business is consumer services," he says. "The assumption is U.S. companies come in with powerhouse technology that will steamroll① the industry. But in some cases that's not the deciding factor in the market. It's understanding the consumer and being able to adapt to consumer tastes here."

Combining two successes won't be a worry for Monster. The company first invested in ChinaHR in 2005 and has been closely involved with its Chinese partner since then. "It's a long-lasting kind of relationship," he says. "We know the people. We like the people. We are just combining the two success stories into one." While Lo says the Monster-ChinaHR combination will become tops in the market, it faces plenty of competition. ChinaHR, launched eight years ago, is No. 2 in the recruiting market, with 24% share, behind Nasdaq-listed 51job. Another

---

① steamroll [ˈstiːmrəul] *vt.* 粉碎,压倒

问题通常在于美国企业的执行官在理解如何迎合中国消费者方面显得无能为力。他说，"因为这些问题发生在网上，所以人们认为他们是技术公司的事情，但是商业在很多方面是消费性劳务。人们通常假设，美国企业以强势的技术挺进中国，以摧枯拉朽之势进入网络行业。但在某些案例中，这并不是市场的决定性因素。关键在于了解消费者，并能够适合这里的消费者口味"。

两种成功的相互合作不会成为怪兽公司的烦恼。怪兽公司在 2005 年首次对中华英才网投资，从此与他的中国搭档保持着紧密的沟通和联系。他说，"这是一种长期持续的关系，我们了解这儿的人民，我们喜欢这些人。我们只是在将两个成功的故事结合成一个"。尽管罗认为怪兽公司—中国英才网的合作将成为市场中的佼佼者，但它也面临无数的竞争。8 年前创立的中华英才网拥有 24% 的市场份额，名列招聘市场第二，仅次于在纳斯达克挂牌的 51Job 网。另一个竞争对手智联招聘网，由于澳大利亚网络招聘专家 SEEK 的投资，注入了 10 500 万美元的现金，该澳大利亚公司拥有智联招聘 43% 的股权，而澳洲麦格里银行拥有 29% 的股权。

根据总部位于北京的市场调查公司易观国际的分析，中国的网络招聘市场相对较小，但正在增长。易观国际发布的一份报告表明，今年第一季度推定市场规模为 4 400 万美元。无论如何，这也是在前一季度的基础上增长了 8%，与去年同期相比增长了 37%。

rival, Zhaopin, received a $105 million influx of cash thanks to investments from Australian online recruiting specialist SEEK, which owns 43% of the company, and Macquarie Group, which owns 29%.

According to Beijing-based market research firm Analysys International, the online recruiting market in China is small but growing. In a released report, Analysys put the size of the market at just $44 million in the first quarter of this year. However, that was an 8% increase over the previous quarter and a 38% increase over the same quarter of last year. According to Analysys, 51Job has 29% market share, ChinaHR has 24%, and Zhaopin 15%.

(767 words)

根据易观国际的数据，51Job 网占有 29% 的市场份额，中华英才网占有 27% 的市场份额，而智联招聘占有 15% 的市场份额。

知识链接

TOM 为中国之领先业界的无线互联网公司，为广大用户提供多媒体增值产品及服务。作为中国知名的互联网品牌公司，TOM 在线专注于向年轻时尚的群体提供包括无线互联网业务和网络广告在内的服务。公司业务范围覆盖了包括短信、彩信、WAP、无线音讯互动服务(IVR)、内容频道、搜索、分类信息，免费及付费电邮服务等网络游戏的多个领域。

Monster Worldwide 怪兽公司是全球最大的专业招聘网站，也是全球最大的招聘服务供应商，其访问量长期位居 30 位内，提供由招聘代理、线上招聘、猎头服务和招聘黄页广告四项构成的全方位的全球招聘解决方案。作为全球互联网招聘行业的第一品牌，Monster 公司招聘收入占整个美国网络招聘市场近 50%的份额。Monster 分支机构密布全球，已在全球 26 个国家设立了分公司并使用 22 种不同语言设立服务专区。

题 记

数字化营销与在线广告在过去几年中飞速增长，就像大海里温暖的盐水一样扩散到整个互联网。与传统的营销投资相比，数字化营销与在线广告提供了更便宜的商品流通、更大的个性化、更高的回报和产品跟踪。数字化营销是基于紧俏的网络化市场创建可能性的营销模式，而在线广告是一种主要基于传统韵律学和思想的在线模式，包括网页横幅广告和网络站点或内容资助。在可供选择、变幻莫测的商海中，各种形状和格式的网页横幅广告，生存在网络世界的沙漠中，就像在干燥、被遗忘的高速公路上孤独延伸的广告牌，一旦他们与数字化营销结合起来，就仿佛提供了一个景色优美的甲板，在这个平台上，共同交流驱动交易的产生和关系的推进，市场商人的预算很快反映在现金和信息交流存在的地方。

Digital Marketing vs. Online Advertising

The Internet marketing landscape has grown rapidly over the past few years, spreading out over the Internet like warm saltwater in the sea. Initially focused on banner advertising and search engine submissions, the environment has grown considerably in terms of tools and sophistication① of the techniques that Internet marketers are employing. Jupiter Media Metrix② has spotted a recent shift in advertising/marketing dollars into online channels that deliver less expensive distribution, greater personalization, and higher response and tracking rates than traditional marketing dollars are able to capture.

What is emerging in the online marketing space is part digital marketing and part online advertising. Online advertising is an online marketing model based largely on traditional metrics③ and thinking. Online advertising learns its lessons from television, print, and radio. Examples of online advertising are banner ads and website/content sponsorships. Digital marketing is a model based on the possibilities

① sophistication [səˌfistiˈkeiʃən] 强词夺理，诡辩

② metrix 神曲系列

③ metrics [ˈmetriks] *n.* 韵律学

数字化营销与在线广告

互联网营销前景在过去的几年中一直飞速增长，就像大海里温暖的盐水一样扩散到整个互联网。 网络环境起初只集中在网页横幅广告和搜索引擎提交领域，但是根据互联网市场商人采用技术的工具和复杂性，它已处于成熟状态。 Jupiter Media Metrix 研究公司已经注意到，广告或营销投资近期转向在线渠道，它与传统的营销投资相比，提供更便宜的商品流通，更大的个性化，更高的回报和产品跟踪。

在线营销空间出现的是部分数字营销和部分在线广告。 在线广告是一种主要基于传统韵律学和思想的在线模式。 在线广告从电视、印刷品和无线广播中吸取经验。 在线广告的例子有网页横幅广告和网络站点或内容资助。 数字化营销是基于紧俏的网络化市场创建可能性的营销模式。 例如，在接下来的 24 小时内，网络冲浪者将会搜索大约 36 507 次 “二手车” 相关信息。 市场商人能用一种前所未有的方式把自己的信息加入在线市场。 即使在一个充满垃圾邮件的世界里，消费者和供应商也可以在互联网上用一种不引人注目的方式找到彼此。

采用数字化营销策略的公司积极地运作，以确保客户获得订货

created by tightly networked markets. For example, in the next 24 hours web surfers will search for "used cars" an estimated 36, 507 times. Marketers are able to insert themselves into these online markets in ways they never could before. Even in a world filled with spam, consumers and businesses are finding each other on the Internet in unobtrusive① ways.

Companies employing digital marketing tactics are actively working to ensure their customers are getting the best and most relevant information that they need to make purchases. Digital marketing consists of search engine optimization, permission-based email marketing, and online coupons②. Marketers were led into online advertising first because it most matched the traditional marketing channels they were accustomed to and the tools for effective digital marketing didn't exist yet. Like exploring new coasts with dated maps, it was only a matter of time before those marketing online gained better tools and information to make them more successful. According to Jupiter, spending in online advertising in the United States grew by only 5 percent. Once the economy settles down, they expect it to bounce back③ and grow at a compound rate of 22 percent over the next five years, reaching a total of more than $ 15 billion. During the same time period, Jupiter predicts that spending on digital marketing initiatives such as search engine optimization, e-mail, and coupons will surpass that of advertising and reach more than $ 19 billion. The growth for online marketers will be huge. According to Jupiter's Internet Advertising Model, online advertising and digital

① unobtrusive [ˈʌnəbˈtruːsiv] *adj.* 不显眼,不引人注目的

② coupon [ˈkuːpɔn] *n.* 优惠券,订货单

③ bounce back 受挫后恢复原状

所需的最好和最相关的信息。数字化营销包括搜索引擎最优化、基于电子邮件许可的营销以及在线优惠券。市场商人首先被导入在线广告，因为在线广告与他们习惯的传统营销渠道最相配，而有效的数字化营销工具尚不存在。就像用一张旧地图去探索新海岸一样，使这些营销网络获得更好的工具和信息、取得更大的成功之前，数字化营销只是个时间问题。按照 Jupiter Media Metrix 的统计，美国用于在线广告的支出仅仅增长了5%。他们希望一旦经济稳定，这种发展势头就会反弹，在未来5年综合增长22%，超过150亿美元的消费总量。Jupiter Media Metrix 在同一时期预测，搜索引擎最优化、电子邮件和在线定购等数字化营销的优先投资将超过在线广告支出，达到190多亿美元。在线市场卖主的增长将无限扩大。根据Jupiter公司的在线广告模型，在线广告和数字化营销的广告市场份额将从3%增长到7%。

随着营销网络的成熟，传统模式无法掌控超链接信息与市场战略融合而产生的强大效用。受超链接驱动快速获取信息和背景成为获得成功的一个重要因素。不同程度的信任取决于信息来源。公司必须确保在搜索引擎上找到相关信息，从而吸引非自愿的和有兴趣的客户。NPD 资讯公司发布的一项研究报告显示，涉及品牌回想、良好的评价等级和鼓舞人的购买力时，搜索列表比标准的网页横幅广告或点击广告更有效。该研究发现：独立回想的过程中，搜索列表胜过标题广告和点击广告，其比例达到3:1；超过两倍的人给予搜索列表排名前三的公司更好的评价；55%的在线购买通过搜索列表网站达成交易，只有9%的在线购买通过标题广告

marketing will account for 7 percent of the total advertising market, up from 3 percent.

As marketing online matures, traditional models didn't grasp how powerful combining hyperlinked information and marketing tactics could be. Driven quickly through hyperlinks to information, context becomes an important factor for success. Varying levels of trust are created depending on where information is found. Companies must ensure they are being found in search engines in order to attract a captive and interested audience. A study from the NPD Group released found that search listings are more effective than standard banner or button advertisements when it comes to brand recall, favorable opinion rating① and inspiring purchases. The study found that in unaided recall, search listings outperformed② banners and buttons by three to one, more than twice as many people gave a more favorable opinion of companies in the top three search positions, 55 percent of online purchases were made on websites found through search listings, and only 9 percent of online purchases were on websites found through banner ads

These studies suggest that people are inclined to trust services like search engines much like they trust a librarian, a trust that people would not be lead wrong by those who would choose to lead them. Search engines work because they are a passive tool, awaiting input from the user to find what they want. Email works because it takes the concept of direct marketing and turns it into an active communication channel driven by valuable information and transactions. Research released from DoubleClick,

---

① opinion rating 评价等级

② outperform [autpəˈfɔːm] *vt.* 做得更好,比……更有效

完成。

这些研究表明，人们就像信任图书馆管理员一样倾向于相信搜索引擎之类的服务，这是一种不会被选择引导他们的人误导的信任。搜索引擎有效是因为它们属于一种被动的工具，期待使用者发现他们想要的输入。电子邮件有效是因为它采用直接营销的理念，并将其转换成由有价值的信息和交易驱动的有效沟通渠道。DoubleClick发布的研究报告显示，超过88%的在线消费者收到许可邮件后即做出购买决定。该研究还发现，37%的消费者通过邮件做出即时购买决定。彭尼百货公司就是一个使用电子邮件促销的例子。在两年之间，彭尼百货的在线销售从1 500万美元增长到29 400万美元。彭尼百货没有公布近期的销售数据，但预测销售量超过4亿美元。该公司的业务怎么会增长得这么快呢？就是集中关注来自4 500多万志愿消费者的目标电邮清单。有孩子的家庭返校时将得到突出彭尼百货返校特价的促销品。

快捷丰富的媒体网页横幅广告不能以这样的方式开始工作。它可能有相关信息或吸引力，但只存在大约千分之一的时间。各种形状和格式的网页横幅广告，生存在网络世界的沙漠中，就像在干燥、被遗忘的高速公路上孤独延伸的广告牌。搜索引擎优化和电子邮件之类的数字化营销填充你的肚子并对你满腹牢骚，因为你渴望得到它。这就是你所想要的……而不是有人察觉到你想要什么。当一个人使用搜索引擎搜索特定的产品或服务的时候，他们就已经具备了潜在客户的资格。在线广告提醒你，一个公司没有消失，坚持单方面的、高频率的信息刺激就像灯塔一样吸引人们

indicates that over 88 percent of online consumers have made a purchase as a result of receiving permission-based email. The research also found that 37 percent had clicked through an email and purchased immediately. JCPenney is an example of a company that is using email to drive sales. During the two years, JCPenney's online sales rose from $ 15 million to $ 294 million. JCPenney hasn't released online sales figures recently, but projections were for sales over $ 400 million. How has the business grown that much? By focusing on targeted email lists from a willing audience of over 4.5 million shoppers. A family with children headed back to school will get promotions that highlight JCPenney's back to school specials.

A blinking rich media banner ad can't begin to work that way. It might have relevant information or appeal, but only about one one-thousandth of the time. Banners, in all shapes and formats, live in the desert of the online world like billboards on a lonely stretch of dry, forgotten highway. Digital marketing, like search engine optimization and email, fills your belly and growls at you because you're hungry for it. It's what you want...not what someone perceives you to want. When a person searches on a search engine for a specific product or service, they are qualifying themselves as a potential customer. Online advertising reminds you that a company has not faded away, sticking to a one-sided, high-frequency push of information will draw people to it like a lighthouse. Digital marketing looks to meet you up on scenic deck, where mutual conversations drive transactions and relationships. In a shifting sea of choices, marketers' budgets will soon reflect where the real money and conversations live.

(945 words)

走进公司。数字化营销似乎给你提供了一个景色优美的甲板，在这个平台上，共同交流驱动交易的产生和关系的推进。在变幻莫测的商海中，市场商人的预算将很快反映在现金和信息交流存在的地方。

知识链接

DoubleClick 成立于 1996 年，有 500 多家企业客户。2005 年以 11 亿美元的价格被 Hellman & Friedman 收购。2008 年 3 月 11 日 Google 正式宣布完成了对网络广告公司 DoubleClick 的收购，最终以 32. 4 亿美元的价格成交。这次收购使 Google 成为网络广告行业绝对的领导者。

美国彭尼公司 （J. C. Penney Company Inc.），也被译为杰西潘尼公司。彭尼公司是美国最大的商店和药品商店零售商，在美国 50 个州和波多黎各、墨西哥、智利经营 1 230 多家商店。公司销售男女和儿童服装，为中等收入和中高等收入家庭提供家具；同时，彭尼公司还经营人寿保险业、重大事故、健康和信用卡保险，该公司经营的药店是美国最大的药品连锁店，拥有 2 600 家药店，主要集中在美国和南北美地区，销售制药和相关产品。公司雇员人数达到 30 678 人。

The NPD Group NPD 集团通过给出事实的真相而帮助 1 700 多家客户投资赚钱。作为全球市场调查公司，NPD 集团通过现金注册的 300 多万名消费者和电子传播面板，跟踪消费者的在线和实体店购买行为。它提供不同行业的市场洞察力，包括服饰、消费者电子学、食品服务、音乐、软件和电子游戏。此外，它的显示器搜索部分提供市场搜索分析，擅长于平面显示产业。NPD 集团在北美、欧洲和亚太地区约有 25 家分公司。

题 记

虚拟企业以临时的合作方式为基础，实现合作方单独无法实现或无法最大程度实现的短期商业机会的价值。英国领先的管理机构预测，2018 年劳动力将从传统的工作场所大批流向虚拟企业，人们依靠发达的信息技术，依靠信息网络，跨越空间界限，广泛地选择自己的合作伙伴，并开展网络销售。人们通过高速宽带进行交流，或许辅以全息技术虚拟出席会议。许多有才华的人“多重就业”，有些在公司或家庭办公室以外的“第三地点”每周工作一天或两天。事实上，虚拟企业已经催生了一部分与传统供应链完全不同的独立的新的产业结构，比如电信产业、数字产业和以虚拟市场渠道为基础的电子虚拟市场等。当价值驱动虚拟运营的结构调整时，一种新的、个体公司的专业化模式正在席卷全球并在互联网经济中确立其卓越的地位。

Saying Hello to Virtual Enterprise

Within a decade millions of workers will be at home juggling their careers with caring for children and older relatives, Britain's leading management institute forecast. Dreams of a future when technological advances would liberate us from the daily drudge[1] and allow more time for leisure appear to be fading, with futurologists predicting less talk about "work-life balance" and more about "work-life integration". A report on the nature of employment in 2018 predicts an exodus[2] from the traditional workplace caused partly by environmental pressure to reduce the carbon footprint of commuting and partly by the demographic pressure of an ageing population, with fewer employees able to avoid looking after older relatives, leading to a blurring of boundaries between family and career.

In a list of scenarios drawn up by the Chartered Management Institute and launched at a seminar in London by Sir John Sunderland, chairman of Cadbury Schweppes, many companies were warned to prepare for a

---

① drudge [drʌdʒ] *n.* 做苦工的人,劳碌的人

② exodus [ˈeksədəs] *n.* 出走,仓促逃离

向虚拟企业致敬

英国的主要管理机构预测，数以百万计的工人在10年内将在家里边忙碌自己的事业边照顾儿童和老人。未来的技术进步将把我们从日常单调乏味的工作中解放出来、从而有更多的时间休闲这个梦想似乎正在逐渐消失，因为未来学家的预测较少谈论“工作与生活的平衡”，而更多的是涉及“工作与生活的融合”。一份关于2018年就业性质的报告预测，劳动力从传统的工作场所大批外流，部分原因是减少交通用碳量的环境压力，部分原因是人口老龄化的压力，只有较少的员工可以不用照顾老年亲属，从而导致家庭和事业之间的界限模糊化。

在皇家特许管理协会起草、吉百利·史威士股份有限公司主席约翰·桑德兰爵士在伦敦研讨会上提出的一系列设想中，很多公司受到警告，要求它们为一系列极小的可能性做好准备，包括网络攻击下的世界、工作人员之间使用全息图进行沟通，以及在雇员的大脑中植入芯片以控制他们的行为。更有可能的设想包

range of remote possibilities, including a world under cyber attack, the use of holograms[1] for communication between staff, and controlling employee behaviour by implanting microchips in their brains. More probable scenarios included a polarisation[2] of businesses, with large corporations consolidating global control and becoming more powerful than the governments of some big countries. But there would also be a proliferation[3] of "virtual" companies, often small community-based enterprises without conventional business premises. These enterprises would have to compete for employees, who will become more footloose[4] and less inclined to work for an organisation that does not allow individuals to tailor the working day to meet their personal requirements. "Organisations will have to address the growing power of the employee," the report said.

Whether or not workers enjoy this extra flexibility, they will not be allowed to cling to traditional patterns of employment. "On all levels there will be a move towards upskilling and multi-skilling. Employees will be required to be more flexible with regard to organisational needs," the report said. This may mean workers abandoning traditional shifts. People may work from home on assignments during specific time slots, or be available on call when work needs to be done. They will communicate by

---

① hologram [ˈhɔləugræm] *n.* 全息摄影,全息图
② polarisation [ˌpəuləraiˈzeiʃən] *n.* 极化,分化
③ proliferation [prəuˈlifəˌreiʃən] *n.* 增殖,繁殖
④ footloose [ˈfutluːs] *adj.* 自由自在的,无拘束的

括企业的两极分化，大型企业巩固全球控制，比某些大国的政府更强大。但“虚拟”公司也将迅速扩散，通常是以小团体为基础、没有传统营业场所的企业。这些企业将不得不为雇员竞争，雇员的流动更加自由，并不太愿意为那些不允许根据个人需求、度身订造工作日的机构工作。报告说，“企业将不得不应付不断增长的职工权利”。

无论工人是否享有这种额外的灵活性，他们将不会被允许固守传统的就业模式。报告说，“各个层级都将朝着提高技能和多重技能运行。雇员将被要求具备更大的灵活性，以满足企业的需要”。这可能意味着工人放弃传统的工作方式。人们可以利用特定的时间空当在家安排工作，或者有工作需要做时可以通过电话随叫随到。他们通过高速宽带进行交流，或许辅以全息技术虚拟出席会议。许多有才华的人“多重就业”，有些在公司或家庭办公室以外的“第三地点”每周工作一天或两天。由于工作变得更加以项目为基础，人们需要使用专门的服务，将自己投放到个人特设项目市场。管理人员将创建多元文化工作团队，将老工人和年轻工人的技能相结合，进行远程操作。由于过去的30年间的社会变化根深蒂固，妇女将进入更高的管理职位。情商和鉴别人的价值能力与技术能力一样，将越来越受到招聘者的重视。

未来学家可能已经预测到这些变化，但皇家特许管理协会认为，

high-speed broadband, perhaps supplemented by hologram technology permitting virtual presence at meetings. Many talented people would become "multi-employed", some working for a day or two a week in "third place locations" outside their organisations or home office. As work becomes more project-based, people will need to use specialised services to market themselves for individual ad hoc projects. Managers will have to create multicultural work teams, operating remotely, combining the skills of older and younger workers. As social changes from the past 30 years take root, women will move into higher management positions. Emotional intelligence and the ability to appreciate people's values as much as their technical competencies will be seen by recruiters as increasingly important.

Futurologists may have predicted some of these changes, but the institute said its report was the first attempt by captains of industry and commerce to predict how their organisations may look 10 years in the future. It said collaborative working would become so important that companies should consider abolishing positions and job titles. "Instead each employee should be seen as a valuable resource, to be employed according to specific organisational needs." Companies would come to regard wisdom as a valuable resource. Some would try to nurture an organisational memory by arranging rituals and storytelling, and listening to the accounts of long-term employees.

The institute put findings from the report to more than 1,000 senior executives. It found 74% expected "virtual teams of employees",

这份报告是工商界首脑第一次尝试预测其机构在 10 年后会是一种什么模样。据说，协同工作将变得非常重要，以至于公司应该考虑取消职位和职称。“每个员工都应该被视为有价值的资源，根据特定的组织需求被雇佣。”公司将逐渐把智慧视作宝贵的资源。有些公司将安排例会和讲故事，倾听长期雇员的建议，尝试培养一种企业记忆。

皇家特许管理协会将报告的研究结果应用于 1 000 多名高级管理人员。结果发现 74% 的人期待“雇员虚拟团队”，相互之间的工作保持距离，这将成为 2018 年的规范。约 64% 的人认为有才能的人将会“多重就业”，59% 的人表示跳槽将变得很普遍，56% 的人表示大部分的常规工作将自动完成。三分之二的经理主管人员期待全球企业发挥的影响力超过政府。几乎同样多的人期待客户更多地参与企业决策和创造更长生命周期的产品，以满足公司的环境需求。较少的人支持未来学家的科技预测。仅有 31% 的人期待与工作人员通过全息图进行沟通，12% 的人认为公司在他们的大脑中植入微芯片将提高工作人员的能力。

皇家特许管理协会的首席执行官玛丽·查普曼说：“展望未来 10 年里，可以清楚地看到，成功的企业将是那些更能把握变革的组织——他们会预测、鉴别和推动变革。管理人员和领导者将被要求更高程度的情商，以使他们能够理解人们的工作方式和人们对变革的可能反应。他们还需要从今天的输入驱动方式转向产出、成功和

working at a distance from each other, to become the norm by 2018. About 64% thought talented people would become "multi-employed," 59% said job hopping would be commonplace and 56% said most routine tasks would be automated. Two-thirds of the executives expected global corporations to exert more influence than governments. Almost as many forecast an increase in customer participation in business decisions and the creation of products with longer life cycles to meet environmental concerns. There was less support for the futurologists' technological projections. Only 31% expected to communicate with staff by hologram and 12% thought companies would enhance the capabilities of staff by implanting microchips in their brains.

Mary Chapman, the institute's chief executive, said: "Looking ahead 10 years, it is clear that the successful organisations will be those who can do more than embrace change-they will anticipate, identify and drive it. A greater degree of emotional intelligence will be required by managers and leaders so they can understand how people work and their likely reaction to change. They will also need to shift from today's input-driven approach to a focus on output, achievement and a better integration between work and personal lives."

(800 words)

工作与个人生活之间更好整合的集中。”

知识链接

The Chartered Management Institute 英国皇家特许管理协会是唯一的特许职业机构，致力于管理和领导工作，并授予特许管理人员身份。协会通过支持管理、给个人或组织提供建议、参与政策制定、给政府施加影响力和职业化等手段来提高商业表现。特许管理人员技能包括：领导才干，管理创新和改革，满足客户需求，建立信息和交际体系，管理项目和资源，开发有效的人事网络。

Cadbury Schweppes 吉百利·史威士股份有限公司创立于1824年，是英国伯明翰老牌糖果制造商，是英国历史最悠久的巧克力品牌之一，也是英国最大的巧克力生产商，更是目前全球最大的糖果公司、第二大口香糖公司、第三大软饮料公司，也是唯一一家同时拥有巧克力、糖果及口香糖产品的公司。吉百利主要生产吉百利巧克力、怡口莲太妃糖、天宝粒粒糖、魄力口香糖、荷氏系列及维果C系列。集团公司总部设在英国伦敦，在世界范围内共拥有36 000多名员工，在10个国家中拥有自己的装瓶厂和合作厂，并在21个国家中与当地企业签订许可证经营和分销合同。

题　记

网络购物已经成为网络经济中增长最快的行业之一。随着网购商品种类的丰富、购物平台、购物体验及服务的完善和网购对网民日常生活的渗透加深，网络购物市场吸引着越来越多的企业用户和个人用户加入，也吸引了资本市场更多的关注。按照现行法律，从亚马逊和 eBay 等网站上购买的商品似乎可以享受到免税政策。不过，按照法律规定，消费者需要按照所在州的消费税率缴纳税金。美国人对网上购物征收销售税的观点已经翻来覆去地讨论了将近 10 年，却一直与最初承诺的简化税收渐行渐远。当美国国会拟对此推出新法案之时，人们仍然期盼着一场游说战争，网购免税时代或将终结，从而为卖家简化流程提供补偿。

Web Sales Tax Looms

Tight state budgets and a new Congress could bring sales taxes to the Web. Attention, online shoppers! This may be the last holiday season you can dodge sales taxes by buying presents on the Web. State legislators, retailers and lawyers say there may be the Internet taxes finally come to pass recently. The idea, which would levy① sales tax on most goods bought online, has been tossed around for nearly a decade. A perfect storm of factors, including record state budget deficits, a new Congress and continued e-commerce growth, appear likely to rekindle② the issue. Experts say that cash-strapped③ states view this revenue, estimated to be several billions of dollars, as money left on the table.

Spotting an opportunity, legislators and other proponents of Internet taxation are renewing their efforts. Scott Peterson, executive director of the Streamlined Sales Tax Governing Board (SSTGB), a group that oversees states' efforts to simplify and modernize sales tax issues, says legislators from Florida, Illinois, Massachusetts, Texas and Virginia, among others, have recently contacted him about the issue. The plan: to

---

① levy [ˈlevi] *vt.* 征收(税等),强索

② rekindle [riˈkindl] *vt.* 再点(火)

③ cash-strapped *adj.* 现金短缺的

网购税若隐若现

紧缩的国家预算和新一届国会可能颁布网购税。网上的购物者们，注意！也许这是你们上网购买免税礼物的最后一个假期了。国家的立法者、零售商和律师认为，网购税可能最终在近期得以通过。对网上购买的大多数商品征收销售税的观点已经翻来覆去地讨论了将近10年。创纪录的国家预算赤字、新一届国会和电子商务的持续增长等因素的完美风暴，显示这个问题很可能被再次提起。专家说，现金短缺的政府把这预计几十亿美元的收入当做放在桌子上的钱。

立法者和其他支持网购税的人正继续努力抓住这个机会。简化销售税理事会（SSTGB——负责监督各州努力简化和使销售税现代化问题的一个团体）的执行董事斯科特·彼得森认为，其中来自佛罗里达州、伊利诺伊州、马萨诸塞州、得克萨斯州和弗吉尼亚州的立法者最近已经就此问题与他联系。他们的计划是：尽早在新一届国会到任的一月份再次提出立法。世界最大的零售商联盟、全美零售商联合会（NRF）副会长莫林·瑞尔说，“我们希望白宫和参议院给予全面的关注，并且我们能够得到提交给新总统的法案”。立法的途径是必要的，因为最高法院在20世纪90年代裁定，各州不能要

reintroduce legislation as early as January when the new Congress takes office. "We're hoping that the House and Senate will give this their full attention and we can get a bill to our new president," says Maureen Riehl, vice president and government and industry relations counsel of the National Retail Federation (NRF), the world's largest retail trade association. The legislative route is necessary because the Supreme Court ruled in the 1990s that states can't require out-of-state retailers to collect sales tax on online sales. Proponents believe that making their case to Congress would be faster and more practical than wending their way through the courts. That has supporters, including the NRF, the SSTGB and the National Conference of State Legislatures (NCSL), mulling① over how to revamp② two bills, both called the "Sales Tax Fairness and Simplification Act," which have been pending③ in the House and the Senate. At issue is how to exempt "small sellers" from the policy and how states plan to reimburse④ vendors who have to collect sales tax. even defining who qualifies as a "small" seller is tricky. To bolster⑤ the need for the tax, the groups also plan to highlight the steady growth of e-commerce and the ways that new technology, such as tax software, could make it easier to collect taxes. They have drafted several professors from the University of Tennessee to calculate how much tax revenue states are currently losing. Once legislation is passed, changes could roll out in

---

① mull [mʌl] *vi.* 深思熟虑

② revamp [riˈvæmp] *vt.* 修补,改写

③ pending [ˈpendiŋ] *adj.* 悬而未决的,迫近的

④ reimburse [ˌriimˈbəːs] *vt.* 偿还,归还

⑤ bolster [ˈbəulstə] *vt.* 援助,支持

求外州零售商收取在线销售的销售税。支持者认为，向国会反映此事比通过法院这种途径更快也更实际。这样做有包括全美零售商联合会、简化销售税理事会以及国家立法机构全国会议（NCSL）在内的支持者，他们在仔细琢磨如何修改两个一直被搁置在白宫和参议院的都被称为“销售税公平和简化法案”。问题在于如何从政策上免除“小型营业者”的税收，以及国家如何计划偿还不得不交付销售税的小贩们，甚至如何定义“小型”营业者也需要技巧。为了支持税收的需要，这些集团还计划强调，电子商务的稳定增长和新技术的方式，如税收软件，能够使征税更容易。他们已经挑选了几名田纳西大学的教授计算政府已经失去多少税收。一旦法案通过，变革将在6个月内小范围实施。

对消费者而言，这种法案意味着网上免税销售的终结。目前存在大量的漏洞。例如，亚马逊网站的购物者只有购买实体公司（如分流中心）所在的五个特殊的州（堪萨斯州、肯塔基州、纽约州、北达科他州和华盛顿）才会缴税。新法律显然能够大大增加这个数目。亚马逊目前正面临着纽约裁决，并由于正在进行的诉讼而拒绝评论这一事件。易趣是另一家大型网上卖家，多年来一直反对网购税。在行业协会见面会上，易趣的间接税高级主管、零售商和州议员威廉·拉舍争辩说，新法律将伤害该公司的数百万卖家，造成收入净额比国家期望的更少。拉舍说，虽然易趣每年在美国有270亿美元商品的销售量，大约110亿美元至140亿美元的交易是对其他

as little as six months.

For consumers, such a law would mean an end to sales tax freeloading online. Plenty of loopholes① currently exist. Shoppers at Amazon.com, for instance, currently pay tax only if they ship purchases to five specific states (Kansas, Kentucky, New York, North Dakota and Washington) where the company has a physical presence, such as a distribution center. A new law could significantly increase that number. Amazon is currently challenging the New York ruling and declined to comment for this story due to the ongoing litigation. Ebay, another large online seller, has opposed Internet taxation for years. In a presentation given to industry associations, retailers and state legislators, William Lasher, an eBay senior director of indirect taxes, argued that a new law would hurt the company's millions of sellers and generate less net revenue than states might expect. Though eBay moved $ 27 billion in merchandise in the U.S. every year, Lasher said that approximately $ 11 billion to $ 14 billion of those transactions were services or sold to consumers in other countries or tax-exempt entities-thus nontaxable or subject only to low taxes. He also said a new law would make business complicated and costly for small sellers. Both companies have found public support from the Direct Marketing Association (DMA), which counts eBay and Amazon among its members. Internet taxation laws are an attempt to make marketers "unpaid tax collectors for the state," says Jerry Cerasale, DMA's senior vice president of government affairs. The trade association has long refuted the numbers touted by taxation supporters.

---

① loophole [ˈluphəul] *n.*（法律等的）漏洞

国家消费者或免税实体的服务或销售，因此免税或仅缴纳低税。他还表示，新法律将使商业复杂化，并令小卖家成本剧增。两家公司已经得到直接营销联盟的公众支持，包括易趣和亚马逊的会员。直接营销联盟的政府事务高级副总裁杰里·瑟拉塞尔说，网购税法案企图使市场上的卖主成为“州政府不领取报酬的缴税者”。该交易联盟长期反对网购税支持者吹捧的群体。

人们期盼一场游说战争。直接营销联盟计划将其信息提交国会山，即销售税的报告和收集对其他州的企业仍然显得过于复杂。它还将对新规则用于电子商务的效果提出警告。瑟拉塞尔说，“这是个追逐长线销售的错误时间。在经济衰退期，我们应该鼓励消费者消费”。很难预测新国会将怎样反应。专家认为，这个问题完全不触及党派原则。全美零售商联合会的瑞尔指出：“它必须与你的州政府和网络销售观相结合。民主党可能会对国家预算更敏感，而共和党可能把它看做一个商业公平的问题”。而兼听则明。蒙哈特律师认为，新的国会代表将更倾向于关注这个问题。

当选总统巴拉克·奥巴马似乎意识到这个问题，但并未暗示他倾向哪种方式。他的竞选运动没有把网购税纳入技术举措包含广泛的名单之中，但据报道，早在他作为伊利诺伊州参议员的日子，他就投了这个法案的赞成票。一些州已经做出了选择。彼得森说，22 个州是他的简化销售税项目成员，另外 22 个州“正在积极讨论”。随着预算越来越吃紧，一切都会改变。彼得森指出，州政府

Expect a lobbying① war. The DMA plans to take its message-that sales tax reporting and collection is still too complicated for out-of-state firms-to Capitol Hill. It will also warn of the effects new rules may have on e-commerce. "It's a bad time to go after remote sales," says Cerasale. "In this economic slowdown, we need to bolster consumer spending." How the new Congress will react is hard to predict. Experts say the issue doesn't split neatly along party lines. "It has to do with your idea of state government and the Internet," notes NRF's Riehl, "Democrats may be more sensitive to state budgetary concerns whereas Republicans might see it as a question of business fairness." Fresh ears make a difference, too. Menhart, the lawyer, thinks new congressional representatives will be more inclined to pay attention to the issue.

President-elect Barack Obama appears to be aware of the issue but hasn't signaled which way he'd lean. His campaign did not include Internet taxation in its broad list of technology initiatives, but he reportedly voted in favor of investigating the issue back in his days as an Illinois state senator. A number of states have yet to choose a side. Peterson says 22 states are members of his streamlined sales tax project and 22 others are "in active discussions." That could change as budgets get tighter. States hate raising taxes, notes Peterson. "Internet taxation gives them a way to go after tax that's already owed."

(933 words)

---

① lobbying [ˈlɔbiiŋ] *n.* 游说

讨厌加税，“网购税给了他们追讨已经欠下的税款的方法”。

知识链接

National Retail Federation 全美零售商联合会是世界最大的零售商联盟，其成员包括百货公司、特产、折扣、目录册、互联网、独立经营的零售商、连锁餐厅和杂货店，以及给零售商提供商品和服务的企业。全美零售商联合会在美国和全球有 160 多万家零售组织，2 400 多万名雇员，年销售量达到 440 亿美元。

The Direct Marketing Association 直接营销联盟是领先的全球贸易联盟，也是非盈利组织，其营销手段是使用和资助多渠道直接营销工具和技术。直接营销联盟提倡可靠的营销标准，以称心如意的出价为核心来满足顾客的需求，提供时尚最前沿的研究、教育和网络机会，改善端到端直接营销过程中的结果。1917 年成立的直接营销联盟今天已有 3 400 多家公司，遍及美国和其他 48 个国家，包括财富 100 强的公司和非营利组织。

题　记

网络交易时代已经完全进入第二个10年，它以强大的势力正在改变着全球消费者的购买习惯和消费行为，也预示着一个新消费时代来临。然而，诞生于“黄金时代”的规则——“只有奢侈的品牌才能创造奢侈的利润”似乎正在成为全球消费品企业品牌策略的明日黄花，英国精品协会举办的“奢侈品在线”研讨会上的多数代表都显示出低水平的在线商务知识和志向，在线销售长期潜力在理论上的接受与具体实施也仍然存在巨大的差距。无论喜欢还是不喜欢，我们生活在一个电子商务的世界里。奢侈品企业迟早将让消费者在任何他们喜欢的渠道——无论是实体店购物、电话购物或在线购物——购买商品和互动，以便消费者享受无缝购物体验。

Web Remains a World away for Luxury Brands

Web commerce may be well into its second decade, but as few as a third of global luxury brands are selling online and half of those who currently do not sell online have no plans to do so. This is one of the findings of a survey in which Walpole, the trade association for the British luxury industry, worked with independent technology and market research company, Forrester Research, to probe what executives in luxury businesses really think about online business. Among the reasons given by respondents is that e-commerce is "inappropriate" and their customers prefer the physical retail experience.

These findings surprised us and may alarm others in the luxury sector. They come at a time when the received wisdom is that the past 12 months has seen an increase in luxury online activity, with more e-commerce capabilities, better digital marketing strategies, and new web start-ups. Two years ago, a majority of delegates① at a Walpole

① delegate [ˈdeligət] *n.* 代表,代表团成员

网络游离于奢侈品牌之外

网络商业已经完全进入第二个 10 年，但只有三分之一的全球奢侈品牌在网上交易，其中有一半目前没有在网上销售的人还没有打算这样做。 这是英国精品协会沃波尔与独立的技术和市场研究公司——弗雷斯特研究公司——共同调查的结果之一，目的是探讨奢侈品交易中主管人员究竟如何思考网上的业务。 回答者给出的理由之一是：电子商务“不合时宜”，他们的客户更喜欢实体零售体验。

这些调查结果令我们感到惊讶，并可能引起奢侈品行业其他人的警觉。 他们在这样一个时期到来：一般人的明智看法是，过去 12 个月中奢侈品的网上活动已经明显增加，涌现出更多的电子商务功能，更好的数字市场战略和新的网络企业。 两年前，英国精品协会举办的“奢侈品在线”研讨会上的多数代表都显示出低水平的在线商务知识和志向。 如果电子商务活动从那时开始爆发，这似乎是一个合理的设想，到现在为止，奢侈品行业可能更接近数码技术的最前沿，这种辩论也可能已经有所进展。然而，这项研究表明，这可

Seminar, Luxury Online, demonstrated low levels of online business knowledge and ambition. Given the explosion of e-commerce activity since then, it seemed a reasonable assumption that, by now, the luxury sector would be closer to the digital cutting edge and the debate might have moved on. This research suggests, however, that this may take some time. Forrester surveyed 178 executives across a diverse group and luxury manufacturers, retailers, and service organisations worldwide, and interviewed 20 companies individually. When some of these had previously tried to sell online, they structured their websites to mimic① the in-store experience and experienced lacklustre② results. This seems to have coloured their view of the web for the future.

However understandable, this remains a missed opportunity for the industry, given that Forrester's e-commerce forecast research shows overall online sales continuing to grow in double digits. Internet revenues in Western Europe, for example, increased by 58 per cent to reach € 54bn ($ 85bn). In addition, Forrester's Consumer Technographics data shows eight out of 10 high net worth consumers use the internet daily and actively research and buy luxury goods and services online on a regular basis. The firms surveyed that do sell online report booming business, on average expecting their e-commerce sales to grow 17 per cent this year and 111 per cent over the next five years, representing 22

---

① mimic [ˈmimik] *vt.* (尤指为了逗乐而)模仿,酷似

② lacklustre [ˈlæklʌstə] *adj.* 无光泽的,无生气的

能需要一些时间。佛雷斯特公司调查了全球178位不同企业的经理主管、奢侈品制造商、零售商和服务机构，还单独采访了20家公司。其中一些公司以前曾尝试在网上销售，他们建构网站，模仿实体店的销售方式，但结果却不尽如人意。这似乎影响了他们对未来网络的见解。

不管用何种方法理解，考虑到佛雷斯特公司电子商务预测研究显示的总体在线销售持续以两位数增长，这仍然是奢侈品行业一个错失的机会。例如西欧的互联网税收增加了58%，达到了540亿欧元（850亿美元）。此外，佛雷斯特公司的消费技术图表数据显示，10名消费者中至少有8名每天使用互联网，并积极研究和在网上定期购买奢侈商品和服务。该公司的调查报告指出，网上销售业务发展迅速，他们今年的电子商务销售额预期平均增长17%，未来五年增长111%，到那时，22%的销售额来自所有的渠道。他们成功的关键是成功地履行卓越的在线客户经验。例如，福特纳姆与马森奢侈品店，哈罗德百货公司，只在网络销售的酷钻石珠宝之类的零售商等，他们在所有的渠道上具备综合性的购物经验，为回头客户提供现场客户支持和姓名辨别等功能。这些企业知道，现在的富裕客户在线时受方便、产品选择、订货和购物速度的驱动。关于未来问题的问卷也引出了有启迪作用的调查结果。当受访者被问及是否认为从现在起到未来的10年中，他们更多的产品将在网上销售而不是在商店销售时，41%的人积极响应，43%的人持怀疑态度，16%的人表

per cent of sales from all channels by then. The key to their success is delivering a superior online customer experience. For example, Fortnum & Mason, Harrods, and pure-play[1] online retailers such as Cool Diamonds, have integrated shopping experiences across all their channels, and offer features such as live customer support and name recognition[2] for repeat customers. These businesses know that today's affluent customers are motivated by convenience, product choice, and speed of shopping and ordering when online. Questions about the future also elicited[3] revealing findings. When respondents were asked if they thought more of their products would be sold online 10 years from now rather than in-store, 41 percent responded positively, 43 per cent doubted it, and 16 per cent did not know; 60 per cent of those who have not taken the plunge[4] when it comes to online shopping see it as a potential channel for products or services. Yet half of these companies have no specific plans for developing this capability and only 22 per cent plan to create an e-commerce site in the next year.

Manifestly[5], there is not only nervousness about a new medium, but also a gulf between the acceptance of the long-term potential of online selling in theory, and making it happen. A question often posed by Walpole is whether the classic luxury business model is flawed in some

---

① pure-play *n.* 单一业务公司
② recognition [ˌrekəgˈniʃən] *n.* 认可
③ elicit [iˈlisit] *vt.* 引出,探出
④ plunge [plʌndʒ] *n.* 猛跌,骤降
⑤ manifestly [ˈmænifestli] *adv.* 明白地

示不知道。当提到在线购物时，60% 尚未上网销售的人将其视作产品或服务的一个潜在渠道。然而，一半以上的公司没有为开发这种能力做出具体的计划，只有 22% 的公司计划来年建立电子商务网站。

显然，新媒介的产生不仅会造成焦虑感，在线销售长期潜力在理论上的接受与具体实施也仍然存在巨大的差距。英国精品协会经常担心的问题是：尽管奢侈品行业长久以来销售良好，经典的奢侈品商业模式是否在某些方面还有缺陷。网络的出现也曝光了这些使人不安的悬念。例如，对传统零售和广告高成本的现行保障也许就是网络低投资的原因之一。同样的，也许某些企业对消费者数据缺乏兴趣妨碍了全面的评价，即很多新贵在传统商店购物总是觉得不舒适，他们享受网上购物的便捷。许多公司开发在线模式的方式不仅表明他们对目前的在线零售最优方法缺乏正确判断，而且暴露了他们渴望控制品牌，将其置于消费者便捷之上，FLASH 技术的过度使用就是一个特别的例子。最后，除电子商务之外，极少数奢侈品公司有把握认为，也许有一天能证明网络可以带来最大的利益——与客户互动、并聆听他们声音的机会。这表明奢侈品行业游离于以消费者为中心的观点究竟到什么程度。

无论喜欢还是不喜欢，我们生活在一个电子商务的世界里。奢侈品企业迟早将让消费者在任何他们喜欢的渠道——无论是实体店购物、电话购物或在线购物——购买商品和互动，以便消费者享受无缝购物体验。有些理解这一点的奢侈品企业，他们正在忙于塑造

respects despite having served the industry so well for so long. The emergence of the web exposes some of these tensions. For example, an existing commitment to the high costs of traditional retail and advertising may be one of the reasons for low investment online. Likewise, maybe the lack of interest in consumer data by some businesses has delayed full appreciation that many of the newly wealthy do not always feel comfortable in traditional stores, and enjoy the convenience of online shopping. The way many firms develop their online presence not only demonstrates a lack of appreciation of current online retailing best practices, but also exposes a desire to put control of the brand above customer convenience, the overuse of Flash technology being a particular example. Finally, e-commerce aside, few luxury companies grasp what may one day prove to be the greatest of the web's benefits-the opportunity to interact with and listen to customers. This shows how far the industry has drifted from a consumer-centric point of view.

Like it or not, we live in an e-world. Sooner or later luxury businesses will have to allow customers to buy and interact in whatever channel they prefer, whether in-store, by telephone, or online, so that the consumer enjoys a seamless shopping experience. There are luxury businesses that understand this and are busy shaping a new shopping experience online. Hopefully it will be their innovations that help the sector break out of catch-up mode and show that it is as capable of technological creativity and leadership as it was 100 years ago.

(875 words)

新的网上购物体验。希望这将是他们的创新，以帮助奢侈品行业摆脱追赶模式，展示它在100年前就已经具备的技术创新和领导能力。

知识链接

Walpole（英国精品协会）英国精品协会是一家英国私营非盈利的奢侈品品牌组织，创建于1992年，其宗旨是促进各国对英国奢侈品品牌的认知。Walpole这一名称源自于伟大的政治家罗伯特·沃波尔（Robert Walpole）爵士（1676—1745），他是一位受人尊敬的商业部长，因积极推动海外贸易而闻名，为英国的一个繁荣和平时代打下了坚实的基础。沃波尔先生热衷于资助艺术和建筑，为手工艺和制造业的黄金时代做出了极大的贡献。英国精品协会目前拥有约100家成员公司，包括巴宝莉、克莱夫基斯汀、芝华士兄弟、Church & Co、登喜路、《金融时报》、格拉夫钻石、Links of London、皇家道尔顿和罗尔斯·罗伊斯。所有英国精品协会成员均拥护和推广英国精品协会的核心价值：质量、时尚、设计、手工艺、创意、服务和创新。

Forrester Research 佛雷斯特公司是一家独立的技术和市场调研公司，于1983年以IT战略服务进入IT调查的市场。从那以后，佛雷斯特公司一直在不断地扩张，针对技术给业务和客户所带来的影响提供务实和具有前瞻性的建议。与它的竞争者不同，佛雷斯特公司的调查不包含高水平的市场增长或是复杂的财务模型方面的研究，但是它却持续地对技术给予长期的关注。分析师完全依靠直觉和佛雷斯特公司的原则即“向适当的人问适当的问题”进行工作。历经市场的检验，佛雷斯特公司已经被公认为思想的领导者和可信赖的咨询商，它通过所从事的研究、咨询、市场活动和高层对等交流计划，帮助那些全球性的企业用户建立起市场领导地位。

题　记

电子商务爆发出巨大的商机，创新的模式和服务带给企业一个增值的平台，给网购市场快速发展创造了机会，成为购物资讯综合平台。网上购物的便捷性使得需求从最大的商品到最小的商品几乎无所不包，增长最快的两类商品是汽车和百货，最大的卖家是机票、图书、音乐制品和礼品。人们常用的“独立自建模式”由企业建立电子商务公司管理，依据公司自有成熟品牌资源，建立网购平台，形成线上线下立体化销售渠道。越来越多的商家发现，与在购物广场开店相比，网上开店明显是一笔具有吸引力的投资，正在快速超出计算机产品的需求。

Recreating the Experience of Internet shopping

This holiday season may be the first in which consumers respond by showing businesses that offer goods and services on line a significant amount of sales. Many Internet merchants have found that volume is up sharply this year as more consumers learn how to find what they want and become comfortable that they will not be defrauded① when they do. The American Express Company calculates that $ 4 billion to $ 6 billion will be spent making credit card purchases over the Internet this year, with sales increasing at more than a 400 percent pace annually. More conservatively②, Forrester Research puts the figure at $ 2.4 billion, double last year's total. "Nineteen ninety-seven has been a watershed③ year for many merchants on line," said Kate Delhagen, an analyst with Forrester Research. Its recent survey found that 25 percent of what it estimates to be 40 million Internet users had bought something on line.

Of course, Internet sales are still only a tiny part of the overall economy. And many shoppers will always want to see, feel and carry

---

① defraud [di'frɔːd] *v.* 欺骗

② conservatively [kən'səːvətivli] *adv.* 保守的,守旧的

③ watershed ['wɔːtəʃed] *n.* 流域,分水岭

重塑网络购物体验

这个假期也许是消费者对网络商品和服务销售额猛增的首次反应。许多互联网商家发现，由于越来越多的消费者认识到如何找到他们想要的东西，如何舒适地在网上购物避免受骗上当，今年的销售额急剧上升。美国运通公司提供的数据表明，今年有 40 亿到 60 亿美元的信用卡消费用于网络购物，销售额还在以每年 400% 的速度递增。佛雷斯特公司更保守的数据估计为 24 亿美元，是去年总额的一倍。佛雷斯特公司的分析师凯特·戴哈根说："1997 年已经成为许多网络商家的分水岭。"最近的调查表明，据估计，400 万的网络用户中有 25% 的人已经上网购物。

当然，网络销售仍然仅仅只是整个经济中很小的一部分。大多数的消费者总是喜欢购物时亲自看、摸和搬回家。Tandy 公司大型超级市场部电脑商城的总裁内森·莫顿说："早在 20 世纪 80 年代，当家庭购物网首次在网络出现的时候，我还记得许多华尔街的人说'零售业完蛋了，所有人都会转向电视购物'。几十年过去了，这一切还没有发生。"但是，电脑商城察觉到大批技术敏锐的消费者的存在，设立了自己的网站并加入到网络销售这一趋势中来。网络商家将这个假期的网上销售需求看做一次关键的测试。美国在线的电

home what they buy. "Back in the early 1980's, when the Home Shopping Network first came on line, I can remember people on Wall Street said, 'Retail is dead and everyone will be buying on their TV's,'" said Nathan Morton, chief executive of Computer City, the superstore unit of the Tandy Corporation. "Well, a couple of decades later that hasn't happened." Nonetheless, Computer City, looking at the number of technology-savvy① consumers, is joining the rush to sell on the Internet with a site of its own. Internet merchants see this holiday season as a critical test of the appeal of buying on line. "Seventy-eight percent of our members are window shopping on line, but only 12 percent have made a purchase," said Wendy Brown, vice president for electronic commerce at America Online Inc., which offers links to dozens of merchants that collectively are making one million sales a month. "Our job this holiday is to convert more shoppers to buyers."

Even without a lift from holiday sales, the Internet is rapidly growing important to certain businesses. Already, 2 percent to 3 percent of the computer hardware in the country is purchased on line, Forrester estimates. The Dell Computer Corporation, a pioneer, is selling more than $ 3 million worth of personal computers a day on its World Wide Web site, triple the pace of eight months ago. But on-line shopping is rapidly moving beyond the obvious appeal of computer products. The next biggest sellers are airline tickets, books, and music and gift items. The convenience of on-line shopping has appeal from the biggest to the smallest purchases. Two of the fastest-growing categories② are on-line purchases of automobiles and groceries. Though some of the initial department store efforts to sell fashion on line have been flops, some

---

① savvy [ˈsævi] *v.&n.* 机智,悟性

② category [ˈkætigəri] *n.* 种类,类别

子商业部副总裁温迪·布朗说："我们有78%的会员在网上查看商品，但仅有12%的人购买。我们在这个假期的任务就是设法让更多网上逛店的人成为购买者。"美国在线为很多商家提供链接，月销售总量达100万批次。

虽然节假日的销售高潮还没有到来，网上销售现已迅速增长为重要的购物方式。佛雷斯特公司估计，美国2%~3%的电脑硬件已经采取了网络销售模式。网络先锋戴尔电脑公司在环球网一天销售的个人电脑总值超过300万美元，是8个月前的3倍。但是，在线购物很明显正在快速超出计算机产品的需求。接下来最大的卖家是机票、图书、音乐制品和礼品。网上购物的便捷性使得需求从最大的商品到最小的商品几乎无所不包。网上购买增长最快的两类商品就是汽车和百货。尽管某些初建的店铺在线销售服装的努力未能成功，但仍然有一些商家发现，他们能够挺进同样的市场，根据目录购衣。美国在线的布朗女士说："如果你知道自己穿多大尺码的埃迪·鲍尔的牛仔裤的话，就用不着到商店去买。"正是对便捷的同样追求推动着过去20年间的电邮购物，并驱使大量的人上网。网上商店24小时开放，全世界的人能够平等地进入网络。

杰普公司主席罗伯特·费希尔说："大型购物广场正变得越来越拥挤，消费者会来到网上，寻找一个轻松的地方购物。"杰普公司两周前开始在自己的网站上销售牛仔裤和礼品。杰普公司的网站利用计算机直观显示部分重塑了某些商店购物体验，让用户观看衬衣、裤子和鞋子的各种不同搭配的整体效果。网上购物的高峰期是上午

merchants are finding that they can tap into the same market that buys clothes from catalogues. "If you know how a pair of Eddie Bauer jeans fits, you don't need to go to the store to buy it," said Ms. Brown of America Online. It is that same quest for convenience that propelled the mail-order business over the last two decades and that is driving many people on line. Internet stores are open around the clock and are equally accessible to people around the world.

"The malls are getting more and more crowded," said Robert Fisher, president of Gap Inc., which started selling jeans and gifts on its Web site two weeks ago. "Customers will come on line and find an easy place to shop." The Gap's site re-creates some of the experience of store shopping with a computer animation① section that allows users to see how various combinations of shirts, pants and shoes will look together. The peak shopping hours are late morning to early afternoon, as buyers take advantage of the faster Internet access offered on many office computers. But the Internet caters② to night owls, as well. Forty percent of the purchases on America Online occur after 9 P.M. Another appeal of online shopping is the prospect of finding a bargain. With lower operating costs, some companies are offering significant discounts. Amazon.com Inc., the online bookseller, offers some titles at 40 percent off the list price. A series of searches conducted by the accounting firm Ernst & Young found that for 90 percent of a basket of gifts—ranging from cordless drills to cameras to bunches of roses—the Internet offers better deals than traditional stores.

Yet not everyone can find all those bargains. For many; online shopping

---

① animation [æni'meiʃən] *n.* 卡通制作

② cater ['keitə] *v.* 迎合,满足需要

的晚些时候和下午的早些时候，因为购物者利用很多办公室电脑进行更快捷的网络搜索。但网络也迎合“夜猫子”的需求。40% 美国在线的购物者晚上 9 点以后上线。网上购物的另一个吸引力就是有希望找到便宜货。因为运营费较低，有些公司提供高额折扣。在线图书销售公司亚马逊对有些图书打六折。安永会计师事务所进行的一系列调查表明，90% 的礼品（包括无线电钻、摄像机、玫瑰花等），网上店面都能比传统店面提供更好的条件。

然而，并非每个人都能找到所有的这些便宜货。对许多人来说，网上购物令他们怨声载道。网上购物者通常抱怨最多的就是寻找商品和购物的过程既慢又复杂，部分是因为固有的互联网连接延迟效应，特别是在家通过调制解调器上网的用户速度缓慢。购物者说，许多网店上的商品排序混乱，购物效率就像使用没有按字母排序的电话簿一样。管理 CUC 国际公司（消费性劳务公司）旗下的一家网上大型购物广场的斯科特·梅兰德说：“速度是问题的实质。”CUC 国际公司发布了一个新的网站版本，剔除了一些移动短信之类的、使购物速度放慢的初期华丽特征。

一批近期崭露头角的网上商店引起了最大的商业连锁店的注意，最为人所熟知的可能还是亚马逊网站，它今年第三季度的销售额达 3 800 万美元，比第二季度增长 32%。所以，许多在典型的商业广场或闹市区耳熟能详的名字，如 Barnes & Noble 有限公司，杰普公司以及 Toys "R" Us 有限公司，已经在互联网开设了自己的网站，给在线购物增加了能见度，使其更接近主流。美国最大的零售商沃

is filled with all the exasperation[①]. The most frequent complaint from online shoppers is that finding and buying things is slow and complex. Some of that is caused by the delays inherent in Internet connections, particularly the slow speed of the modems that people use to connect from home. But many sites, shoppers say, are so poorly organized that shopping can be about as efficient as using a phone book that is not in alphabetical[②] order. "Speed is the name of the game," said Scot Melland, who runs the Net Market Internet shopping mall for CUC International Inc., the consumer services company. CUC is releasing a new version of the site that removes some of the initial fancy features, such as moving messages, that slowed shopping.

The most recent batch of Internet start-up companies has caught the attention of the biggest store chains. Perhaps the best known of these has been Amazon. com, which had sales of $38 million in the third quarter, up 32 percent from the second quarter of this year. Thus, many of the names in the typical mall or strip center—like Barnes & Noble Inc., the Gap and Toys "R" Us Inc., have started to open sites on the Internet, giving online shopping added visibility and pushing it closer to the mainstream. The nation's largest retailer, Wal-Mart Stores Inc., is replicating its endless aisles with a Web store selling everything from computers to corn flakes. And even if Internet sales are small, more and more merchants are finding that opening a store on the Internet is an attractive investment compared with a store in a mall.

(1,046 words)

---

① exasperation [igzɑːspəˈreiʃən] *n.* 恼怒

② alphabetical [ælfəˈbetikəl] *adj.* 按字母表顺序的

尔玛百货有限公司正在复制网络商店无穷尽的货架，销售从计算机到玉米片等各式商品。即使网络销售量很少，但越来越多的商家发现，与在购物广场开店相比，网上开店是一笔具有吸引力的投资。

知识链接

American Express Company 美国运通为全球最大的旅行社，并以其美国运通记账卡闻名全球。其业务主要可分为旅行、财务顾问和银行等部分，分别以 Travel Related Services、American Express Financial Advisors 及 American Express Bank 为主体。Travel Related Services 提供包括记账卡、卡友贷款、旅行支票、个人及企业旅行服务；American Express Financial Advisors 服务内容有财务规划和建议、投资建议、保险及年金和共同基金；American Express Bank 有企业金融、私人银行、个人金融服务和全球交易等服务项目。

American Online 美国在线是美国时代华纳的子公司，著名的互联网服务提供商，可提供电子邮件、新闻组、教育和娱乐服务，并支持对互联网访问。2000 年美国在线服务(AOL)公司与媒体巨人华纳时代公司合并，旨在扩展品牌内容服务以及通信服务的大众市场，合并后的公司形成了一个通信和媒体大公司，这个大公司拥有因特网最大用户群体，并有娱乐、出版和有线电视领域的广泛基础。

题 记

网站本身不会为你的生意做什么贡献，也不会自我组织。它的使用价值取决于交易，而交易又取决于营销。没有营销计划的网站，其用途如同一个无人知晓的免费长途电话号码。网站的竞争优势随着时间的流逝依托在行业的整体平台上，其领先的技术实现了前台的页面拼装、内容搜索等服务。快速加载网页、新颖的内容、营销的杠杆作用和对网站的信赖都是增强网站竞争优势的基本策略。功利是网站的特性，而赢利则是网站用户得到的积极价值。功利一旦和赢利结合，就可以利用电子商务的竞争优势开辟一个又一个朝气蓬勃的市场。

Web Competitive Edge

One of the biggest and most widespread fallacies of the late 20th century Internet boom in the United States was the idea that a website would or could create business on its own. This outrageous[①] idea was populated by messages such as the television commercial, watched by millions in the late 1990s, showing two women who invented an improvement on sunglasses while on the beach, and in a subsequent scene they were still happily on the beach but at that point living off of their website. In truth it just doesn't happen like that. Here are some basic truths to offset common myths:

1. Websites without traffic offer no business or organizational purpose: Sad but true, this is just pure myth. If you build a beautiful website and nobody comes, no matter how useful or artistic the website, it is useless. Think of a website as a new version of the toll free telephone number; just like a toll free number is useless if nobody calls it, so too a website is useless if nobody visits it.

2. Websites don't get traffic by themselves: If you build it, and do nothing else, they will come. That's also a myth. Websites don't generate

---

① outrageous [aʊtˈreidʒəs] *adj.* 骇人的,残暴的

网站竞争优势

美国20世纪网络繁荣的最大和流传最广的谬论之一是这样一种观点：网站自身即将或能够创造交易。这个令人不可容忍的想法由于20世纪90年代末一个被数百万观众收看的电视商业广告而广为流传。节目中的两位女士在沙滩上对太阳镜做了一些改进，接下来的画面是她们仍然快乐地坐在沙滩上，但这时已经在用网站营生。事实上，这类事情并不会发生。这里有些基本的事实回应这些庸俗的神话：

1. 没有交易的网站提供不了商机或组织效用：很悲哀但却是事实，这只是纯粹的神话。如果你建造了一个完美的网站却无人来访，网站无论多么实用、多么有艺术感也毫无价值。把网站当做一个免费的长途电话号码来思考，就像无人呼叫的免费长途电话号码一样，如果无人访问网站，它就毫无价值。

2. 网站自身不会招揽交易：如果你除了建网站什么也不干，生意自然会来。这也是神话。目前，网站并不再仅仅因为有益或者实用而产生交易。

3. 交易需要营销：需要营销在网站创造交易。成功的网站通过传统营销模式的新应用做生意，包括广告、公共关系和口碑。他们还通过新的网络营销做生意，强调细致的搜索策略管理。

traffic anymore just because they are good, or useful.

3. Traffic takes marketing: It takes marketing to generate traffic on a website. Successful websites generate traffic by new applications of old-fashioned marketing, including advertising, public relations, and word of mouth. They also generate traffic through new Internet marketing, highlighted by careful management of searcher strategies.

4. The Internet gold rush is over: Times have changed for the Internet, investors are no longer going to invest in traffic alone. These days plans have to be complete, from marketing to revenues and expenses, with business sense.

What is your website's competitive edge? How are you different from all others? In what way does it stand out? Is there sustainable value that you can maintain and develop over time? The most classic of the competitive edges are those based on proprietary technology and protected by patents. A patent, an algorithm, even deeply entrenched know-how, can be a solid competitive edge. In services, however, the edge can be as simple as having the phone number 1 (800), which is an actual case. A successful company was built around that phone number. Sometimes market share and brand acceptance are just as important. Know-how① does not have to be protected by patent to offer a competitive edge. For example, some of these values might lead to competitive edge:

• Quick loading pages-2 seconds vs. 12 seconds, 8 seconds being the average. For example, Buy.com's average load time is 2-4 seconds. This has certainly been the case with Yahoo!, it consistently loads in a very

① Know-how 专门知识,技术诀窍

4. 网络淘金热已经结束：时代因为网络而改变，投资者们不再仅仅投资贸易。现在计划肯定要完善，从营销到税收和开支都需要商业理念。

什么是你网站的竞争优势？ 你和其他人有什么不同？ 哪种方法能使之脱颖而出？ 你能随着时间的流逝维持和发展持续的价值吗？ 最典型的竞争优势基于专利技术，并受到专利权的保护。一项专利，一组编码，甚至根深蒂固的专门技术，都能成为坚实的竞争优势。然而在服务行业，这种优势可以像拥有电话号码 1（800）一样简单，这就是现存的例子。一个成功的企业就建在这个电话号码的周围。有时，市场份额和品牌的认可度也同样重要。专门技术没有必要受专利权的保护而提供竞争优势。例如，下列价值中的一部分可能导致竞争优势：

· 快速加载网页——2 比 12 秒，平均 8 秒钟。例如，购买网的平均载入时间是 2 至 4 秒。雅虎当然也是如此，它一贯都在很短的时间内载入。

· 内容新颖：例如重大新闻站点。洋葱头网和电子杂志网的读者很少关注这一问题，他们期待网页的内容每周、每月或每季度更新。

· 营销的杠杆作用：例如，聚焦网隶属于 NBCi 公司，它是最大的美国全国广播公司的子公司。美国全国广播公司根据 NBCi 公司的指导进行交易。NFL.com 网站上的美国足球联盟通过链接足球实况转播互动达成交易。

· 信赖：一个人们感觉能够自由地发表想法和担忧的社区将拥有基于信赖的竞争优势。新帖子和新想法使网民再次登录你的网站。

small amount of time.

• Fresh content. e.g., major news sites. This is less of a concern to readers of theonion.com or e-zine sites, where the expectation is that content will be updated on a weekly, monthly, or quarterly basis.

• Marketing leverage. For example, zoom.com is owned by NBCi, a subsidiary of NBC the major national television network. NBC directs traffic in NBCi's direction. The National Football League site at NFL.com generates traffic by linking to football broadcasts with live interaction.

• Trust. A community where people feel free to post their thoughts and concerns will have a competitive advantage based on trust. New posts and new ideas bring them back to your site. Fool.com, for example, has mastered the art of building a network of users. They have dozens of custom email newsletters①, some of which feature the most popular message board posts for that day.

The competitive edge might be different for any given company, even between one company and another in the same industry. You don't have to have a competitive edge to run a successful business-hard work, integrity, and customer satisfaction can substitute for it-but any edge will certainly give you a head start if you need to bring in new investment. Maybe it's your customer base, as in the case with Hewlett-Packard's traditional relationship with engineers and technicians, or maybe it's image and awareness, such as with Dell. Maybe your competitive edge is quality control and consistency, like that of IBM. A good website strategy first identifies a market need, which indicates a target market, and then

① newsletter [ˈnjuːzˌletə(r)] *n.* 简报;业务通讯

例如，愚人网已经掌握了建造用户网络的艺术。他们拥有很多客户电邮时事通讯，其中有些展示当天最受欢迎的留言板帖子中的要点。

竞争优势可能与任何特定的企业不同，甚至同一行业中的公司与公司之间也不同。你不一定要有竞争优势才能经营成功的事业——勤劳、正直和客户的满意度都可以取代竞争优势——但是，如果你想引进新投资，任何优势都肯定会让你领先。或许这种优势是你的客户基础，就像惠普公司与工程师和技术人员的传统关系。或者可能是形象和知名度，比如戴尔公司。或许你的竞争优势是质量控制和持续性，就像 IBM。好的网站策略首先要识别市场需求，当然指目标市场，然后满足那种需求。如今，20 世纪末的网络发展已经结束，如果考虑谁将会花费多少来满足需求，你的策略通常会增加一点基本的商业收益。

功利是网站的特性，而赢利则是网站用户所得到的积极价值。功利作为工具给预期用户提供赢利。通常，人们购买的赢利多于功利。网站有能力让人们相信它的成功所在，他们的计划无懈可击，能够答疑、解惑和实施详尽的步骤。网站设计人员创造功利，但是人们购买赢利。好的市场商人理解功利，但是强调赢利。他们利用功利解释和提高赢利。常规也存在例外。有些网站，有些市场，甚至有些行业都受到功利的驱动。对买者而言，计算机和个人电子器件都有这种倾向。功利有时和赢利结合。例如，在线交易网站中，广告经常销售相关的可靠性和专门知识赢利，而不是特定的网站功利。当你考察在线代理营销时，可以考虑将此作为背景。这些广告大多数推动赢利，但有些只强调价格，还有一些推销功利。想一想你所了解

fills that need. Now that the Internet boom of the late 20th century is over, your strategy usually has to add an element of basic business revenue, considering who will pay how much to have that need filled.

Features are characteristics of the site, while benefits are positive values to the person who uses the site. The features serve as a means to offer the intended customer benefit. Usually people buy benefits more than features. The site's ability to give people reassurance① that their plan is okay, answers to questions, resolve doubts, and specific how-to steps is why it's successful. Site designers create features, but people buy benefits. Good marketers understand features, but emphasize benefits. They use features to explain and develop benefits. There are exceptions to the general rule. Some websites, some markets, and even some industries are feature-driven. For some buyers, computers and personal electronics have this tendency. Sometimes the features and benefits merge together. Among online trading websites, for example, advertising often sells benefits related to reliability and expertise, more than specific website features. As you look at the online brokers marketing, think about this as background. Most of these ads push benefits, but some push price alone, and some push features. Think about ads you know and how they suggest benefits and specifically inform about features.

(951 words)

---

① reassurance [ˌriːəˈʃuərəns] *n.* 消除恐惧或疑惑，恢复信心

的广告，考察他们如何表达赢利和明确地鼓吹功利。

知识链接

NBC （National Broadcasting Company）美国全国广播公司是美国一家主流广播电视网络公司，总部设在纽约的洛克菲勒中心，以孔雀为标记。NBC1926 年由美国无线电公司（RCA）成立，1986 年被通用电气公司（GE，General Electric Corp.）收购，2004 年与法国的维旺迪环球旗下的娱乐部门合并之后，变更为“NBC 环球”（NBC Universal，Inc.），但在一些节目中 NBC 仍会使用它“全国广播公司”的全称。NBC 目前是传媒联合大企业 NBC Universal 的一部分，向下属 200 多家美国电视台提供大量的新闻、体育娱乐节目及电视剧等节目。

题　记

随着互联网的不断发展，越来越多的人开始尝试在线交易。然而病毒、黑客、网络钓鱼以及网页仿冒诈骗等恶意威胁，给在线交易的安全性带来了极大的挑战。公司和金融机构实施了无数的安全措施来解决身份认证问题，使用端到端身份认证构造和多因素身份认证法就是排除隐患的重要手段。使用端到端方法的公司能够依靠数字署名认证购买订单、发票和其他单据，允许他们自动操作，最终到达财政供应链的终端。身份认证是公司的首选，因为这可以获得商业利益，如加速收据流通；还可以享有决策收益，如推动新的市场。强大的网络身份认证使电子商务的能动性发挥出前所未有的安全水平，给双方的攻击性和防御性都提供了新的机会。

E-Commerce Authentication

While the global community goes about its daily business, a sinister force—the e—criminal—lurks[①] as close as a web browser, threatening to stop e-commerce in its tracks. Business and consumers have capitalized on[②] the convenience and cost-effectiveness of trading online, but it could come to a crashing halt if companies and their banks stop insuring losses because of online fraud—as some have hinted they might. The assurance that both parties in a transaction are secure is essential to thwarting rampant[③] fraud, which places identity authentication at the heart of the battle for the future of e-commerce.

While e-criminals' tactics have evolved, many corporations have not responded in kind, at least when it comes to identity authentication strategies. Times are a-changing. As businesses face critical decisions about whether or how to insure losses that result from e-crime, many are focusing on reducing their risk outright by fortifying[④] the role of identity authentication. They are taking an end-to-end approach in partnership with their financial institutions. Corporations and their financial

---

① lurk [lə:k] *v.* 潜伏,潜在
② capitalize on 充分利用某事物
③ rampant [ˈræmpənt] *adj.* 猖獗的,无法控制的
④ fortify [ˈfɔːtifai] *vt.* 增强,强化

电子商务身份认证

当全球的公众忙于日常业务时，一股险恶的势力——电子罪犯——像网络浏览器一样就近潜伏，在其通道上构成威胁，堵塞电子商务。商家和消费者已经在利用网上交易的便利和成本效率，但如果公司和银行由于网络诈骗停止对损失的投保，这种便利就会突然中止，正如有些公司和银行暗示的，他们有可能这样做。交易双方的安全保障对阻止网络诈骗的横行很有必要，它把身份认证置于未来电子商务竞争的核心。

随着网络罪犯手段的演变，很多公司至少在进行身份认证策略时不履行以货代款。网络时代风云变幻。当公司面临关键性的决策，是否或如何确保网络犯罪造成的损失，很多公司完全通过增强身份认证的作用来集中减少风险。他们与金融机构一道采取端到端的方法。公司和金融机构近年来已经实施了无数的安全措施来解决身份认证问题，但通常采纳零散与整体规划的方法。很多公司已经得知，依赖一系列互不相干的解决方案的难处是无法提供客户和商家的能见度或解除所有的恶兆。比如，一个通常使用的认证方

institutions through the years have implemented countless security measures to address identity issues, but generally have pursued a piecemeal versus an enterprise approach. Many have learned the hard way that relying on a series of discrete point solutions cannot provide end-to-end visibility or address the total threat. For example, two-factor authentication, a frequently deployed① identity authentication method that couples a password with another type of identification, has proved to be fallible—when used alone—at thwarting man-in-the-middle attacks, when a hacker intercepts confidential messages, using the information to access accounts. When the link between the user and their internet service provider is phished or hacked into, the hacker can insert fraudulent② sites into the workflow, collect password and personal information and use that information to access accounts or commit other identity fraud crimes.

The piecemeal approach falls short because most point solutions focus on access versus authentication. Thus, as long as an individual has the appropriate Pin/password or token combined with a user name or site key, he/she can gain access to a site or data. This approach is short-sighted because companies need to understand and vet the way in which credentials are granted before they can rely upon them. Solutions that simply authenticate a user's credentials, and not who the user really is—while noble first attempts—do not guarantee a trusted infrastructure, and only meet basic compliance with domestic and international identity authentication guidelines and regulations. To provide security of the highest level possible, organizations must perform multi-factor authentication across the enterprise, using a single comprehensive

---

① deploy [di'plɔi] *v.* 施展,部署

② fraudulent ['frɔːdjulənt] *a.* 欺骗的,不诚实的

法——密码和另一类型认证相结合的两因素认证，在防止中间人攻击时单独使用就会出错，黑客截取机密消息时，即利用该信息访问账户。一旦用户和网络提供商的联系被中断或被黑客侵入，黑客可以通过工作流插入欺诈网站，收集密码和个人信息，并用这些信息获取账户或对其他身份认证作案。

大部分端点方案集中在进入方法和身份认证，零散的方法并不适用。所以，只要个人有合适的个人身份号码或密码，或带有用户名或网站密码，他或她都有权使用网站或数据库。这种方法缺乏远见，因为公司需要推敲和审查认证资格的方法才能对其信任。仅仅鉴别用户资格、不了解用户真实身份的方案，尽管初衷高尚，也不能保证值得信赖的防御结构，只不过基本符合国内和国际身份认证的指导方针和规则。为了尽可能提供最高水平的安全，企业之间必须使用多因素身份认证法，使用将各种各样的端点方案整体化、形成多方保护的单独综合法，交叉认证网络用户，确保两者通过数字认证，待双方仔细审查后才能公布。同样关键的是验证认证信息，而不是实时更新显示认证信息是否到期或已被撤销的数据清单。

身份认证方法的全球通用性是另一个严肃的问题。企业需要跨国认证保护和国内外都接受的法律体制。另外，如果引发安全缺口或数字化签名文件不被捆绑接受，就会呈现费用昂贵和

solution that integrates various point solutions for all-round protection; cross-authenticates the user with the site; and secures the two through digital certificates, which have been issued only after the parties have been fully vetted. It is also critical to validate certificates against a real-time updated list that indicates whether or not the certificate has expired or been revoked①.

Global interoperability② of identity authentication solutions is another serious concern. Enterprises need authentication protection across international borders and a legal framework that is acceptable domestically and internationally. Otherwise, a corporation or its financial institution could face the prospect of adjudicating③ disputes in jurisdictions around the world should a security breach arise or a digitally signed document not be accepted as binding—an expensive and cumbersome prospect. Financial institutions have a unique role and opportunity in an end-to-end infrastructure that incorporates digital certificates as the identity authentication vehicle. They can leverage their position as a trusted third-party in the traditional off-line world and offer new services as a third-party issuer of online digital certificates, simplifying the delivery for customers and eliminating the need to expand the number of parties trusted with personal and confidential information.

For corporations, the benefits of an end-to-end identity authentication infrastructure extend far beyond protection from cyber criminals. They can drive new revenue opportunities and operational efficiencies. Corporations using an end-to-end approach can rely on the

---

① revoke [riˈvəuk] *v.* 撤销,取消

② interoperability [ˈintərɔpərəˈbiləti] *n.* 协同工作的能力

③ adjudicate [əˈdʒuːdikeit] *v.* 判决,裁定

公司运转不灵的前景，公司或其金融机构将面临世界司法裁决争议。金融机构在并购作为身份认证媒介的端对端数字认证构造中，具有独特的角色和机会。它们在传统的脱机世界中，能够作为监管的第三方提高地位，并作为网络数字认证的第三方发行者提供新的服务，简化了消费者传递，排除了扩大私人和机密信息托管方数目的需要。

对公司而言，端到端身份认证构造的好处远远超过对网络罪犯的防卫。他们能创造新的税收机会和经营效率。使用端到端方法的公司能够依靠数字署名认证购买订单、发票和其他单据，允许他们自动操作，最终到达财政供应链的终端。公司对于综合性身份认证方法的潜力持乐观态度，以帮助他们获取新的商业机会。对商业主管们近期进行的一项“经济学家智能单元”调查表明，246 名回答者中的 45% 认为，有效的身份认证能让他们的业务在未来三年更加快速地增长。三分之二的公司说，身份认证是他们公司的首选，因为这可以获得商业利益，如加速收据流通；还可享有决策收益，如推动新的市场。当访问者声称代表客户的银行时，大部分消费者不会在电话中公开他们的银行账户密码，但很多金融机构和消费者在网上做生意时却鲁莽行事。很多公司急于扩大网上的店面，集中关注使用的轻松安逸，而将安全束之高阁，并事后追悔，从而让金融机构和他们的客户容易

authenticity of digital signatures for purchase orders, invoices, and other documents, allowing them to automate—finally—the last legs of the financial supply chain. Businesses are optimistic about the potential of comprehensive identity authentication solutions to help them capture new business opportunities. A recent Economist Intelligence Unit survey of business executives revealed that 45 per cent of the 246 respondents said that effective identity authentication would enable their businesses to grow more rapidly over the next three years. Two-thirds said identity authentication was a priority for their companies because it could deliver business benefits, such as expediting receipts, as well as strategic benefits, such as facilitating entry into new markets. Most consumers will not share their bank account passwords over the phone with a caller claiming to represent their bank, but many financial institutions and consumers adopt reckless privacy practices when doing business online. In the rush to expand their online storefronts, many organisations have focused on ease of use while relegating① security to an afterthought—leaving the institutions and their customers vulnerable to financial losses and critical damage to their reputations. A strong online identity authentication strategy, however, does not require businesses to sacrifice ease-of-use or replace their current data security infrastructures. Rather, companies taking the leap from a point solution to an enterprise approach stand to gain unprecedented levels of assurance for their e-commerce initiatives as well as new opportunities for efficiency and expansion—a win on both the offensive and defensive fronts.

(923 words)

---

① relegate [ˈreligeit] *v.* 使降级,使降职

蒙受金融损失，严重损害了他们的信誉。然而，强大的网络身份认证策略并不要求商家牺牲使用的便利性或者取代他们目前使用数据的安全构造。宁可采用从端点方案到企业规划的公司一定获利，电子商务能动性前所未有的安全水平以及效率和扩展的新机会，影响着双方攻击性和防御性的态度。

知识链接

计算机及网络系统中常用的身份认证方式主要有以下几种：

1. 用户名/密码。这是基于"what you know"的验证手段。每个用户的密码由用户自己设定，只有用户自己才知道。只要能够正确输入密码，计算机就认为操作者是合法用户。
2. 智能卡认证。智能卡是一种内置集成电路的芯片，芯片中存有与用户身份相关的数据，是不可复制的硬件。智能卡由合法用户随身携带，登录时必须将智能卡插入专用的读卡器读取其中的信息，以验证用户的身份。
3. 动态口令 USB Key 认证。

题 记

如果说电的发明为工业提供了历史机遇，使资本主义在不到100年的时间里创造的生产力远远超过了以前几个世纪的总和，给人类带来了进步和幸福，那么电子商务是人类文明史上科技领域里信息控制技术革命的又一次重大飞跃。这次科技革命极大地推动了人类社会经济、政治、文化领域的变革，使人类社会生活和人的现代化向更高境界发展。在线阀门销售把人们的经商方式和思维模式推向了崭新的互联网时代：通过载有照片的目录页和产品的具体信息，提供实时信贷和处理联系人姓名和电话号码的网站、为客户购买产品的方式、创建定制的“添加”到“购物车”，使用信用卡支付产品价格和运输费用，及时发货到位。在线阀门销售的虚拟技术和交互式收集和反馈信息处理技术已经呈现出一种史无前例的科学技术的生命力。

Selling Valves Online

The world of electronic commerce is no longer limited to books, gifts and knickknacks. The power of the Internet is as vital to commerce now as electricity was to industry a hundred years ago and the future of nearly every commercial enterprise depends on the ability of leaders to harness[1] the opportunities provided by innovative sales protocols[2], to implement them effectively and to secure them for consistent, easy use. While the valve industry is slowly embracing an Internet method for buying and selling valves actuators, that situation will change as online sales channels become more sophisticated[3], flexible and cost-effective. Expanding the reach of a relatively small company is easily attainable with online sales and distribution—enabling valve providers to do business around the globe. Online sales accounted for more than $100 billion at present and the number will only grow.

A successful e-commerce website and business depends upon several interrelated factors. It should have the capacity to display catalog pages containing photos and product specific information, a real-time credit and

---

① harness [ˈhɑːnis] *vt.* 利用

② protocol [ˈprəutəkɔl] *n.* 草案,议定书

③ sophisticated [səˈfistikeitid] *adj.* 老练的,老于世故的

在线阀门销售

全球电子商务不再局限于书本、礼品和小玩意。互联网现在对于商业的力量与100年前电对于工业的力量一样至关重要，几乎每一个商业公司的前途都依靠领导的能力，利用创新销售协议所提供的机会，有效地执行协议，并且确保它们的一致性和便利使用。虽然阀门行业正以逐渐渗透互联网的方法购买和出售阀门制动器，但是随着网上销售渠道更为成熟、灵活和划算，这种情况将发生改变。利用在线销售和分销很容易扩大相对较小公司的范围，使阀门供应商能够在世界各地做生意。在线销售额目前已超过1 000亿美元，这一数据将只会增长。

成功的电子商务网站和商业取决于若干相互关联的因素。它应该有能力显示载有照片的目录页和产品的具体信息，提供实时信贷和处理联系人姓名和电话号码的网站、为客户购买产品的方式、创建定制的“添加”到“购物车”，及时发货到位，以展示产品、价格和运输费用。用户搜索特定的零件，或滚动数据库寻找他们需要的零件。他们拿到报价并订购控制阀、零件、制动装置和仪器。电

processing site with a contact name and phone number, and a way for customers to purchase products and have them delivered to their place of business in a timely fashion by creating a customized① "add to" shopping cart, displaying products, prices and shipping costs. Customers search for specific parts, or scroll a database to find the parts they need. They get quotes and order control valves, parts, actuators and instrumentation. The e-commerce angle expedites the ordering process by reducing the need for paper catalogs and allows customers to get product quotes and to order parts around the clock without having to make numerous phone calls and talk to multiple layers in a sales department. This e-commerce capability means that operating companies now have access to an extensive inventory of repair kits: new, aftermarket, and remanufactured parts for valves and assemblies; actuators; gaskets②; instruments and seal kits. Customers can search for specific parts, find the parts they need, get quotes and order them for delivery. A customer enters the online catalog through a website and begins selecting items. After making selections, the customer is presented a webpage showing the total amount to be paid for the items. The customer is then given an option for paying using a credit card. A reputable payment provider must be authorized to accept credit cards on behalf of the merchant. It may be a bank or authorized company who can accept and process these credit cards online. Finally, this payment gateway needs to be integrated within a website to carry online transactions safely and securely.

---

① customize [ˈkʌstəmaiz] *vt.* 定做,定制

② gasket [ˈgæskit] *n.* 垫圈,衬垫

子商务通过减少纸质目录的需要加快了定购流程，让客户在24小时内获取产品报价和订购零部件，不需要与销售部门进行无数的电话沟通和多层次的交谈。这种电子商务的能力意味着运营公司现在已经有权使用范围广泛的套装修理工具清单：新的配件市场和改装阀门零件与组装、制动器、垫圈、器械和密封的全套元件。用户可以搜索特定的零件，寻找他们需要的零件，获得报价和定购交货。客户通过网站进入在线目录，并开始选择项目。客户选择之后，得到一个显示所选商品应付款的总额网页。客户获得使用信用卡支付的权利。有信誉的付款商必须得到授权，代表商家接受信用卡。它可能是银行或经授权的公司，能够在线接受和处理这些信用卡。最后，这种付款通道需要在一个网站整合，以便安全可靠地进行网上交易。

另一个吸引和维持业务的好办法是提供只有在线才可利用的机会，如销售、折扣和散装率。网络促销方法可以比现实世界的促销更具成本效益，他们可以增加商业合作伙伴之间的信用，同时与尊贵的客户长期保持联系。美国和其他28个经济合作与发展组织成员签署了新的准则，目的是保护和通知用户有关国际电子商务销售的信息。由于这个原因，美国的电子商务销售受到全球信赖，被认为是最高标准。据美国联邦贸易委员会的规定，企业应遵守下列指导原则：使用公平的交易、广告和营销业务；提供公司和商品或服务准确、清晰和容易获得的信息；充分披露条款、条件和交易费用

Another good way to attract and maintain business is to offer online opportunities that are not available otherwise—such as sales, discounts, and bulk rates. Online promotional methods can be much more cost-effective than their real-world counterparts, and they can increase confidence between business partners while at the same time staying in touch with valued customers in a long-term way. The U.S. and 28 other countries have signed new guidelines as members of the Organization for Economic Cooperation and Development in order to protect and inform users about international e-commerce sales. For this reason, American e-commerce sales are trusted globally and held to the highest standard. According to the Federal Trade Commission, businesses that adhere to these guidelines: Use fair business, advertising and marketing practices; Provide accurate, clear and easily accessible information about the company and the goods or services; Disclose full information about the terms, conditions, and costs of the transaction; Ensure that consumers know they are making a commitment to buy before closing the deal; Provide an easy-to-use and secure method for online payments; Protect consumer privacy during electronic commerce transactions; Address consumer complaints and difficulties; Adopt fair, effective and easy-to-understand self-regulatory policies and procedures, and; Help educate consumers about electronic commerce. Following these guidelines is an effective method for building trust here and abroad. With something like e-commerce, dependability is incredibly important, and one bad deal can sour a client forever.

The ability to track orders, examine trends, and deal directly with customers is invaluable to a retailer. The difference between a retailer in

信息；确保消费者了解他们在交易结束之前正在承诺购买商品；为在线支付提供一个易于使用和安全的方法；在电子商务交易的过程中保护消费者的隐私；处理消费者的投诉和困难；采取公平、有效和易于理解的自律政策和程序；帮助指导消费者进行电子商务。遵循这些指导方针是在国内外建立信任的一种有效方法。随着电子商务的出现，可靠性毋庸置疑变得尤为重要，不利的交易可以使客户永远失去兴趣。

跟踪订单、审查发展趋势、直接与客户打交道的能力对零售商来说非常宝贵。在阀门产业利用商业机会的零售商和从零开始建立商业网站的人之间的区别是：阀门零售商有固定的客户基数，只不过是给他们提供更多的机会和更容易的方式来经商。他们毫无风险，只是换一种方式及时给那些需要的人交付优质产品。公司销售队伍的规模不再是问题，公司将由产品和服务的质量做出裁决。距离和时间不再是问题，总部设在美国东南部的企业能够毫无麻烦或障碍地处理欧洲和亚洲的业务。此外，如果客户的订单始终是同一个产品，或者订单几乎没有变化，将能够建立在线的个人资料，使再次订购几乎易如反掌。

未来总是无法预测的，但全球电子商务通道注定将保存下来。阀门产业获利的领导者将是那些抓住现有机会，建立坚固基础设施的人，这种基础设施不仅有效，而且易于导航。商业本身并没有改

the valve industry utilizing the opportunity of ecommerce and somebody starting up an e-commerce site from scratch① is that the valve retailer has a built-in customer base that is merely being offered more opportunities and an easier way to do business. There is no risk; merely an alternate method for delivering quality products to those who need them in a timely fashion. The size of a company's sales team will no longer matter, a company will be judged only by the quality of products and services. Distance and time will no longer be an issue, and businesses based in the American southeast will be able to deal with businesses in Europe and Asia without hassle② or snags③. Additionally, a client that consistently orders the same thing, or the same thing with very few variations, will be able to create an online profile that will make reordering nearly effortless.

The future is always unpredictable, but the global e-commerce channels are here to stay. The leaders in the valve industry who profit will be those who seize the opportunities presented, and build a solid infrastructure that is not only stable, but is also effective and easy to navigate④. Business itself is not changing, but the way people do business is always in flux⑤, and it is important to be one step ahead at all times.

(941 words)

---

① scratch [skrætʃ] *vt.* 抓,挠(from scratch:从零做起)
② hassle [ˈhæsəl] *n.* 困难的事情
③ snag [snæg] *n.* 障碍,阻碍
④ navigate [ˈnævigeit] *vt.* 引导
⑤ flux [flʌks] *n.* 不断的变动,变迁

变，但人们经商的方式总在不断变化，重要的是在任何时候都要领先一步。

知识链接

the Organization for Economic Cooperation and Development （OECD）经济合作与发展组织。它成立于 1961 年，其前身是欧洲经济合作组织（OEEC），目前共有 30 个成员，国民生产总值占全世界三分之二，包括几乎所有的发达国家：澳大利亚、奥地利、比利时、加拿大、捷克、丹麦、芬兰、法国、德国、希腊、匈牙利、冰岛、爱尔兰、意大利、日本、韩国、卢森堡、墨西哥、荷兰、新西兰、挪威、波兰、葡萄牙、斯洛伐克、西班牙、瑞典、瑞士、土耳其、英国和美国等。它还包括国际能源代理机构、核能代理机构、欧洲交通部长会议、发展中心、教育研究和创新、Club du Sahel 等 6 个半自治的代理机构。OECD 的职能主要是研究分析和预测世界经济的发展走向，协调成员关系，促进成员合作，经常为成员制定国内政策和确定在区域性、国际性组织中的立场提供帮助。

题　记

互联网零售业的国际化正以迅雷不及掩耳之势席卷全球。百货商场——20世纪初期的成功神话——正在衰落；购物中心和超市——20世纪后期的成功神话——正面临巨大的挑战，网络零售商掀起了一场零售业的革命。“无店铺销售”让人们走进“虚拟现实”，在这里，“电子概念商店”之类的时髦网站，能使购物者移动鼠标、滚动网页、启动超链接的各种方式去接近目标商品，从不同的角度对他们进行考察。网络购物的两种不同发展趋势拥有各自的客户群体，一种销售物美价廉的低档商品，另一种提供高档消费商品服务。网络销售给传统零售商带来压力的同时也带来了全新的机会：一方面，他们通过网络的力量不断扩大自己品牌的知名度，获取利润；另一方面，网络商家通过网络商店做出自己的品牌后，通过一些传统方式进行网下交易，建立一种美妙的客户体验。

A Retailing Revolution

The road to the online retailing future is littered with the wrecks of internet start-ups① once hailed as the pioneers of a retailing revolution. Yet, after the internet bubble burst, online retailing is thriving—set to be the fastest-growing area of retailing this Christmas shopping season. ComScore Networks, a research firm, predicts that online sales—excluding travel sales and auction sites—will grow 23 to 26 per cent to about $ 15bn in the US, still by far the largest market. ComScore forecasts that US internet spending will leap 25 per cent from $ 52.9bn last year to about $ 66bn this year, driven by the spread of broadband connections and growing consumer confidence in shopping online. This trend is reflected in other developed markets, notably the UK and Japan, where companies show that innovative internet retailing is a global phenomenon.

The shape of e-retail, however, is very different from what was predicted a few years ago. Apart from Amazon and eBay—the web's biggest forum for buying and selling, though it is an auction house not a

① start-up 新创办的小公司

零售业的革命

通往网络零售业未来的道路上杂乱无章地堆满了互联网创业之初遗弃的残骸，他们曾受到零售业革命的先驱者喝彩欢呼。然而，互联网泡沫过后，网络零售业正在繁荣稳定地发展：今年圣诞购物期间成为零售业中增长最快的领域。市场调查公司康姆斯克网预言，网络销售除旅行销售和拍卖网络外，到目前为止仍然是美国最庞大的市场，将增长 23% 到 26%，达到 150 亿美元的销售额。康姆斯克网预言，受宽带网普及和消费者不断增强的网络购物信心的驱动，美国互联网消费将迅速提升 25%，从去年的 529 亿美元一跃成为今年的约 660 亿美元。这种趋势在其他发达国家的市场中也有反映，英国和日本尤为明显，这些国家的公司显示，创新性的互联网零售是一种全球性的现象。

然而，电子销售的形式与几年前的预测大相径庭。除了亚马逊和易购两个最大的网络销售论坛之外（尽管它们是网络拍卖场而不

retailer—most of the biggest online retailers are not internet start-ups but traditional shop or mail-order groups. Retailers have brought their investment capacity and trusted brand names to bear on internet shopping—thus boosting public confidence. Many have integrated online sales into a "multichannel①" strategy that may link a website, shops and a mail-order catalogue. "There was a time when everybody said the internet was going to steal purchases from shops. But the opposite is happening: multichannel retailing is the reality today," says Darrell Rigby, head of the global retail practice at Bain & Co, the management consultants. "Many classic bricks-and-mortar retailers actually started making money on their online operations long before Amazon did."

A prime example of the fusion of the online and so-called "offline" retail worlds is Amazon itself. The company has expanded well beyond its roots as a seller of books and CDs, acting as an online mall selling everything from gourmet② foods to clothing. Evolving from pure retailer to "retail platform", it now conducts its online commerce in partnership with bricks-and-mortar retailers such as Target, Nordstrom, Borders and Circuit City. That blending of online and offline is offering consumers new ways to shop. They may research and order their purchase online, but have it delivered to a nearby shop—a service offered by retailers such as Sears Roebuck and Circuit City—so as to avoid delivery charges and allow

① multichannel [ˌmʌltiˈtʃænl] *a.* 多通话线路的,多波段的

② gourmet [ˈguəmei] *n.* 美食者

是零售商），多数大的网络零售商不是互联网企业而是传统的商店或邮购团队。零售商具有投资能力和令人信赖的品牌上网开店，所以增强了公众的信心。很多零售商已经将在线销售综合成连接网站、商店、邮购目录的“多渠道”策略。全球领先的零售业贝恩咨询公司的管理咨询顾问达雷尔·鲁比说：“大家曾经一度认为互联网将窃取商店的销售量，但恰恰相反：多渠道零售业在今天成为现实。事实上，许多一流的实体零售企业早在亚马逊出现之前就已经通过网络营销赚钱了。”

网络零售和号称“脱机”零售相融合的一个最佳范例就是亚马逊自己。亚马逊公司在书籍和CD销售商的基础上已经充分扩展，担当网络大型商场的职责，销售从美食到衣物等所有商品。亚马逊从纯粹的零售商到“零售平台”，现在已将在线商务与塔吉特、诺思通、博德斯和电路城等实体零售商合股经营。联机与脱机的结合正在给消费者提供新的购物方式。他们可以上网搜索和订购，但要求商品送到一家附近的商店，如西尔斯·罗巴克公司和电路城都会提供此类服务，以便避免送货到户费，让顾客先看货或试用一下。顾客可以浏览“陶瓷谷仓”或“板条箱和桶”等零售商寄来的小册子，发现他们喜欢的沙发，然后去商店查看，仔细考虑后上网定

them to see or try it on first. They may see a sofa they like in a brochure they received in the mail from retailers such as Pottery Barn or Crate and Barrel, go and look at it in a shop, mull it over① , then order online. Williams Sonoma, the kitchenware chain that is Pottery Barn's parent, is generating much of its new business online.

Recreational Equipment Inc, better known as REI, is another highly integrated multichannel retailer. A member-owned co-operative—which sells outdoor gear and clothing and has a heritage as a shop and catalogue retailer—it embraced the internet in the mid-1990s, putting internet kiosks② in its shops. It now offers 40,000 products online—more than its biggest shop could stock. Direct sales—four-fifths online, one-fifth by phone—account for 15 per cent of total orders. About 35 per cent of people ordering online will pick up their purchase in one of REI's 76 shops, and about one-third of those will buy something else in the shop at the same time. Sally Jewell, REI's chief operating officer, says that in this way the company's website, with 50,000 pages of product information, drives online and in-store sales. Even retail customers are frequently coming to the stores with a print-out from our website where they have done some pre-screening. Ms Jewell admits that shoppers may research purchases on its website, and then use an online price comparison service to buy the product cheaper from a cut-price retailer.

---

① mull...over 慎重考虑

② kiosk [ˈkiːɔsk] *n.* 凉亭，报摊

购。"陶瓷谷仓"的母公司、威廉斯·索诺玛厨具连锁店正在网上经营它的新业务。

REI 作为运动休闲器材公司，是另一个通过多渠道高度整合的零售商。它是卖户外运动设备和服装的会员合伙制企业，继承了商店和零售商人的特质，它于 20 世纪 90 年代中期进入互联网开始网络店铺设计。现在它已在网络上提供了 40 000 个产品，超过其最大商店的库存量。五分之四网购和五分之一邮购的直销商品占需求总量的 15%。大约 35% 的人上网定购就会增加他们在 REI 76 个分店中一个分店的销售额，同时有大约三分之一的人在商店购买其他产品。REI 的首席营运官萨莉·杰威尔说，公司用这种方式在网站提供了与产品信息相关的 50 000 个网页，推动了在线和商场销售。甚至零售顾客也会频繁地拿着他们预先筛选、从网页上打印的信息光顾商店。杰威尔女士承认，顾客也许会先在网站研究产品，然后使用在线价格比较服务，在廉价零售商店购买更便宜的商品。

一些美国最大的零售商正在发展一体化经营。百年老店、连锁百货彭尼公司，去年的互联网销售额达到 6 亿美元。它提供 200 000多种产品，可以直接送到客户家中或 1 020 家连锁店中的任

Some of the biggest US retailers are developing integrated operations. JC Penney, the century-old department store chain, saw its internet sales reach $600m last year. It offers 200,000 items that can be delivered to customers' homes or any of its 1,020 shops. Steve Riordan, a consultant at AT Kearney, says traditional retailers that have not yet embraced the online world face heavy investment and some tough choices. Are they going to run online operations themselves or outsource them? Do they use the same sourcing model from the same factories? Do they have different distribution centres? "There is not yet an emerging best practice," Mr Riordan says. "Things are sort of at the gawky① teenager stage." While the US still leads the way, it does not have a monopoly on successful internet retailers. Tesco has the world's biggest online grocery business. It has helped Safeway, the third-largest US supermarket chain, set up its internet operations.

Some pure-play internet retailers are also continuing to grow. Yoox.com, which sells end-of-season and exclusive goods from designers such as Armani, Prada and Dolce & Gabbana, has proved that designer labels will sell online and that European e-retailers can succeed internationally. It chose to launch in Europe first, close to the designers whose goods it sells, beginning operations as the air was already escaping from the internet bubble. Yoox now sells in seven languages to 25 countries in Europe, North America and Japan. Its stylish site, which it calls an "e-

---

① gawky [ˈgɔːki] *n.* 笨人;*a.* 笨拙的

何一个。科尔尼公司的一位咨询顾问史蒂夫·莱尔登认为，还没有参与网络销售的传统零售商面临巨额投资和一些艰难的抉择。他们打算自己经营网络营销还是采取外包的方式呢？他们使用来自相同工厂的相同资源模型吗？他们有不同的配给中心吗？莱尔登先生说：“暂时还没有最佳方案。事情仍处于青涩的少年期。”尽管美国仍然处于领导地位，但它却没有对成功的网络零售商实施垄断。特易购有全球最大的网络杂货生意。它帮助美国第三大连锁超市西夫韦建立了互联网销售。

一些纯玩家的网络零售商也在继续成长。放心买代购网销售阿玛尼、普拉达和多尔切与哥班等设计商的换季商品和奢侈品，它证明设计师的标签将上网销售，欧洲的网络零售商能在国际上取得成功。它首选欧洲作为投放市场，以更接近被销商品的设计师，随着从互联网泡沫成功逃离的氛围开始经营。放心买代购网现在用 7 种语言在欧洲、北美、日本等 25 个国家销售商品。它称为“电子概念商店”的时髦网站，能使购物者“移近目标”服装，从不同的角度对他们进行考察，包括视频和音乐。如亚马逊一样，它正在对他人出售电子商务专门技术。放心买代购网的创建者和首席执行官、意大利前投资银行家费得里

concept store", enables shoppers to "zoom" in on clothes and see them from different angles, and includes video and music. Like Amazon, it is now selling its e-commerce expertise to others. Federico Marchetti, the Italian former investment banker who is Yoox's founder and chief executive, says that anyone selling online does not just have to get the technology and orders right. They also have to provide fun and entertainment. "What we have been trying to do with Yoox is build a very nice customer experience," he says. "The online retailer always has to be doing something interesting and different."

(1,007 words)

哥·玛切蒂认为，任何网络营销者不应该仅仅只有从网络获得的技术和订单权。他们还必须提供娱乐和消遣。他说：“我们一直试图与放心买代购网建立一种美妙的客户体验。网络零售商必须经常做有趣和不同的事情。”

知识链接

Bain & Company 贝恩是一家全球领先的战略咨询公司，致力于帮助企业提升价值，其客户的业绩超出市场平均水平4倍之多。自1973年成立以来，基于“咨询顾问为客户提供的应该是结果，而非报告”的理念，贝恩咨询公司在全球有超过2 400人的专业咨询顾问团队，已经为全世界各行各业超过3 300家客户提供了专业的咨询服务。贝恩咨询公司的主要业务领域包括：战略决策、电子商务战略、客户关系、企业成长、企业运作管理优化、供应链管理、组织与变革管理和兼并重组。贝恩咨询公司1993年在北京设立代表处。

Sears Roebuck 西尔斯公司是美国，也是世界最大的私人零售企业之一，它对美国消费者的购物及生活方式，都产生了很大影响，在西方商业界享有“零售业科学院”之誉。西尔斯公司在100多年的发展中经历了美国社会生活的几次大变革，跟上了潮流，在稳定中增长和发展，目前拥有30多万名职工，仅仅印刷在商品目录上的连锁商店就有1 600多家，另外还有800多家供应契约商，其子公司遍布欧美各大城市。

题　记

网上购物在推动国家经济增长方面是一支崭新的力量，它的模式已经在更大的范围内、更广的层面上以更高的效率实现着资源配置。但是，消费者通过零售商网站进行在线购物的关键因素仍然是网上购物的安全性问题。在网购过程中，因为消费者的个人隐私会受到带进攻性的市场技术的侵犯，也会受到供方给消费者的不足和不适当的信息的侵犯，以及要面对用信用卡支付时可能带来的欺诈和错误风险，所以，他们需要得到特别的保护。警惕价格诱惑、关注网站的产品描述、检查联系信息、防范共享电脑的信息泄露、使用信用卡付费、保存网上购物记录、经常审查信用卡报表以及确保商品安全送达等网上购物安全常识，帮助消费者在电子商务环境中愉快体验网上购物的消费信心和消费意愿。

Tips for Shopping Safely Online

Shopping online offers many benefits that you don't find at the mall. Stores on the Internet are always open—7 days a week, 24 hours a day—so you can research your purchases thoroughly, and bargain-hunt and comparison shop in your pajamas. There are no lines, lots of selection, and often great prices on the Web. Many companies even offer special deals on shipping and lenient① return policies to ease your mind further.

But before you take advantage of the Web to shop online, be sure you've educated yourself about it. Shopping on the Internet is technically no less safe than shopping in a store or by mail. As long as you are dealing with a reputable company, online transactions are actually far more secure than face-to-face transactions, since online purchasing eliminates the middle man—like the waiter or cashier who processes your credit card payment. On the Web, your private information is actually exposed to fewer people. But criminals do prey on the ignorant, so acquaint yourself with the techniques they use and be smart when shopping online. There are tips for protecting yourself when shopping online.

---

① lenient [ˈliːnjənt] *adj.* 宽大的,仁慈的

网上购物安全常识

网上购物提供了许多你在购物中心无法得到的好处。互联网上的商店总在营业之中：一周 7 天、每天 24 小时，所以你可以穿着睡衣透彻地研究网上商品、搜索便宜货和比较网络店铺。网上商店没有商业机构的人员，但有很多选择，通常物美价廉。很多公司甚至提供特殊的送货方式和宽松的退货政策，进一步减轻你的负担。

但在你利用网络优势购物之前，请务必了解网上购物的常识。从技术上讲，互联网购物与商店购物和邮购一样安全。只要你与一个有信誉的公司做生意，在线交易的安全性实际上远远超过面对面的交易，因为网上购物无须考虑中间人，如操作你的信用卡付款的侍者或收银员。在网络上，您的个人信息其实透露给更少的人。但是，罪犯就是抢劫无知的人，所以你要熟知他们使用的技巧，漂亮潇洒地网上购物。网上购物时有一些自

Tips for Shopping Safely Online

Be skeptical①. If a deal sounds too good to be true—say, $20 for that new iPod—it probably is. It's probably an attempt to trick you into divulging personal information. On the other hand, consider carefully whether you may be paying too much for an item, particularly if you're bidding through an auction site like eBay. You may want to comparison shop, online or offline, before you buy.

Read between the lines. Pay close attention to the look of the merchant's site. Is it amateurish②? Are there spelling or grammatical errors? Do the prices seem unusually low? Read the seller's description of the product closely, especially the fine print. Words like "refurbished," "vintage," or "close-out" may indicate that a product is in less-than-mint condition—or counterfeit③.

When in doubt, check them out. If you are shopping with a merchant you've never heard of, or on a little-known Web site, look around the site before you make a purchase. Do they have clearly posted information about shipping rates, return policies, warranties, and privacy protection? Can you find contact information easily? Beware if the site doesn't list phone numbers and only includes an email address—or worse, just a post office box. If you're still in doubt and the site does specify a phone number, call it and see if you get a human being on the

---

① skeptical [ˈskeptikəl] *a.* 好怀疑的

② amateurish [ˈæmətəriʃ] *a.* 外行的，不熟练的

③ counterfeit [ˈkauntəfit] *n.* 仿制品，伪造物

我保护的小技巧。

保持警惕。如果一笔交易听起来很便宜而令人难以置信，如一个新的 iPod 只需 20 美元，它或许就是如此，这可能是企图诱使你泄露个人信息。另一方面，购物时出价过高就应该仔细考虑，特别是在易趣之类的拍卖网站竞价。无论是联机还是脱机，你都应该先去比价商店后再决定是否购买。

体会言外之意。密切关注店主的网站外观。网站是业余的吗？有拼写或语法错误吗？价格似乎异常低？仔细阅读卖家对产品的描述，特别是精致的印刷品。“翻新的”、“老式的”、或“抛售”一类字眼可能表明，这个产品不再完好无损，或者是赝品。

如有疑问，认真检查。如果你与一个从未听说过的商家打交道或在不出名的网站购物，购物前需要认真查看。他们清楚地公布了运货比率、获利政策、保修证书和隐私保护吗？你能很容易找到联系信息吗？如果网站没有列出电话号码，只有电子邮箱地址，或更糟糕的是，只有一个邮政信箱，你就要警惕。如果你仍有疑问，而网站确实指定了一个电话号码，那么你就拨打这个电话，看看是否有人接听。任何人都可以安置语音信箱。如果你对听到的或没有听到的仍然忧心忡忡，就去别处购物。

line. Anyone can have voicemail set up. If you're uneasy about what you're hearing or not hearing, shop somewhere else.

Sharing can be a bad thing. Save your online shopping lists and checking your bank account balance for your own computer. Conducting your private business on shared computers, such as the ones available at Internet cafés, libraries, hotels, and other public places, can be very dangerous. The risk is that hackers can install keylogger hardware or software on the computer. The keylogger captures everything you type before it's encrypted—and it can be very difficult to detect. Or, scammers could just "shoulder surf," watching you type logins, passwords, and account information—even using their cell phone camera to photograph your screen!

Say "no" to public, unsecured wireless. Avoid conducting your private business on wireless networks that are available to the public in places like airports, bookstores, and coffee shops. While pubic wireless networks are convenient, there is no guarantee that someone isn't "shoulder surfing"—watching over your shoulder—or launching a "man-in-the-middle attack," logging the sensitive information you send over the network, such as your bank account login or credit card number.

Pay with a credit card. In the event that a criminal does get hold of your card number when you shop online, you're safer if you've been using a credit card than if you used a debit card. That's because debit cards immediately withdraw money directly from your checking account — so

共享是一件坏事。在个人电脑上保存你的网络购物清单和检查银行账户余额。在诸如能够上网的咖啡馆、图书馆、旅馆以及其他公共场所使用公用电脑操作私人交易非常危险。风险在于黑客可以在电脑上安装键盘记录程序硬件或软件。键盘记录程序在信息加密之前捕获你输入的一切，而且该程序很难被发现。或者，欺诈伪造者能做的只是“背后偷窥”：监视你登录信息、密码和账户信息，甚至用他们的手机摄像拍摄你的屏幕。

对公用的、不安全的无线网络说“不”。避免在机场、书店和咖啡厅等提供无线网络的公共场所输入个人信息。尽管公共无线网络很方便，但是它不能保证有人在“背后偷窥”，即从背后监视你的信息，或发动“中间人攻击”，记录你通过网络发送的敏感信息，如你的银行账户注册或信用卡号码。

使用信用卡付费。上网购物时在犯罪分子的确掌握了你的卡号的情况下，如果使用信用卡就比使用借记卡更安全。这是因为犯罪分子可以立即从你的借记卡中把现金取走，这种欺诈交易更难抵制，因为你的钱也已经被消费完了。即使你再次看到借记卡，也需要好几个月才能把钱追回来。但是，如果犯罪分子使用你的信用卡进行犯罪，信用卡公司将帮助你解决这个问题。联邦法律将信用卡

fraudulent[1] transactions are tougher to fight since the money has already been spent. It can take months to get your money back, if you ever see it again at all. But if your credit card was used by a criminal, the credit card company will help you resolve the issue. Federal law limits your liability to $ 50 in fraudulent charges on your credit card, and many companies won't hold you responsible for any use by imposters. If you are reluctant to give out your credit card number over the Internet, you can use a third-party escrow[2] service such as PayPal.

Suspect the suspicious. If you're on a checkout page and the site asks for your date of birth and Social Security number, be very careful. Such information is generally not required for online shopping transactions, and the combination of your birth date and your SSN can give a wrongdoer sufficient information to start applying for new credit cards in your name. If anything seems suspicious, call the company and ask questions before you buy.

Keep a paper trail. Print and save records of your online transactions, including the product description and price, the online receipt, and copies of any email you exchange with the seller. You can also create a folder on your computer to save all such emails and receipts.

Review your credit card statements frequently. Read your statements as you receive them , particularly if you shop often online . Stay on the

① fraudulent [ˈfrɔːdjulənt] *adj.* 欺骗的,不诚实的
② escrow [ˈeskrəu] *n.* 由第三者保存附带条件委付盖印的契约

冒用额度限制在50美元以内，许多公司对任何冒用也不追究你的责任。如果你不愿意在互联网上给出信用卡号，你可以利用贝宝之类的第三者支付服务。

对可疑之处保持警惕。如果你在结账网页，网站要求你输入出生日期和社保号码，就必须非常小心。这些资料一般在进行网上购物交易时是不需要的，你的出生日期和社保号码一起给做坏事的人足够的信息，开始以你的名义申请新的信用卡。如果有任何看似可疑的情况，购物之前给公司打电话和提问。

保存网上购物记录。打印并保存在线交易记录，包括产品描述和价格，网上收据，并复制任何与卖方交流的电子邮件。也可以在计算机上创建一个文件夹来保存所有这些电子邮件和收据。

经常审查信用卡报表。收到报表后立即阅读，特别是如果你经常在线购物。对未经授权的交易保持警惕。骗子有时从10美元或20美元以下的小件购物开始，观察你对账户的监视有多严密。如果他们能消费小件，就会花费更多。尽早发现这一点将为你节省大量的时间、金钱和随后的扼腕叹息。还要每年监控你的信用报告。

确保商品安全送达。点击“提交”时，你的网上购物体验并没

lookout for unauthorized charges. Scammers sometimes start with small purchases, under $ 10 or $ 20, to see how closely you watch your account. If they can get away with something small, they will spend more. Catching it early will save you a lot of time, money, and heartache later. Monitor your credit report annually, too.

Ensure the safe delivery of your item. Your online shopping experience doesn't end when you click "Submit." Inspect your purchase as soon as you receive it. Contact the seller as soon as possible if you discover a problem with it, because federal law limits seller liability after a short time. Tell the seller in writing about any problems you have, ask for a repair or refund, and again, keep a copy of your correspondence. Report any problems you have to the Better Business Bureau.

(1,047 words)

有结束。收到货物就要尽快检查。如果你发现商品有问题，尽快联系卖家，因为联邦法律限定了卖方的短期责任期限。将你的问题以书面形式告诉卖方，要求修理或偿还，还要保存双方互通的信函。最好向商业服务监督局报告任何你遇到的问题。

知识链接

Better Business Bureau 商业服务监督局(BBB)成立于 1912 年，是由美国和加拿大的几家私营商业机构联合组成的一个商业社团，在商业服务监督局委员会(CBBB)的统一领导下开展工作。商业服务监督局的目标是鼓励一个公正和有效的市场机制，买卖双方能够互相信任(Start with Trust)。它收集和报告可靠的商务信息，提醒公众对消费者和商业机构诈骗保持警惕，提供商业道德规范信息，担当消费者和企业共同信任的仲裁人解决纷争。公众可以随时通过商业服务监督局的网站在线访问他们的服务。

题　记

婚礼是人生重要的时刻，每一位新娘都期待完美的礼服将自己装扮得漂亮可人、优雅浪漫；每一位伴娘都希望以个性鲜明、超凡脱俗的品位着装帮助新娘打造这最幸福的时刻。今天，当准新郎、新娘或家庭要计划美妙独特的婚礼之时，他们首先要访问的是最近的虚拟市场，这里信息量大，款式多样。互联网为他们在线挑选最合适的结婚礼服提供了引领现代都会的流行节奏。在这里，技术使这一切成为可能，各种创作灵感的结婚礼服五彩纷呈，时尚和概念你追我赶。而在线选购婚礼服装最重要的决定因素是价廉物美和安心方便，低成本和折扣优惠券吸引了无数顾客，剪辑礼服的图像并让所有宾客欣赏和酝酿也将成为婚礼回味无穷的话题之一。

Choose Your Wedding Dress Online

Is that polyester① lavender② number still hanging way in the back of the closet? Or the lumpy pink chiffon③? Or the fussy flowered frock that cost a small fortune? Fortunately, the bridesmaid dress—unwearable in the real world—is being supplanted by chic, even snazzy, garb that doesn't evoke pity when women walk down the aisle ahead of the bride.

The Internet is helping to drive the shift to fashionable bridal attendant wear. Web sites of companies like Ann Taylor, J. Crew, Target and Disney are offering a broad choice of styles and fabrics, ease of purchase and, when necessary, returns. Most online vendors also offer accessories, including shoes, clutches④ and sashes⑤. "You can do gown research online, take a group vote, then order from home," said Kathleen A. Murray, deputy editor of TheKnot.com, a wedding site. Two-thirds of bridal and bridesmaids dresses are still custom-ordered in a local

---

① polyester [pɔli'estə] *n.* 多元酯
② lavender ['lævində] *adj.* 淡紫色的
③ chiffon [ʃi'fɔn] *n.* 薄纱,饰边
④ clutch [klʌtʃ] *n.* 离合器
⑤ sash [sæʃ] *n.* 肩带,腰带

在线选购婚礼服装

那件淡紫色的聚酯服装还挂在衣橱后面吗？ 那件飘逸的粉红色薄纱褶皱裙呢？ 还有那件花了一笔巨款、堆满装饰花的外衣呢？幸运的是，不适合在现实生活中穿戴的伴娘礼服正在被别致、甚至是时髦的服装取代，这样的打扮使女士们在新娘前面走过通道时毫不逊色。

互联网正在促使婚礼出席者的装束转向时尚。 安·泰勒，J. Crew，塔吉特及迪士尼等公司的网站都提供了多种不同的款式和面料，供顾客选择，购买极为方便，必要时还可以退货。 大多数网上销售商还提供鞋子、女用无带皮包和腰带等配件。 TheKnot.com 婚礼网站的代理主编凯思琳·A·穆雷说："你可以上网调查礼服，进行小组表决，然后在家里下订单。" 据康德纳斯特婚纱集团的调查显示，三分之二的新娘和伴娘礼服仍然按习俗在当地婚纱店定制。 绝大多数婚礼出席者仍然穿着同样的礼服——这是从中世纪就开始的一个风俗，康德纳斯特新娘杂志主编米莉·玛蒂尼·布拉特说："这些离新娘最近的人穿着同样，以迷惑邪恶的幽灵，保护新娘。" 但是，更多的新娘受好莱坞红地毯最新式样的影响，伴娘们也越来越有时尚意识。 另一个婚礼网站 brides.com 的主编特丽莎·迪玛希说："礼服越来越倾向时尚，现在已经不可能再有适合所有人的一刀

bridal salon, according to research by Condé Nast Bridal Group. And a majority of attendants still wear identical outfits—a custom that began in medieval times. "Those closest to the bride dressed up identically to confuse evil spirits and protect the bride," said Millie Martini Bratten, editor in chief of Condé Nast Brides magazine. But more brides are taking their cues from the latest on Hollywood's red carpet, and bridesmaids are becoming more fashion-conscious, too. "Dresses are more fashion-forward," said Theresa DiMasi, editor in chief of brides.com, another wedding site. "It's not the one-size-fits-all cookie-cutter wedding anymore."

Many clothing retailers have posted lower sales, but one segment is bucking the trend: weddings. At Ann Taylor, whose overall sales dipped in the year, it is full speed ahead in the bridal area. "It's been double-digit growth," said Maria Sceppaguercio, a company spokeswoman. The company, which had $2.3 billion in overall sales in the fiscal year ended, does not release numbers for online or bridal sales, she said. Trish Donnelly, head of direct merchandising at J. Crew, said the company responded to customer demand by introducing four bridesmaid styles online. "We found there was a great void out there for a classic timeless dress," she said. "And it just took off." The company now offers bridal and bridesmaid collections in the spring and fall, and updates both online and by catalog. The company can keep prices relatively low, she said, because it contracts directly for the gowns to be made in Asia.

切式的婚礼模式。”

许多服装零售商纷纷推出降价信息，但有一种商品却与之背道而驰：那就是婚纱。在安·泰勒，虽然公司的年度总销售额下降，新娘礼服领域却在全速发展。公司的女发言人玛丽亚·斯帕古尔欧说：“它正以两位数的速度增长。”她认为，公司在财政年度结束时的总销售已达23亿美元，但没有放松在线或婚礼服的销售。J. Crew的直销部的负责人崔西·唐娜丽说，公司为了迎合顾客的需要，在线推出了四种风格的伴娘礼服。她说，“我们发现经典、永不过时的礼服还有很大的发展空间，它还处于起步阶段”。该公司目前在春秋两季推出新娘礼服和伴娘礼服的收藏版，同时更新网上信息和销售目录。她认为，公司能够保持相对低的价格是因为礼服是直接外包到亚洲生产。

迪士尼公司推出了以灰姑娘、白雪公主、圣诞公主等为创作灵感的结婚礼服。它开始在disneybridal.com上销售这些童话故事伴娘礼服，迪士尼消费者产品部的财务副总裁雪莉·A·隆贝拉说，23种款式的礼服价格从200美元到450美元不等。塔吉特百货公司加入了这场竞争，一直为零售商创作服装的艾萨克·兹拉希设计了首个新娘礼服专营网站。他提供了3款设计，包括价格在89.99美元到159.99美元之间的一款贴身丝绸蓬裙，目标消费群是那些既想好看又不想花太多钱的新娘。伴娘服装也运用了同样的设计理念，她们可以从成打的礼服中挑选，价格从39.99美元起始，还另加配件。康德纳斯特数据显示，新娘礼服的平均成本现在为800美元，近期一个典型的婚礼有五位伴娘，每位的礼服花费大约140美元。

尽管更多的设计师倾向于将新娘和伴娘礼服设计得更为时尚，

The Disney Company unveiled wedding apparel inspired by characters including Cinderella, Snow White and Ariel. It will begin selling its fairy-tale bridesmaid dresses on disneybridal.com, with 23 offerings priced from $ 200 to $ 450, said Sherri A. Lombra, vice president for finance at Disney Consumer Products. Target joined the fray, introducing a Web-only bridal line—its first—designed by Isaac Mizrahi, who has been creating clothing for the retailer. He is offering three designs, including a figure-hugging silk cowl dress, for $ 89.99 to $ 159.99, aimed at brides who want a good look but don't want to break the bank. The same idea goes for the bridesmaids, who can select from dozens of dresses, at prices that start at $ 39.99—plus the accessories. The average bridal gown now costs $ 800, and bridesmaids—a typical number per wedding these days is five—spend about $ 140 each, according to Condé Nast figures.

While more designers are zipping bridesmaids as well as brides into more fashionable looks, many couples are also looking to cut costs for their attendants. "I couldn't justify asking my girls, who are all in different life stages—single, married, kids—but who are all watching their wallets for good reason, to cough up $ 275 for a bridesmaid dress they will wear once, primarily for my amusement," said Megan Ferington, 27, who works for a Cleveland greeting card company and plans to marry. "Ultimately, price was the deciding factor for me; our wedding isn't about putting anyone in debt, except maybe us." Her first choice, she said, was J. Crew, which offers many options for $ 165 to $ 425. To save money, she canvassed the site's clearance section at the

在线选购婚礼服装

许多新婚夫妇也在寻找降低婚礼参与者成本的方法。计划结婚的骑士贺卡公司的员工、27岁的梅根说:“我不能理直气壮地要求我的那些女伴只是为了取悦我，花275美元去买一件她们只穿一次的伴娘礼服。他们全都处于不同的人生阶段:有的单身，有的已婚，有的已生儿育女。他们全都有足够的理由看紧自己的钱包。价格基本上对我来说是最重要的决定因素。我们的婚礼除了我们自己，不会让任何人背负债务。”她的首选就是J. Crew，因为它提供了价格从165到425美元不等的多种选择。为了省钱，她仔细查看了该网站的季末清仓，以找到不太昂贵的礼服。但是尽管有J. Crew公司电话咨询的帮助，她也没有找到她想要的价格为100美元的礼服。于是菲瑞顿小姐向安・泰勒求证，因为安・泰勒的庆典收藏中有深咖啡色的及膝礼服，与她秋日主题的婚礼非常契合。由于有一张八折优惠券，所以每套的价格仅为150美元。

但菲瑞顿小姐也说，虽然几乎所有的婚礼安排都是在互联网上完成的，价格并不是上网购物的唯一考虑。她认为，另一个因素是安心和方便，能够剪辑礼服的图像，发送给远在加利福尼亚州、纽约州北部和曼哈顿的宾客，征求他们对该礼服的外形、领口、长度和质地的意见。德克萨斯州奥斯丁一家杂志的编辑米歇尔・R. 考伯特也有相似的经历。她给6位伴娘电邮了她喜欢的6款礼服的照片。她说:“我们采用即时信息，所以很快就做了决定。”这样做比在某个下午把远近的朋友都召集到一个当地的婚纱店更容易。为了筹备婚礼，她决定购买J. Crew的婚纱，因为她发现它的价格合理，而且“提供永恒、经典的裁剪”，与各种实体店里大大的、塔夫绸的样式不同。

end of last season to find less expensive dresses. But even with help from J. Crew phone consultants, she couldn't find four of the $ 100 dresses she wanted. So Ms. Ferington checked Ann Taylor, whose Celebrations collection had knee-length dresses in an espresso color to match her autumn-themed nuptials①. With a coupon for 20 percent off, the price was $ 150 each.

But price isn't the only consideration in shopping online, said Ms. Ferington, who is doing almost all her wedding planning on the Internet. Another factor is the ease and convenience of being able to clip dress images and send them to her far-flung attendants in California, upstate New York and Manhattan to get their opinions on the silhouette, neckline, length and fabric, she said. Michelle R. Colbert, a magazine editor in Austin, Tex., had a similar experience. She e-mailed images of dresses she liked to her six bridesmaids. "We did instant-messaging, and, lickety-split, the decision was made," she said. That was easier than trying to convene her friends, near and far, for an afternoon at a local bridal salon. For her wedding, she decided to go with J. Crew because she found the prices to be reasonable, and because "they offer a timeless, classic cut" that was different from the big, taffeta at various brick-and- mortar stores.

Online purchases do come with a downside: there are no alterations; those are the buyer's responsibility. But J. Crew and Ann

---

① nuptial [ˈnʌpʃəl] *n.* 婚礼

在线购物也有不利的一面：不能更改。这是买方的责任。但是J. Crew和安·泰勒的主管表示，任何人都可以进入他们店铺，试穿不同尺码的服装。菲瑞顿小姐说，轻松退货非常重要，她选择的伴娘有一个因为家庭问题不得不退出："她没有受到任何处罚就退还了礼服，这与顾客定制的高级服装店不同，他们是不能退货的。"最重要的，在线购物有时帮助伴娘避免既费力又令人失望的经历。27岁的艾琳·莱德也是菲瑞顿小姐的伴娘之一。她说："我曾为了参加我妹妹的婚礼而试穿了30套礼服。而梅根的婚礼通过网络向我们展示了她想要什么。我买下了礼服，它被送到我的家门口，而且完全合身。"洛杉矶的电视制作人赖德女士说："它的颜色是如此的漂亮，我可以穿着它再参加另外的婚礼。它不会像我已经堆在衣橱里的其他礼服一样被闲置了。"

知识链接

Ann Taylor 安·泰勒1954年建立，是美国著名时尚服装品牌、最大的女性产品制造商之一，其产品包括衣服、礼服、女式鞋子和装饰品。安·泰勒奉行以优雅为制胜的秘诀，专门针对25岁至55岁年龄层、受过高等教育的专业知识女性顾客，与Polo Ralph Lauren、Calvin Klein等居美国高档品牌销量前五名，有"美国第一行政品牌"之称。它的设计不张扬，不夸张，稳重但不老成，漂亮但不轻佻，以经典而轻松的样式备受欢迎，稳重得可以上班穿，轻松得可以下班也穿。安·泰勒在全美有800个专卖店，旗下有五个品牌：Ann Taylor，Ann Taylor LOFT，Ann Taylor Studiond，Ann Taylor Petites，Ann Taylor Factory。

Taylor executives note that anyone can go into their stores and try on a dress for size. Ease of return is also important, said Ms. Ferington, noting that one of her chosen bridesmaids had to bow out because of a family problem: "She returned the dress without any penalty—which is different from a salon where things are custom-ordered and there are no returns." Above all, shopping online helps the bridesmaids avoid what can sometimes be an arduous① and disappointing experience. "I tried on 30 dresses for my sister's wedding," said Erin Ryder, 27, who will also be a bridesmaid for Ms. Ferington. "But for Megan's, she showed us what she wanted online. I bought it, it arrived on my doorstep and it fits close to perfectly." "Because it's such a great color, I can wear it again to some other weddings," said Ms. Ryder, a television producer based in Los Angeles. "It won't be sitting in my closet like the others I've accumulated."

(1,082 words)

① arduous [ˈɑːdjuəs] *a.* 费力的,辛勤的

J. Crew 属于“简练优雅+典型美式休闲+职业风格”的100%美国血统，是美国民众狂热追捧的中高档品牌之一。自1983年成立以来，J. Crew已由制作代表美国精神、趣味性的服饰及生活、工作、休闲、甚至结婚相关服饰及配件发展成为目前闻名全球的美国品牌。J. Crew以做工考究在市场占得一席之地，它的面料上乘，用料和剪裁都不偷工减料，多用开司米和绸缎，还缀以手工珠饰，定价却只有大牌的十分之一。J. Crew的服饰风格流露出贴近大自然的动人色调和简约纯美的清新气息，体现了热爱生活、追求潮流、内敛含蓄的个性，以及重视品质和品位细节的完美结合。

Target 塔吉特百货公司位于美国明尼苏达州明尼阿波利斯市，是美国第四大零售商，全球500强企业之第33名，在美国47个州设有1330家商店，提供时尚前沿的零售服务，市场定位是高级折扣零售店。“期待更多，花费更少”(Expect More，Spend Less）是塔吉特百货公司的口号，公司是更追求品位、品质和舒适的购物环境的人们购买平价时尚商品之所。不管是实体店还是在线商场(Target. com)，塔吉特都提供数千件风格独特的商品，让顾客享受乐趣横生、简单方便的购物体验。

题　记

假日消费季的美国零售业形势依然低迷，但在线零售商通过使用价格折扣、免费寄送和其他网络促销手段使网络销售大幅上升，零售商兴建网站使互联网成为主要的购物天堂。越来越多的在线零售商开始实施上网购物但店内取货的方式，让顾客不必支付运货到取货门市的费用，同时提供更多产品让顾客上网选购。零售商们不约而同展开降价战术以刺激消费，因为他们并没有看到假日消费季预期的火爆场面。吸引上网买便宜货的人成为小型零售商的最大希望，让购物者在寻找网络商品的价值、搜索价格信息和价格比照的过程中形成客流量的回归。在线零售商在感受假日消费季出现的一丝清冷寒意之时，仍然绞尽脑汁制定详尽而极具攻击性的重塑计划，期待摆脱低迷的市场表现。

Retailers Push for Online Sales

The holiday outlook is gloomy, but online retailers can react faster with discounts, free shipping, and other Web promotions than stores can. Nicole DeBoom watched online sales at her women's sportswear company drop 25% in early November—a sign that buyers were pulling back just when holiday shopping should have started. So DeBoom, who is chief executive of SkirtSports, a five-person company she founded three years ago in Boulder, Colo., planned to cut prices 30% on old inventory at the company's online outlet, SkirtSportsOutlet. com, starting the Monday after Thanksgiving. "We think it'll spark a major feeding frenzy① . Our margins are going to take a hit, but at this point, we just need volume," DeBoom says. She hopes the discount will keep sales on a level with the last holiday season, even as her profits shrink because of those thinner margins.

Small retailers like SkirtSports that sell online aren't waiting to see whether recession-spooked② consumers will dampen online growth.

---

① frenzy [ˈfrenzi] *n.* 狂乱

② spook [spuːk] *vt.* 吓;吓唬

零售商力推在线销售

假日购物季的前景令人沮丧，但在线零售商通过使用价格折扣、免费寄送和其他网络促销手段比实体店的行动更为迅速。尼克尔·迪波姆留意到女士运动装公司的在线销售 11 月初下降了 25%，假日购物理应开始之时，消费者却正在发出撤离的信号。因此，作为 3 年前在科罗拉多州博尔德市注册的 5 人公司 SkirtSports 的首席执行官迪波姆，计划在感恩节的首个周一之后，将公司网上经销点 SkirtSportsOutlet.com 的存货价格削减 30%。迪波姆说："我们认为这将引起一个购物狂潮。我们的利润会受损，但是在这个时候，我们只是需要销售量。"她希望折扣能使销售量与去年假日购物季持平，即使利润由于盈余更低而缩水。

类似 SkirtSports 的小型网络零售商并不期望看到受经济危机吓唬的消费者抑制在线销售的增长。他们正在采取措施尽可能地维持同等数量的销售额。过去的假日购物季，在线销售年复一年持续增长 20% 或更多，即使更广泛意义上的零售增长要慢得多。但这种情况可能改变。市场研究公司 TNS Retail Forward 预测，网络假日销售将比去年增长 9%，但是佛雷斯特研究公司（FORR）预报，将有

They're taking steps now to shore up[1] as much business as possible. In the past, online sales have sustained year-over-year increases of 20% or more during the holidays, even as broader retail sales grew much more slowly. But that's likely to change. Market researcher TNS Retail Forward predicted online holiday sales will grow 9% over last year, while Forrester Research (FORR) forecast 12% growth. ComScore (SCOR) reported six consecutive[2] months of slowing growth in online retail. In the third quarter, online retail sales grew just 0.3% over the second quarter. That beat the broader retail sector, which shrank 1.4% in the same period, which is preceded the financial crisis that began to snowball.

Still, small retailers with an online presence recognize they are better positioned to drive sales than their brick-and-mortar counterparts facing the prospect of empty stores. "The general mood we've seen is that online retail is resilient[3] but not immune to the economic downturn," says Larry Joseloff, vice-president for content at Shop.org, the digital arm of the National Retail Federation. Joseloff says online retailers can adjust strategy in response to shoppers, as DeBoom did with her clearance sale. "From an online perspective, you can change your promotions very quickly," he says. Just as SkirtSports is betting on discounts to jump-start

---

① shore up 支撑住
② consecutive [kən'sekjutiv] *adj.* 连续的
③ resilient [ri'ziliənt] *adj.* 弹性的;有弹力的

12% 的增长。ComScore（SCOR）报告了在线零售 6 个月持续缓慢上升，第三季度的在线销售比上季度只增长了 0.3%。这种情况对零售业形成了更广泛的打击，同期减缩 1.4%，这是滚雪球似的经济危机开始的前奏。

当然，在线开店的小型零售商承认，他们比实体零售商面对空店铺时能更好地定位，推动销售。有全美零售商联合会数字武器之称的 Shop.org 公司的副总裁拉里·杰塞佛说，“我们看到的常见状态是网络零售的反弹，但无法避免经济低迷”。杰塞佛认为，在线零售商应该与迪波姆做清仓削价销售一样，适应购物者做出战略调整。他说：“从网络的角度看，你可以迅速调整促销手段”。正如 SkirtSports 为拉升销售量打赌折扣一样，吸引上网买便宜货的人成为小型零售商的最大希望。TNS Retail Forward 公司的高级经济师弗兰克·班迪洛说：“购物者正在寻找网络商品的价值，更多的可能是搜索价格信息和价格比照。”零售商目前针对节俭购物者采用的促销手段更加积极进取。例如，在线美食零售商 Zenobia Nuts 的电子商务总监扎克·巴布克说，该公司开始向游离他们网页的顾客提供 10% 的折扣代码，从而将浏览者变为购买者。本季度到目前为止，来自销售商 UpSellit 的服务已经帮助纽约布朗克斯家族公司增加了 10% 的订单。该公司去年也开展了为期 2 天的免费寄送活动。巴布克认为，这显然导致了假日购物季订单的增加。并不是所有的小型零售商都能支付得起在线购物免费寄送服务。马萨诸塞州杜克

sales, appealing to bargain hunters online may be the best hope for small retailers. "Shoppers are looking for value and more likely to be searching for price information and price comparisons," says Frank Badillo, senior economist at TNS Retail Forward. Retailers are becoming more aggressive at present with Internet promotions aimed at frugal shoppers. For example, online gourmet retailer Zenobia Nuts on the Net started offering customers who try to navigate away from their page a 10% discount code, which helps convert browsers to buyers, according to Zach Bobker, the company's e-commerce director. The service, from a vendor called UpSellit, has helped the Bronx (N.Y.) family business boost orders 10% so far this season. The company also began free two-day shipping last year, which Bobker says increased sales particularly for holiday orders. Not all small businesses can afford to offer free shipping online. Cindy Nichols-Cheever, owner of the Duxbury (Mass.) gift shop Mermaids at Duxbury Bay, says the cost of shipping is the biggest concern for her online customers, who make up about 15% of her business. "The freight I'm not making any money on," she says. "The freight they pay is really what it costs me to ship the box."

Companies that can't afford to absorb shipping costs should be up front about the fees, because seeing charges tacked on at checkout can repel shoppers, says Eddie Davis, head of small business merchant services at PayPal (EBAY). "People actually do abandon carts when they see an extra line" for shipping costs, he points out. Likewise, small companies selling online need to be clear about return policies to reassure

斯贝尔湾礼品店老板辛迪·尼古拉斯·其福尔说，在线购物者最关心邮寄成本，这项支出占生意额的 15%。她说："我在运费上没赚一分钱。顾客支付的运费真的就是货运箱费用。"

易趣公司贝宝贸易经济服务部的埃迪·戴维斯认为，无力承担免费邮寄的小型零售商应该提前收费，因为顾客看到商品上的加价有可能流失。他指出，因为运输费用，"顾客留意到另一网站时就会真的放弃购物车"。戴维斯说，小型在线销售公司同样需要解释清楚退货政策，打消顾客的疑虑。根据加利福尼亚州阳光谷公司 Shipwire 网站提供的客户数据，货运量的增长更趋缓慢，每件商品的货运开支实际下降了 30%，该公司提供仓储外包和网络零售运输服务，是拥有数百家小型企业的代理商。Shipwire 的首席执行官达蒙·斯科特说："人们总是将陆路货运拖到第二天，他们选择第二天取货而不是第一天。"他还说，小型零售商在全国范围内的仓库贮存货运更灵活，使商品更靠近消费者，并降低了成本。斯科特确认，在线零售商在这个假日购物季高兴的一件事是出口。他说，代理商一年前在国际上只有 2% 的订单，现在这个数字增加到了 15%，刺激 Shipwire 公司在多伦多、温哥华和伦敦开设仓库。贝宝的戴维斯同样说，小型企业的国际化销售日益增长，受顺汇率的部分影响，美国商品成为廉价货。

除努力扩大国际影响和争取难以驾驭的购物者之外，在线零售商正在为电子商务有史以来最低迷的假日购物季做准备。SkirtSports 的迪波姆为紧缩利润和训练顾客对廉价预期的担忧，但她觉得除了

buyers, Davis says. Shipping volume is growing more slowly, and spending on shipping has actually gone down 30% per item shipped, according to client data from Shipwire, a Sunnyvale (Calif.) company that offers outsourced warehousing and shipping services for online retailers and says it has hundreds of small business clients. "People are picking ground shipping over second day, and they're picking second day over first day," says Shipwire Chief Executive Damon Schechter. He also says small business clients are becoming more adept about shipping by warehousing goods across the country to get products closer to customers and reduce costs. One bright spot for online retailers Schechter identified this holiday season is exporting. He says clients a year ago were shipping only 2% of orders internationally, but that figure is now up to 15%, spurring Shipwire to open warehouses in Toronto, Vancouver, and London. Davis of PayPal likewise says small businesses are increasingly selling globally, spurred in part by favorable exchange rates that make buying U.S. goods a bargain.

Despite efforts to expand internationally and woo reluctant shoppers, online retailers are preparing for what might be the gloomiest holiday season since e-commerce began. DeBoom of SkirtSports worries about shrinking margins and training her customers to expect sales, but she feels like she has no choice but to cut prices. "If something's not on sale, people are not buying," she says.

(875 words)

削价别无他法。她说，“有些商品如果不廉价销售就无人购买”。

知识链接

comScore Networks 康姆斯克在线用户测量公司是测量数字世界和数字营销智能首选资源的全球领导者。康姆斯克通过行为和测量洞察力的有力结合，使客户从快速发展的全球网络和移动论坛更好地理解、发挥优势和获益。康姆斯克为企业组合和客户提供解决方案，包括在线网民测量、电子商务、广告、搜索、视频和移动装置。康姆斯克采用数字营销和精准的纵向联合行业专门技术来提供专注的分析。广告商、出版商、市场商人和分析师求助于康姆斯克，谨慎地构建行业领先的解决方案，以及成功的数字、营销、生产发展和贸易策略。

题　记

在电脑显示器的方寸之间敲击键盘和移动鼠标，“凭空”多出了一个不受时空限制的购物渠道，网店的魅力正吸引着越来越多的普通百姓。随着互联网的普及，中国的在线购物交易量持续迅速地增长。人们感受到在线购物的方便快捷：在线选择商品，签署订购单，商品通过物流渠道送到家门口，省去逛商场的时间。商家发现了巨大的商机和经营成本的低廉：在线商店不需要租店面，商品价格相对便宜，汽车之类的耐用消费品、房屋之类的大宗消费品以及钻石之类的奢侈品开始走俏网络。在线购物代表信息时代商品交易的发展方向，越来越受到人们的青睐，迅速成为一种时尚的生活方式。

Online shopping gets popular with ordinary folks

In recent years, the e-shopping via Internet has been developed rapidly and has become an innegligible component in the e-business. E-shopping is a kind of online purchasing behavior of terminal purchasers, and consumers' shopping occupies most. The fast development of e-shopping indicates that the core of e-shopping begins to transfer from B2B (business to business) to B2C (business to consumer) and C2C (consumer to consumer), and the e-shopping shows a new trend of popularization.

For most of e-shopping, commodities will be chosen online, purchase orders will be signed and commodities will be delivered to customers' doorsteps via logistics① distribution, so the transaction cost is low. The e-shopping is convenient and prompt, and consumers will save the time of looking around marketplaces. As there is no need to rent storefronts for online shops, the operating cost is low and the price of

① logistics [ləˈdʒistiks] *n.* 后勤学;物流

百姓热捧在线购物

近年来，互联网电子购物迅猛发展，已经成为电子商务不可忽略的组成部分。在线购物是终端用户在线购物的一种行为，消费者购物占多数。快速发展的网上购物表明，在线购物的核心开始从商家对商家（B2B）模式转向商家对消费者（B2C）和消费者对消费者（C2C）模式，在线购物展现出一种新的流行趋势。

对大多数在线购物来说，在线选择商品，签署订购单，商品就将会通过物流渠道送到消费者的门口，因此交易费用低廉。在线购物既方便又快捷，消费者可以省去逛商场的时间。由于在线商店不需要租店面，经营成本低廉，商品价格相对便宜，能使购买者受益。在网络普及率相对较高的大城市，在线购物越来越受到人们的青睐，迅速成为一种时尚的生活方式。

当今中国的在线购物市场具有以下特点：

其一，在线购物的规模不断扩大。根据相关统计数据，中国网民的在线购物比例占 22.1%，购物群体人数达 4 640 万。这些在线购物网民中有硕士学位或更高学历的消费者已占 56.5%。在线购物的市值达 561 亿元人民币，并以每年 117.4% 的速率逐年增长。这

commodities is relatively low, which enable purchasers to enjoy benefits. In large cities with a relatively high Internet penetration① rate, e-shopping is more and more favored by people and becomes a fashionable life style quickly.

For the moment, China's e-shopping market is provided with the following characteristics: Firstly, the e-shopping scale keeps enlarging. According to related statistics, the proportion of netizens' online shopping in China is 22.1 percent, and the purchaser population achieves 46.4 million. And the online shopping proportion of such netizens with Master degree or above has reached 56.5 percent. The scale of e-shopping market is RMB56.1 billion Yuan with the growth rate of 117.4 percent year on year. This indicates that the penetration of Internet drives a rapid growth of e-shopping. E-shopping websites keep improving transaction modes, and consumers' acceptance degree to the e-shopping is enhanced increasingly.

Secondly, the transaction amount of B2C and C2C accounts for the most part of the total transaction amount of e-shopping. E-shopping contains the purchasing of terminal consumers and the commodity transfer between consumers, as well as the online shopping of part of manufacturing operators. The transaction amount of C2C e-shopping hit RMB51.8 billion Yuan at present, up 125.2 percent than before. The transaction amount of taobao.com took up 83.6 percent of C2C e-shopping, paipai.com ranked No.2 with the transaction amount of 8.7

---

① penetration [peniˈtreiʃən] *n.* 渗透,侵入

表明，互联网的渗透推动在线购物的迅速增长。在线购物网站持续不断地改善着交易模式，消费者对在线购物的接受程度正在日益增强。

其二，企业对消费者模式和消费者对消费者模式的交易量占在线购物总交易量的大部分。在线购物包含终端消费者的购买和消费者之间的商品交易，以及在线购物的部分生产经营者。消费者对消费者模式的交易量目前已达518亿元，比往年增长152.2%。淘宝网交易量占消费者对消费者交易模式的83.6%，拍拍网以交易量8.7%排在第二位，易趣网排在第三位。企业对消费者模式的交易量达43亿元，比往年增长92.3%。当当网排在第一位，交易量占83.6%；卓越网排在第二位，北斗手机网排在第三位。这说明消费者的购买力占据在线购物的主要位置。

其三，在线购物的商品范围日益迅速扩展。卓越网和当当网早期主要经营书籍和电子音像产品。他们的经营范围近年一直在不断扩大。卓越网的商品种类已扩展到20大类，超过70万种。当当网除了销售书籍、杂志和电子音像产品，还包括手机、化妆品、服装、鞋帽，商品种类充足丰富。在线购物的商品也已经打破仅仅提供有形商品的限制，扩展到数字产品和服务，所以，很多专业网站根据数字目录和网络服务提供商品。

此外，女性消费者产品占据在线购物市场的重要位置。随着在线购物商品逐渐转向消费产品，化妆品和服装等女性消费品变得十分畅销。根据统计数据，上海网民的网上购物量在中国内地排位第

percent, and eachnet.com ranked No.3. The transaction amount of B2C e-shopping hit RMB4.3 billion Yuan, up 92.3 percent than before. The transaction amount of dangdang.com ranked No.1 with the transaction proportion of 83.6 percent, joyo.com ranked No.2, and 139shop.com No.3. This illustrates that consumers' purchasing takes up a main position in the e-shopping.

Thirdly, the commodity scope① of e-shopping is expanding increasingly. The early joyo.com and dangdang.com mainly operated books and video products. In recent years, their operation scope has been enlarged continuously; joyo.com has expanded its commodity scope to 20 classifications and more than 700 thousand types. Except selling books, magazines and videos, dangdang.com is also involved in selling mobile phones, cosmetics, garments②, shoes and hats, whose commodities have been rich in variety. The commodities of e-shopping have also broken the restriction of only providing tangible③ commodities, and expanded to digital products and services, so many professional websites supply the commodities in terms of digital content and network service.

Additionally, female consumer products occupy an important position in the e-shopping market. With the gradual transferring from e-shopping commodities to consumer products, such female consumer products as cosmetics and garments become well-selling commodities.

---

① scope [skəup] *n.* 范围
② garment [ˈɡɑːmənt] *n.* 衣服
③ tangible [ˈtændʒəbl] *a.* 实体的

一。而被上海在线购物群体买得最多的是化妆品和香水之类的女性美容用品，同时，上海在线购物商品中增长量最快的是女性内衣和女用箱包。这些数据显示，女性在线购物群体的购买力。女性消费产品市场正在受到在线购物网站越来越多的关注。

随着未来互联网的普及，中国的在线购物交易量将会持续迅速地增长，消费者对消费者交易模式将是促使在线购物增长的主要驱动力，在线购物商品的多样化将进一步丰富，在线购物社区对网络用户的吸引力将越来越强。根据中国电子信息产业发展研究院的咨询报告，中国的在线购物交易量将以每年 60% 的速度增长。推动在线购物迅速发展的因素包括：快速的经济增长和居民消费水平的进一步改善；二线和三线城市互联网的普及和网民的增加；在线购物商品种类的逐渐扩大；百度网之类的新经营者的参与；在付款、物流和在线购物等方面安全环境的改善。

同时，在线购物商品分类在目前的基础上将扩展到所有的商业领域。从在线购物市场的热点和趋势来看，在线购物商品分类将在书刊、电子音像、手机、化妆品和服装的基础上完善丰富。在线预订各种各样的商品和服务正开始扩展。在线购物群体发展迅速。汽车之类的耐用消费品、房屋之类的大宗消费品以及钻石之类的奢侈品等也开始在网络购物中扮演重要角色。这些商品将使在线购物的销售量明显地提升。更重要的是，在线购物社区对网络用户的吸引力越来越强。调查显示，越来越多的在线消费者已经开始从单纯

According to the statistics, the transaction amount of e-shopping of Shanghai netizens is ranking No. 1 in China. And the commodities purchased by the Shanghai e-shopping group most are such female beauty supplies as cosmetics and perfume①. Meanwhile, the commodities with the greatest quantity growth of e-shopping in Shanghai are female underwear and lady-used cases and bags; these data throw out female e-shopping group's scale of purchasing power. The female consumer product market is being paid more and more attention to by e-shopping websites.

With the popularity of Internet in the future, China's e-shopping transaction amount will keep a rapid growth, C2C will keep being the main driving power for the e-shopping growth, the commodity variety of e-shopping will be enriched further, and the attraction of online shopping communities to network subscribers will be stronger and stronger. According to the research of CCID Consulting, China's e-shopping transaction amount will be with the annual growth rate of above 60 percent. The driving factors of the rapid development of e-shopping include: a fast economic growth and a further improved residents' consuming level; Internet popularization and netizen increase in the second and third line cities; gradual classification expansion of e-shopping commodities; the participation of such new operators as baidu.com; the improved safety environment in terms of payment, logistics and online shopping, etc.

At the same time, on the present basis, the classification of e-

① perfume [ˈpəːfjuːm] *n.* 香水,香气

商家对消费者交易平台转移到通过消费者对消费者交易平台，而且趋势明显。所以说，在线购物代表信息时代商品交易的发展方向，而且中国的在线购物前途无量。

知识链接

taobao. com 淘宝网是亚洲最大网络零售商圈，致力于打造全球首选网络零售商圈，由阿里巴巴集团于 2003 年 5 月 10 日投资创办，它的使命是“没有淘不到的宝贝，没有卖不出的宝贝”。淘宝网目前的业务跨越 C2C（个人对个人）、B2C（商家对个人）两大部分，注册会员超过 6 200 万人，覆盖中国绝大部分网购人群，占据中国网购市场 70%以上市场份额，C2C 市场占据 80%以上市场份额。淘宝网倡导诚信、活泼、高效的网络交易文化，坚持“宝可不淘，信不能弃”。

paipai. com 拍拍网是腾讯旗下电子商务交易平台，网站于 2005 年 9 月 12 日上线发布，2006 年 3 月 13 日宣布正式运营。拍拍网目前主要有网游、数码、女人、男人、生活、运动、学生、特惠、明星等几大频道，其中的 QQ 特区还包括 QCC、QQ 宠物、QQ 秀、QQ 公仔等腾讯特色产品及服务。拍拍网拥有功能强大的在线支付平台——财付通，为用户提供安全、便捷的在线交易服务。

eachnet. com 易趣网是全球最大的电子商务公司 eBay 和国内领先的门户网站、无线互联网公司 TOM 在线于 2006 年携手组建的一家合资公司。秉承帮助几乎任何人在任何地方能实现任何交易的宗旨，易趣网不仅为卖家提供了一个网上创业、实现自我价值的舞台，品种繁多、价廉物美的商品资源，也给广大买家带来了全新的购物体验和品质购物环境。

shopping commodities will expand to all commercial fields. Seen from the hotspot and the trend in e-shopping market, the classification of e-shopping commodities will be enriched on the basis of such classifications as books and magazines, videos and music, mobile phones, cosmetics, and garments. The online reservation① for various commodities and services just start to expand. The online group purchasing develops rapidly. Such commodities as consumer durables② such as autos, consumer products with a huge amount such as houses and luxury products such as diamonds also start to play important roles in e-shopping. These commodities will show an obvious elevation③ function for the sales volume of e-shopping. What's more important is that the attraction of online shopping communities to network subscribers④ becomes stronger and stronger. Investigation indicates that more and more online consumers have begun to conduct transaction from purely via B2C platform to via C2C platform, and the trend of B2C subscribers' transferring to the C2C community is evident. So to speak, the e-shopping represents the development orientation of commodity transaction in the information era, and China's e-shopping is very promising.

(979 words)

---

① reservation [ˌrezəˈveiʃən] *n.* 预定

② durable [ˈdjuərəbl] *n.* 耐用物品

③ elevation [ˌeliˈveiʃən] *n.* 提高

④ subscriber [sʌbsˈkraibə] *n.* 订户

139*shop. com* 北斗手机网是亚洲地区最大的手机电子商务网站，致力于手机的 B2C 和 B2B 业务，提供完善的电子商务服务。目前，网站注册用户过百万，日浏览量过千万，B2B 业务年交易额数十亿。北斗手机网已经覆盖全国各地，在全国二十多个大、中城市建立了手机销售中心，通过完备的物流配送体系、优质的人性化服务，消费者可以非常安全、便捷地享受到“手机超低价 服务联到家”的全新服务。

题 记

时下快捷方便的在线购物成为新的消费形式，但精明的购物达人发现：网上产品广告宣传与实物不符、商品质量差、送货不及时、网上交易诚信度低。毫无疑问，互联网通常对有计划的购物具有非凡的魅力，对时间短缺的人也是个实惠。但是用它来取代社交活动或休闲娱乐却不太适合，因为这些活动是很多人非常享受的生活。随着经济的发展和社会的进步，人民的生活水平越来越高，消费方式逐渐由购买商品或耐用品转向服务。而各种服务性的商店在网上无法建立，必须由实体商店来提供服务。更重要的是，购物应该是一项社会活动，购物会带来一种愉快的满足感，不仅来自物品本身，也来自获得物品的过程。实体商店的当面交易意味着宽泛、丰富的交换。贸易通道不只是物物交换，还有思想、知识、信仰和技能的全部欲望。

The Perils of Online Shopping

Last week, one of my children said she wanted a copy of Roald Dahl's book Charlie and the Chocolate Factory for her birthday, so I duly logged on to Amazon.com.uk and ordered it. The website told me I should also buy the book's "perfect partner", the Charlie and the Chocolate Factory Gift Book, so being an obedient sort of person, I ordered that too. Amazon said both books were "usually dispatched① within 24 hours". Instead, it took three days. After that, the actual delivery took so long that the books had still not arrived on the eve of my daughter's birthday. So I had to make the trek to a real bookshop, Waterstone's, to get what I wanted. The punchline② is that, when the two Amazon books finally arrived and I set about returning them, I discovered they were exactly the same story, just in slightly different formats, so I would have ended up returning one of them anyway.

That is the perils of online shopping. Probably no big internet retailer has a better reputation than Amazon, yet even this company can let you down. Experiences such as this, however, have not prevented people

① dispatch [dis'pætʃ] *v.* 派遣

② punchline ['pʌntʃlain] *n.* 头条笑料,妙语如珠

在线购物的危险

上周，我的一个孩子说她想要本罗尔德·达尔的《查理和巧克力工厂》作为生日礼物，于是我及时登录亚马逊英国在线网站订购。网站告诉我，还应该购买该书的“完美搭档”——《查理和巧克力工厂寄赠书》，我是个随和的人，也就一并订购。亚马逊说，两本书“通常会在24小时内送出”，但实际3天后才发货。之后，实际交付的时间太长，以致女儿生日的前夜还没到达。所以我只得步行到沃特斯通实体书店，买了本我想要的书。好笑的是，当两本亚马逊的书终于送到、我正打算将其返还之时，我发现它们讲的完全是同样的故事，只是格式略有差别，所以不管怎样我都要拒绝为其中的一本付款。

这就是在线购物的危险。没有哪家大互联网零售商的声誉比亚马逊更好，但即使是这家公司都会让你失望。然而，这类经历对人们在线购物的热情并没有造成更多的妨碍。根据康姆斯克在线用户测量公司发布的调查数据，圣诞期间的两个月，美国互联网零售销售额与上年同期数据相比上升25%，而高盛集团、尼尔森网络评估公司和哈里斯互动调研公司发布的数据为30%。在英国，根据零售

from doing more of their shopping online. In the two-month during the Christmas, internet retail sales in the US rose by 25 per cent year-on-year, according to comScore Networks, or 30 per cent according to Goldman Sachs, Nielsen//NetRatings and Harris Interactive. In Britain, according to the Interactive Media in Retail Group, the figure was nearly 50 per cent. ComScore reckons online sales now account for 6 per cent of US retail spending, and in the UK, IMRG puts the figure at an astonishing 9 per cent. At this rate, how much longer will it be before shops and stores as we know them start to disappear?

A while yet, I suspect. The thing is, there is plenty of scope for spinning the retail figures depending on what story you want to tell. The skill lies in deciding what to include and what to leave out. For example, does spending on new and used cars count as retail? Or on fuel? Do you count spending on entertainment, hotel rooms, restaurant meals, supermarket food, banking, estate agents' commissions, iPod downloads, airline tickets or video games? What about spending on Dell computers, supplied direct by the manufacturer? What about pornography①? What about Ebay?

To give some idea of the latitude, the US commerce department reckons that, even after years of double-digit percentage increases, online sales still account for only 2.3 per cent of the US total- hardly, one would have thought, a basis for declaring the end of shopping as we know it. Perhaps we can agree that the really interesting figures would be those

---

① pornography [pɔːˈnɔgrəfi] *n.* 色情

集团互动媒体发布的数据，增长率接近50%。康姆斯克在线用户测量公司估计，在线销售目前占据美国零售消费的6%；而在英国，零售集团互动媒体发布的数据令人惊讶地达到了9%。照这样下去，商场和店铺多久之后就会开始消失呢？

我猜想仍然需要时间。问题是编造零售数据的余地很大，取决于你想讲述什么样的故事。技巧取决于纳入什么数据和省略什么数据。例如，买新车和二手车算零售吗？买燃料算零售吗？娱乐消遣、酒店住宿、餐馆吃饭、超市购物、银行储蓄、房地产代理佣金、iPod下载、机票或电子游戏算零售吗？购买直接由制造商提供的戴尔电脑算零售吗？购买色情文学算零售吗？上易趣购物算零售吗？

为了界定零售范围，美国商务部估计，即使在线销售几年后以两位数的百分比增长，仍然只占美国总销售额的2.3%——人们几乎很难想象，这就是宣称我们熟悉的购物终结的根据。也许我们可以赞同，显示人们放弃在购物商场或商业街购物、转而在线购买同样商品的范围是真正有趣的数据。不幸的是，据我所知，这样的数据不存在。但只要稍加思考，就足以肯定这个总数不大。例如，想一想网上消费最大的几类：色情资料、赌博、银行业务、经纪业务、航空订票、赛事订票和网上拍卖。不可否认，任何其他地方消费的增长都会减少普通商店可获得的消费量，或许有些银行、赌场、旅行社和色情店铺已经消失，但所有这些消费场所传统上与主

showing the extent to which people were giving up shopping in the mall or on the high street and making the same purchases online instead. Unfortunately, as far as I know, no such figures exist. But a moment's reflection is surely enough to suggest the sums are not large. Think, for example, of some of the biggest categories of internet spending: pornography, gambling, banking, broking, airline ticketing, event ticketing and online auctions. Admittedly, any increase in spending elsewhere could reduce the amount available for spending in conventional stores, and perhaps some banks, betting shops, travel agencies and porn shops have disappeared, but none of these areas of spending are traditionally associated with mainstream shopping. Using a stricter definition of retail, the comScore and GNH[1] surveys say the top three online categories in the Christmas run-up were computer hardware and peripherals[2], consumer electronics and clothing. Well, does this really represent much of a loss to conventional retailing? In computers and consumer electronics, the growth of internet spending has coincided with the rapid growth of the categories and I doubt it has led to many store closures. In clothing, the growth of online spending has coincided with the decline of mail order and catalogue retailing, so again I do not think we are talking about a mass exodus[3] from the stores.

What of the future? I cannot deny the internet is usually marvelous

---

① GNH 国民幸福指数(Gross National Happiness)

② peripheral [pəˈrifərəl] *n.* 外围设备

③ exodus [ˈeksədəs] *n.* 大批的离去

流购物无关。使用一个对零售更精确的定义，康姆斯克在线用户测量公司和国民幸福指数的调查表明，圣诞节前期三类顶级在线销售是计算机硬件及外围设备、家用电器和服装。那么，这就真正代表传统零售业的大量流失吗？在计算机和家用电器行业，互联网消费的增长与各种类别实物的快速增长一致，我对它会导致许多店面倒闭持质疑的态度。在服装业，在线消费的增长与邮购和目录零售业的减少相符，所以我再次重申，我们谈论的不是商店的大批迁离。

未来会怎么样呢？我不能否认，互联网通常对有计划的购物具有非凡的魅力，它对时间短缺的人来说也是个实惠，但是用它来取代社交活动或休闲娱乐却不太适合，因为这些活动是很多人非常享受的生活。为建立这种乐趣，商店应该努力让购物体验更快乐——特别是在英国，客户服务糟糕透顶。更多的零售商们应该仿效约翰·路易斯百货公司连锁店，根据贝恩公司尼可·格林斯潘的观点，它拥有全国最高客户支持水平，也就是说，人们会向其他人推荐这家商店。格林斯潘先生说，约翰·路易斯百货公司连锁店的战略是超额投资客户服务，在每平方英尺的零售空间比任何竞争链雇佣更多的人。

还有一种观点。在发达国家，消费者正将逐渐增长的消费转向服务，而不是商品或耐用品。正如网上赌博的增长显示，有些这样的服务可以在线提供，但很多其他的服务却行不通。你肯定知道文身店外标志牌上的老笑话："等候之时耳已穿洞。"你不能在网上理

for planned purchases. It is also a boon[1] to the time-starved. But it is a poor substitute for shopping as a social activity and/or leisure pursuit, which is how it is enjoyed by many. To build on this, shops should strive to make the shopping experience more pleasurable — particularly in Britain, where customer service is dire[2]. More retailers should emulate the John Lewis department store chain, which according to Nick Greenspan at Bain & Company has the country's highest level of customer advocacy, that is, people recommending the store to others. Mr. Greenspan says John Lewis's tactic is to over-invest in customer service by employing more people per square foot of retail space than any competing chain.

One more point. In developed countries, consumers are switching their incremental[3] spending towards services, not goods or durables. As the growth of internet gambling shows, some such services can be provided online, but many more cannot. You must know that old joke about the sign outside the tattoo parlour: "Ears pierced while you wait." You cannot have your hair cut on the internet, buy a cup of coffee or eat a restaurant meal. So yes, the internet may one day affect the high street and the mall, but my guess is they will change, not die.

(918 words)

---

① boon [buːn] *n.* 恩惠

② dire [ˈdaiə] *adj.* 可怕的,悲惨的

③ incremental [inkriˈmentəl] *adj.* 逐渐增长的

发、买杯咖啡，或者吃一顿餐馆的饭。 所以，互联网也许有一天影响繁华的街道和购物商场，但我的推测是：它们只会改变，不会消失。

知识链接

Amazon. com, Inc. 亚马逊是美国一家电子商务网站，总部设在华盛顿州西雅图。亚马逊也是美国最大的在线零售商，其网络上的销售额大约是美国最大办公用品零售商 Staples 的三倍。卓越亚马逊成立于 2000 年，总部设在北京，为客户提供各类图书、音像、软件、玩具礼品、百货等商品，并成立了上海和广州分公司，成为中国网上零售的领先者。2004 年 8 月，亚马逊全资收购卓越亚马逊，使亚马逊全球领先的网上零售专长与卓越亚马逊深厚的中国市场经验相结合，进一步提升客户体验，并促进中国电子商务的成长。

Goldman Sachs 高盛集团是集投资银行、证券交易和投资管理等业务为一体的国际著名的投资银行。它为全球成千上万个重要客户，包括企业、金融机构、国家政府及富有的个人，提供全方位的高质量金融服务。高盛 1869 年创立于纽约曼哈顿，是华尔街上历史最悠久、经验最丰富、实力最雄厚的投资银行之一，已于 2008 年 9 月 21 日宣布转为银行控股公司。高盛集团总部设在纽约，在全球二十多个国家设有分部，并以香港、伦敦、法兰克福及东京等地作为地区总部。

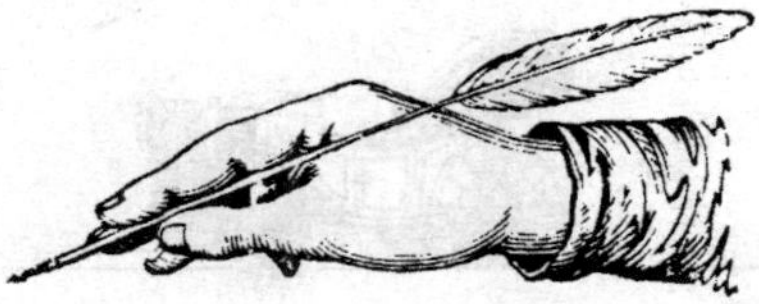

题 记

网络化使人们对商务活动的价值重视已经从“时间、距离和带宽”逐步转向“内容和电子商务”，并进一步追求即时的网上应用、个性化在线服务以及实时交互操作等更加丰富的网络服务。墨西哥西麦克斯水泥公司开发的卫星通信系统，随时跟踪、撤销和变更订单行程，客户只需在终端屏幕前尽职尽责地与之交流；但电子化的嘉信理财让在线业务达到最大流速，而消费者却拒绝接受这种纯粹的虚拟商业模式。思科的客户更是将在线业务排在经济活动的末端运作模式。人们在网络经济时代太过钟情于创新，而未能够捕捉到新思维、产品和服务的价值。因此，在你加入网络数字化之前，请停下来思考：你的公司如何赚钱？你生意的问题是什么？数字化技术如何建立在你拥有的财富之上？

Thinking First before You Webify

Here's some good news for all those corporations still trying to figure out their Internet strategy: It's not too late. Even better, you can learn from those who have tried and failed...or succeeded. One key lesson: E-success may have more to do with execution than brilliant vision. In this e-Corp Special Report, we'll show you how the details doomed one high-profile venture, Whirlpool's experiment with Brandwise, and how they're working in favor of another effort, Kmart's surprising BlueLight subsidiary. And FORTUNE columnist Michael Schrage, author of Serious Play, argues that we have fallen too in love with innovation and not enough with capturing the value of new ideas, products, and services. Digital success is not about technology or cool Websites. Instead, it's about using digital technology to create value that is consistent with your company's core goals. So before you jump into the fray①, stop and think. How does your company make money? What are your business issues? How can digital technology build on what you have? Answer those questions, and you'll be well on your way.

Practically all business people today would tell you that they are bringing their companies into the Internet Age, but there haven't been

① fray [frei] *n.* 打架,争论

网络化前请三思

对那些仍在盘算网络策略的公司来说，好消息接踵而至：网络化为时未晚。更令人兴奋的是，你可以向已经尝试过、并且失败了或成功了的案例人学习。一个重要的教训是：电子化成功与实施行为更有关联，而非卓越的先见之明。在这篇电子企业特别报告中，我们将向你展示细节如何决定一个备受瞩目的风险投资，制造商惠尔普与大型家用电器评价网站 Brandwise 的尝试，他们如何配合其他的有利行动，以及卡马特令人称奇的蓝光子公司等。《财富》杂志的专栏作家、《严肃的游戏》作者迈克尔·斯拉格认为，我们太过钟情于创新，而未能够捕捉到新思维、产品和服务的价值。数字化成功不在于技术或一流的网站，而在于运用数字化技术创造与公司核心目标一致的价值。因此，在你加入这一争论时，请停下来思考：你的公司如何赚钱？你生意的问题是什么？数字化技术如何建立在你拥有的财富之上？解答了这些问题，你前行的道路将会非常顺畅。

实际上如今所有的商人都会告诉你，他们正在引领公司进入互联网时代，但成功的事例尚不多见。那么尚未网络化的公司经理们又错在何处？首先，我们要对有效网络化的数字商业计划和与网络无关、只有未解决的数字商业计划加以区别。许多有义务的大公司对网站的出现心存恐惧，它们认为自己必须立即激活互联网、建立

very many success stories. Where do managers at big existing non-dot-com companies go wrong? First, we would like to make a distinction between those digital business designs that are Internet-enabled vs. those that are just outstanding digital business designs but may not have anything to do with the Internet. A lot of large incumbent① enterprises scared by the presence of the dot-com. They believe they must immediately be Internet-enabled, have a Website, or get into e-commerce. The classic example is the story of Cemex, the Mexican cement company. Cemex developed a communication system that until very recently was internal but was very, very successful in solving its business and customer issues. Their issue was unforecastable demand for cement at construction sites. Before putting the technology to work, they studied very carefully other companies that dealt with this issue—a FedEx, an Exxon rerouting oil tankers. They developed a satellite communication system—put a global positioning satellite system into their trucks. They created a central clearing facility to track and to follow cancellations and rerouting. They basically developed an internal Cemex information system that allowed them to reduce their response time to a customer order from three hours to 20 minutes. Now their next phase is going to be very Internet-intensive because they are trying to figure out how to help their customers at construction sites. So a huge cement company is an advanced digital business.

Big existing companies can take advantage of this shift to a digital business successfully if they go about it the right way. Another example of a company that seems too big and too heterogeneous② to ever make this

① incumbent [in'kʌmbənt] *a.* 负有义务的

② heterogeneous [hetərə'dʒiːniəs] *a.* 异种的,由不同成分形成的

网站或进入电子商务。墨西哥水泥公司——西麦克斯公司——就是一个经典范例。西麦克斯开发了一个通信系统，虽然近期还只是内部系统，但在解决其业务和客户问题上却非常、非常成功。它们的问题是建筑场所不可预见的水泥需求。在运用这项技术之前，它们仔细研究了其他公司对这个问题的处理方式——联邦快递和埃克森改道发送油轮。它们开发了一个卫星通信系统——在卡车上置放全球卫星定位系统。它们创建了一个中央清算设施，跟踪和追随撤销与变更行程。从根本上说，它们开发了一个内部的西麦克斯信息系统，使它们回复客户订单的时间从 3 小时减少到 20 分钟。现在，它们下一阶段的目标是深化网络系统，因为它们正在考虑如何在建筑场所为客户提供帮助。所以，一个巨大的水泥公司就是一个先进的数字商业。

现有的大公司只要遵循正确的模式，都可以成功利用数字商业转化。另一个公司的例子似乎太庞大和异类，以致不可能很好地产生转化，但它却正在这么做，它就是通用电气公司。它们的出发点不是互联网，也不是数字化工具，而是“我们公司面临的最重要的商业问题是什么”？对通用电气公司来说，商业重点是“我们用 18 年建立了世界上最具竞争力的大公司，但是现在环境的改变置我们于风险之中，因为如果我们价格下跌的速度超过成本，利润将会缩水。人们有新的机会介入我们和我们的客户之间，并且比以前有更多的机会让人们攻击我们的金融服务业务”。第一步被称为“摧毁你的商业网站”，这是让每个商人了解门外汉如何进入商业网站并将他们毁灭的开端。然后过渡到“培育你的商业网站”，思考我们如何向客户提供新的和更

transition well, and yet it is doing it, is General Electric. There the point of departure was not the Internet. It wasn't digital tools. The point of departure was "What are the most important business issues facing our company?" For GE the business issue was, "Here we've spent 18 years building the most competitive big company in the world, and now this environmental change is putting us at risk because if our prices fall more quickly than our costs, our margins will get squeezed. There are new opportunities for people to get in between us and our customers, and there are more opportunities than before for people to attack our financial services business." The first step was called "destroy your business.com," which was an initiative all about wanting every business to understand how an outsider could come in and blow them away. And then it transitioned to "grow your business.com", taking those ideas that how we can achieve higher growth by delivering a new and better-value proposition for our customers. The third phase was developing the Web-enabled tools to do that. At first there were many commentators who looked at GE's Websites and said, "They're not very sophisticated; they're not very cool." But they were driven by a very well thought-through business purpose and very well thought-through strategy.

Whether it's smarter to start up a digital initiative in a separate division or as part of the company's core depends on the customer and competitive circumstances. Let's illustrate with two counter-examples. Schwab started e-Schwab separately in 1996. The success and growth of E-Trade defined a pace of growth for that business. Schwab decided that they could achieve the maximum rate of movement for the online part of the business, not as a separate company but as a separate division. And they succeeded in that. But then the customer said to Schwab, I don't want to

有价值的建议以达到更快增长。第三阶段是开发有效的网络工具完成网站建设。很多评论者当初看着通用电气公司的网站说："不够复杂，不够酷。"但这些网站都受到深思熟虑的商业目标和深思熟虑的策略驱使。

到底是从一个独立的部门还是从公司核心的部分启动数字化更明智取决于消费者和竞争环境。让我们来看两个反例：嘉信理财于1996年独立实施电子化的嘉信理财。电子贸易的成功和增长勾勒出业务的增速。嘉信理财断定，作为独立的部门而不是独立的公司，其在线业务能够达到最大流速。它们在这方面也的确成功了。但随后消费者对嘉信理财说，我不想与两个嘉信理财做交易，只想和一个嘉信理财打交道，这又触发了一场艰巨但必要的重新整合。另一个相反的例子是通用电气公司。当时通用电气公司正在迎接竞争，而非有电子贸易的等价物设定步伐。在它们的案例中，从最初的核心业务做起具有可行性，也是最正确的方法。所以，不了解消费者状况和竞争状况，最重要的是，不了解哪一类消费者想要纯粹的虚拟商业模式，就很难事先做出判断。在很多行业中，这只不过是个小数目。

认为思科的成功是完全的数字化，就是一个大大的误解。问一问思科的客户："什么对你最重要"？它们回答的第一点是"可靠性和正常运行时间"；它们说的第二点是技术和商务人士所需的网络特征；第三是全球化服务；第四是杰出的销售代表；第五是在线业务。现在，如果没有在线业务，思科不可能增长40%到60%，但是客户会说，除非正确地拥有前四项，否则在线业务对他们来说毫无价值。因此，从商业问题、灵巧的模式选择开始，然后询问哪些

deal with two Schwabs, I want to deal with one, and that triggered a tough but necessary reintegration. Shift to the other end of the spectrum with GE. GE was anticipating competition, rather than having an equivalent of E-Trade setting the pace. In their case, doing it in the core business at the outset was feasible, and it was the right way to go. So that it is very difficult to be prescriptive① in advance without knowing what's the customer situation, what's the competitive situation, and, most important, which of our customer sets want a purely virtual business model. In a lot of industries that's a very small number.

There's a big misconception about Cisco that its success is entirely digital. You go to a Cisco customer and ask, "What's most important to you?" and the first things they say are "reliability and uptime." The second thing they say is technology and the features for the network my business people need. The third is global service. The fourth is a great sales rep. And the fifth is online presence. Now, without the online presence, Cisco would never have been able to grow at 40% to 60%. But the customer will tell you that unless you get the first four things right, the online doesn't really do very much for them. So starting with the business issues and with smart design choices and then asking about which digital tools and options can help us do a better job on this is a common characteristic of all the people who have done it successfully.

(1,050 words)

---

① prescriptive [priˈskriptiv] *a.* 规定的,惯例的

数字工具和选择能够帮助我们更好地完成工作，这是所有网络化的成功人士共同的特征。

知识链接

DELL 戴尔　总部设在得克萨斯州奥斯汀(Austin)的戴尔公司是全球领先的 IT 产品及服务提供商，其业务包括帮助客户建立自己的信息技术及互联网基础架构。DELL 戴尔通过其“全球客户计划”，向拥有全球业务的用户提供订制的成套服务支持。它为全球客户提供符合行业标准技术的产品和服务的统一订货、结账、订制产品(包括安装专有软件)，以及本地供货和现场服务，不断地致力于提供最佳的客服。戴尔公司目前在全球共有47 800位雇员。

Cisco 思科　思科系统公司(Cisco Systems，Inc.)，是互联网解决方案的领先提供者，其设备和软件产品主要用于连接计算机网络系统。思科系统公司 1984 年 12 月在美国成立，创始人是斯坦福大学的一对教师夫妇。思科系统公司目前已成为公认的全球网络互联解决方案的领先厂商，其提供的解决方案是世界各地成千上万的公司、大学、企业和政府部门建立互联网的基础，用户遍及电信、金融、服务、零售等行业以及政府部门和教育机构等。同时，思科系统公司也是建立网络的中坚力量，互联网上近 80%的信息流量经由思科系统公司的产品传递。思科系统公司目前在全球拥有35 000多名雇员。

题　记

互联网开创的电子商务时代，不仅仅是某种跨越式的技术，而是利用互联网技术创造出前所未有的商业模式。而那些在互联网时代脱颖而出、持续创造利润的企业，也多是由于很好地利用了互联网，或者说将互联网精神融入企业管理之中。在电子商务的直接通道上建立起的信任随着时间的推移和个人的互动而发展；互联网技术改变了人力资源管理、事务处理和信息服务的方式，从劳动力优化的角度实现了最高员工效率；即时报价能力和在线存货供给大大简化了传统交易的流程，打破了时空限制，使客户得到了空前丰富的信息；而流动的办公时间更是促使电子商务用户良性竞争，为网络商机的发展带来了新的契机。在开放、合作、平等和全球化的平台上与电子商务愉快相处已经成为互联网语境下的时尚概念。

Getting Comfortable with E-Commerce

The level of customer service available through an e-commerce site should be considered during the purchasing decision. An e-commerce site's privacy statement should be easy to find and easy to understand. Price quotes for a quantity of stock can be obtained almost instantly online. This information helps manufacturers serve their customers better with more accurate quotes of their own. Being able to check the availability of stock is a beneficial feature of a well-developed online materials purchasing site. Some customers view it as their own "virtual inventory".

For decades, transactions in the steel industry usually involved some sort of personal relationship, usually face-to-face and over the phone. Issues such as security and privacy were rarely a concern, as each party knew one another. Trust was fostered over many years. Even with the advent of call centers and the fax machine, most steel buyers had the assurance that the information needed to complete a transaction would not find its way outside the company. Trust is an essential component of transactions between any two entities. With conventional transactions, it

与电子商务愉快相处

在决定购买商品的过程中，客户通过电子商务网站可能获得的服务水平应该在考虑之列。电子商务网站的隐私声明应该不难找到，也容易理解。绝大多数的股票报价都可以即时上网查询。这些信息帮助厂商更好地服务客户，并提供更准确的自行报价。能够检查股票的有效性是健康发展的在线原料采购网站的一种受益特征。有些客户认为这是他们自己的“虚拟库存”。

几十年来，钢铁行业的交易通常涉及某些个人关系，通常是面对面的交易或电话沟通。因为双方相互了解，人们很少关注安全和隐私之类的问题。信任已承受了多年的历练。即使呼叫中心和传真机时代已经到来，大多数钢铁买家仍然确信：完成交易所需的信息在公司之外无法寻觅。信任对任何两个实体之间的交易是必不可少的组成部分。与传统的交易相比，信任随着时间的推移和个人的互动而发展。电子商务是通道直接、但买卖双方不相谋面。由于采用常规难以培养互信，电子商务网站

develops over time and with personal interaction. However, e-commerce is immediate and can be faceless. With the usual methods for fostering trust unavailable, e-commerce sites have resorted to technological systems that ensure that personal information is protected and safeguarded, and money is transferred fully to and from the correct parties. While no commerce system will ever be fraud-free, today's methods provide an excellent—and trustworthy—foundation for expanding the e-commerce enterprise.

Almost all of the metal buyers noted that buying online improved their efficiency. They reported spending less time on the phone or waiting for a return call or fax. "I don't like talking to people. I don't like dealing with them," says Rick Wagner of San Jose, California-based Sierra Pacific Manufacturing, which makes stainless, aluminum and plastic parts for semiconductor and medical industry. He qualified his response: "I was looking for a way to order materials quickly and easily and this is the way to go. You point and click and it's a done deal. If I can save 5 minutes of my time from writing up a fax or getting on the phone and dealing with someone, then I can be more competitive."

Frank Viola, vice president of manufacturing at Lynton, a manufacturer of screw machine products, fasteners and electronic hardware in Spokane, Washington, says the automation offered through e-commerce avoids common problems associated with conventional ordering methods. "I spend a lot less time making phone calls," he said. "And then you have missed calls. Because ordering online is

已经借助技术体系确保客户的个人信息受到保护和维护，货币在正确的当事人之间转换。尽管没有任何商业系统能够保证永远零欺诈，但今天的方法为扩大电子商务企业的规模提供了卓越和值得信赖的基础。

几乎所有的金属买家都指出，网上购买提高了效率。他们报告说，打电话、等回电和传真的时间较之以前少了很多。位于美国加利福尼亚州圣何塞市塞拉利昂太平洋制造公司的里克·瓦格纳说，“我不喜欢与人交谈。我不喜欢与人打交道”。该公司为半导体和医疗行业生产不锈钢、铝和塑料零件。他振振有词地说：“我一直在寻找快速便捷订购材料的方式，这就是途径。只需要点击和敲打就可成交。如果我可以从写传真或电话交谈和与人交易中节省5分钟的时间，我可以更具竞争力。”

位于林顿市制造螺杆机械、紧固件和电子硬件产品的制造业副总裁弗兰克·维奥拉在华盛顿州斯波坎说，电子商务提供的自动化服务避免了传统订货方式面临的常见问题。他说，“我打电话的时间较少。却又错过了电话。由于网上订购更快，我能够让这个位置上的人做更多的事情”。乔治·汉森来自宾夕法尼亚州的哈利斯维尔东海岸金属公司，这是一家生产螺纹棒和螺栓、U型螺栓、锚杆、钩、螺栓、螺母、垫圈和插座产品的专业

quicker, I'm able to have the person in that position do more things." George Hanson, Jr., from East Coast Metals, a specialty manufacturer of threaded rods and studs, u-bolts, anchor bolts, hooks, bolts, nuts, washers and socket products in Harleysville, Pennsylvania, concurs[①], noting also the reduction in paperwork. "I can place the order right there with a click of the button," he said. "It saves paperwork time. I don't need to find a purchase order, write it up and fax it over. One click and the order is placed. At first, I thought how much quicker could it be, after you turn on the computer, log on, go to the site, and so on. I thought it would be a hindrance rather than a benefit. But the whole process is done in 5 minutes or so."

Metals e-commerce users also laud[②] the ability to obtain instant quotes. Typically, machine shop owners would call or fax a quote request to a particular individual. Responsiveness would vary dramatically: sometimes a sales representative would be on hand to take a call while other times one would reach voice mail or an uninformed assistant. Mr. Wagner says he finds that the improved efficiency has helped him serve customers better. "You don't even have to order the product. If a customer calls and wants me to quote a job, I can have a ballpark[③] quote in my hands while the customer is still on the phone. It allows me to

---

① concur [kən'kəː] *vi.* 同意,赞成

② laud [lɔːd] *vt.* 赞美,褒奖

③ ballpark ['bɔːlpɑːk] *adj.* 大致正确的

制造商。他说，“我可以击键直接整理文件，节省文书工作的时间。我并不需要找订购单，填写和发传真。点击一下就完成订购。起初，我还在想，打开电脑、登录、进入网站等竟如此繁琐，我觉得真像是跨越障碍而不是受益。没想到整个过程5分钟左右就完成了”。

金属电子商务用户还对获得即时报价的能力大加赞赏。机器店主通常将报价致电或传真给某个人。回复可能完全不同：有时销售代表会立即打电话，而有时会语音留言或由不知情的助理接待。瓦格纳先生认为，提高工作效率帮助他更好地为客户服务。他说，“你甚至不必订购产品。如果客户打电话来，希望我介绍一下，我就可以在与客户打电话时随即给他一个大致报价。这让我更好地回复了客户”。同样的，位于伊利诺伊州卡罗尔河谷、专门从事金属和塑料制品的王子工业制造公司的罗伯特·哈恩认为，报价过程的速度和精确性非常有益。他说，“我一整天都在购买金属，在金属电子商务网站上，从请求到订购，包括运费，不到2分钟。然后，10到15分钟内我收到一封确认的电子邮件。很多时候，在线工作比打电话更可取”。

与即时报价一样，存货在线供给也被认为有利可图。有些电子商务网站允许用户获取存货信息，以检查特定合金的尺寸或

be more responsive to my customers," he says. Similarly, Robert Hahn with Prince Industries, a manufacturing company specializing in metal and plastic goods located in Carol Stream, Illinois, said the speed and thoroughness of the quoting process were beneficial. "I purchase metals all day, and with metal e-commerce sites you can go from request to order in less than 2 minutes, including the freight cost," he said. "Then I receive an e-mail confirmation of the order within 10-15 minutes. Many times, it's preferable to work online rather than on the phone."

Along the same lines as instant quotes, online availability of stock is viewed as beneficial. Some e-commerce sites allow users to access information on inventory to check if a particular alloy, size or spec is in stock and ready for delivery. Some customers view it like their own inventory, accessible with a few short keystrokes①. "I can check on very specific items, like stainless 416 and 316 in different shapes and sizes to see if they are available," says Mr. Hahn, adding that it is helpful to know what metals are in stock before he makes the actual purchase. Chiu Moy, president of Concept Manufacturing, Waltham, Massachusetts, says that the instant inventory verification is comforting, but selection can be limited. "You can't access all of the specialty materials now, like those for aeronautic② parts," he says. He offers a

---

① keystroke [ˈkiːstrəuk] *n.* 敲击

② aeronautic [ˌɛərəˈnɔːtik] *adj.* 航空学的，飞行术的

规格是否有库存，并提供现货。有些客户认为它像自己的库存，用几个快捷键就可以得到。哈恩先生说，“我可以检查非常具体的项目，如 416 号不锈钢和 316 号不锈钢的不同形状和尺寸，查看是否有现货”。他补充说，这有助于在实际购买之前了解金属的存货情况。马萨诸塞州沃尔瑟姆概念制造公司的总裁邱·莫埃认为，即时库存核查是一种安慰，但是选择是有限的。他说，“你不能马上访问所有的特种材料，如航空零件”。他提出了一点希望：“如果网站没有这种材料，它应该能够链接有这种材料的其他的网站。”

金属行业的每个人都知道这不是一个朝九晚五的工作。在计算机数字控制下没有“银行时间”，因此，电子商务的使用者报告说，他们喜欢“网上商店”是不足为奇的，因为他们无论什么时候都可以订购金属材料。休斯敦得克萨斯州质量制造商蒂莫勒维耶说，“我可以利用零碎的时间下订单，这是好事，因为我不用在白天考虑采购的事情”。哈恩先生说，“我在办公室一直待到晚上 9 点才完成了订购。早上 6:30 已经下了金属订单，营业部此时根本没有人。以前，我会一直等到有人来开门”。莫埃先生喜欢可移动性，或者说从一个地点到另一地点、仍然无拘无束地进入在线商店的能力。他说，“这很方便。我能一天

wish: "If the site doesn't have the material, it should be able to link to others that do."

Everyone in the metal industry knows this isn't a 9-to-5 job. There are no "banker's hours" amid the CNC[①] machines. So it is no surprise that users of e-commerce report that they enjoy having "online stores" that are open whenever they want to order metals. "I am able to place orders at odd hours, which is good because I don't always think about purchases during the day," says Timothy Levier, of Texas Quality Manufacturing in Houston. "I've been in the office as late as 9 p.m. and have placed an order. I've ordered metals at 6:30 in the morning when no humans would have been in the sales office," says Mr. Hahn. "Before e-commerce, I would have been waiting for the guy to open." In addition to the lack of time restrictions, Mr. Moy welcomes the portability, or ability to move from location to location and still have unfettered[②] access to an online store. "It is convenient. I can access it 24 hours a day and get a response right away," he says. "I use it from my office and my home. If I am at home quoting jobs at night, it's very helpful to be able to access the information I need."

(1,133 words)

---

① CNC [计] Computerized Numerical Control 电脑数值控制
② unfettered [ʌn'fetəd] 自由自在的,无拘束的

24 小时访问，并马上得到回复。我在办公室和家里都使用电子商务。如果我晚上在家工作，能够获取我需要的信息真是受益匪浅”。

知识链接

ASTM American Society for Testing Material 美国试验材料学会是美国负责材料测试及标准制定的学术机构。自 1898 年以来，学会中的技术委员会进行了大量、广泛的调查研究，而后制定出标准。标准号码用分类号、序列号及年号表示。